OXFORD PAPERBACK REFERENCE

The Oxford Dictionary of
Rhyming Slang

John Ayto is an experienced lexicographer, and
author of many books on the English language,
Century Words
dictive

D1335541

XB00 000005 3105

Oxford Paperback Reference

The most authoritative and up-to-date reference books for both students and the general reader.

ABC of Music
Accounting
Allusions
Animal Behaviour
Archaeology
Architecture and Landscape
  Architecture
Art and Artists
Art Terms
Arthurian Legend and
  Literature*
Astronomy
Battles*
Better Wordpower
Bible
Biology
British History
British Place-Names
Buddhism
Business and Management
Card Games
Catchphrases
Celtic Mythology
Chemistry
Christian Art
Christian Church
Chronology of English
  Literature
Chronology of Modern Words*
Classical Literature
Classical Myth and Religion
Classical World*
Computing
Contemporary World History
Countries of the World
Dance
Dynasties of the World
Earth Sciences
Ecology
Economics
Encyclopedia
Engineering*
English Etymology
English Folklore
English Grammar
English Language
English Literature
English Surnames
Euphemisms
Everyday Grammar
Finance and Banking
First Names
Food and Drink
Food and Nutrition
Foreign Words and Phrases
Geography
Humorous Quotations
Idioms
Internet

Islam
Kings and Queens of Britain
Language Toolkit
Law
Law Enforcement*
Linguistics
Literary Terms
Local and Family History
London Place-Names
Mathematics
Medical
Medicinal Drugs
Modern Design
Modern Quotations
Modern Slang
Music
Musical Terms
Musical Works
Nicknames
Nursing
Ologies and Isms
Philosophy
Phrase and Fable
Physics
Plant Sciences
Plays*
Pocket Fowler's Modern English
  Usage
Political Quotations
Politics
Popes
Proverbs
Psychology
Quotations
Quotations by Subject
Reverse Dictionary
Rhymes*
Rhyming Slang
Saints
Science
Shakespeare
Ships and the Sea*
Slang
Sociology
Space Exploration
Statistics
Superstitions
Synonyms and Antonyms
Weather
Weights, Measures, and Units
Word Histories
World History
World Mythology
World Place-Names
World Religions
Zoology

*forthcoming

The Oxford Dictionary of

Rhyming Slang

JOHN AYTO

OXFORD
UNIVERSITY PRESS

OXFORD
UNIVERSITY PRESS

Great Clarendon Street, Oxford OX2 6DP

Oxford University Press is a department of the University of Oxford.
It furthers the University's objective of excellence in research, scholarship,
and education by publishing worldwide in

Oxford New York

Auckland Bangkok Buenos Aires Cape Town
Chennai Dar es Salaam Delhi Hong Kong Istanbul Karachi
Kolkata Kuala Lumpur Madrid Melbourne Mexico City Mumbai Nairobi
São Paulo Shanghai Singapore Taipei Tokyo Toronto

Oxford is a registered trade mark of Oxford University Press
in the UK and in certain other countries

Published in the United States
by Oxford University Pres Inc., New York

© John Ayto, 2002, 2003

First published 2002
First issued as an Oxford University Press paperback 2003

The moral rights of the author have been asserted
Database right Oxford University Press (maker)

British Library Cataloguing in Publication Data
Data available

Library of Congress Cataloging in Publication Data
Data available

ISBN-13: 978-0-19-860751-9

5

Typeset in Swift Light by Footnote Graphics, Warminster, Wiltshire
Printed in Great Britain by Clays Ltd, St Ives plc

Contents

Introduction

Go into any tourist gift shop or newsagent in the centre of London and you are liable to find there, probably displayed next to the cash register for the benefit of the impulse buyer, a small phrase book of London rhyming slang (it might be, for instance, *Rhyming Cockney Slang* by 'Jack Jones', first published in 1971 and into its 27th impression by the year 2000) purporting to interpret for bemused tourists the strange utterances with which they have been greeted by the chirpy but incomprehensible locals: *bees and honey, oily rag, Tom and Dick, Uncle Ned*, and the like.

The likelihood of most tourists encountering more than a tiny fraction of the rhymes in these collections is minimal, but that's beside the point. These little books are more souvenirs than practical dictionaries. Rhyming slang serves as a saleable icon of London life and culture. It has become a commodity, to an extent unparalleled in any other area of language and usage. In the process it has become embalmed, but it has also been given new life. Whiskery rhymes that in the normal course of linguistic evolution might have faded quietly away (*apples and pears, skin and blister, whistle and flute*) are preserved and polished as much-loved heirlooms, and their high profile keeps alive the impulse to create new rhymes (*Britney Spears, Millennium Dome, Pete Tong*).

But how did it all begin? The earliest explicit reference to 'rhyming slang' on record is in John Camden Hotten's *The Slang Dictionary* (1859): 'The cant, which has nothing to do with that spoken by the costermongers, is known in Seven Dials [a noted sink of iniquity in 18th- and 19th-century Holborn] and elsewhere as the Rhyming Slang, or the substitution of words and sentences which rhyme with other words intended to be kept secret. . . I learn that the rhyming slang was introduced about twelve or fifteen years ago.' Note that Hotten refers to it as '*the* Rhyming Slang', implying that it was by this time already an established code with recognized rules and status, in use among the petty criminals and down-and-outs of central London. He identifies it as a comparatively recent innovation, an observation anticipated by Henry Mayhew in his *London Labour and the London Poor* (1851): 'The new style of cadgers' [street sellers' or beggars'] cant is done all on the rhyming principle.' The picture is of a fully elaborated secret vocabulary of the underworld, designed to enable its users to communicate with each other, safe from prying ears. It seems unlikely, though, that rhyming slang had such coherent beginnings. It is much more plausible that it evolved gradually, in the early 19th or even the late 18th century, as one amongst a range of word-play strategies employed by streetwise Londoners partly as class-membership markers and excluders of outsiders, but partly also for the sheer exuberant enjoyment to be got out of inventing and using them. Rhymes and puns appealed to the quick-witted (Francis Grose in his *Classical Dictionary of the Vulgar Tongue* (1796) records one contemporary effort: 'He will have a hearty choak and caper sauce for breakfast: i.e. he will be hanged'), and records of a few possible rhymed synonyms survive from the late 18th century, although their status is debatable (see *hot beef* at CRIME AND PUNISHMENT and *kick* at MONEY AND COMMERCE). These are not very similar to 19th-century rhyming slang, and certainly do not present a picture of a fully developed system, but they are the only evidence of rhyme that is to be found in Grose. A few rhyming items appear in H. Brandon's slang glossary appended to his edition of *Poverty, Mendacity and Crime* (1839), but the first reference book to include significant amounts of rhyming slang—including such sturdy old favourites as *apples and pears, barnet fair*, and *mince pies*—was *The Vulgar Tongue* (1857), by 'Ducange Anglicus' (a still unpenetrated pseudonym).

Superficially rhyming slang is in the tradition of the thieves' cant of the 16th, 17th, and 18th centuries, and Hotten specifically distinguishes it from the specialized talk of street traders. Mayhew, however, linked it with the 'cagders', and by the end of the 19th century it had become firmly associated with the language of London costermongers (J. W. Horsley in *I Remember* (1911) refers to 'the more modern rhyming slang . . . invented and chiefly used by costermongers, to whom "daisy roots" is a substitute for the word boots'), and the seeds of its celebrity as the mainstay of cheekily vivid Cockney repartee had been well and truly sown. In the 1850s it had had little or no public profile (Charles Dickens in an 1853 article on slang in *Household Words* didn't refer to it at all), but by the beginning of the 20th century it was a star.

How did this come about? Part of the explanation is no doubt the greater mobility of the later 19th century, which brought the language of Londoners into ever-increasing contact with people from all over Britain (Eric Partridge, in his *Dictionary of Forces' Slang* (1948), noted the role of dialectal contact within the army: 'Before the First World War, [rhyming slang] was in common use in the Forces, even in Scottish regiments, such was the influence of the Cockney, who is the expert rhyming slangster'). But maybe in the final analysis it was the jollity of rhyming slang that endeared it to people, together with its relative approachability for the uninitiated (as compared with other 'secret language' systems, such as backslang (e.g. *ecilop* for *police*) and Pig Latin (e.g. *amscray* for *scram*), which are almost impossible to decipher without a good deal of practice). Its original role as an impenetrable code, to the extent that it ever existed, was fast fading into the background, as it took up its new career as a comic turn.

A high-water mark appears to have been reached in the first decade of the 20th century, and a decline in rhyming slang's popularity was noted thereafter. George Orwell, for instance, writing many years later in *Down and Out in Paris and London* (1933), observed 'Twenty-five or thirty years ago . . . the "rhyming slang" was all the rage in London. In the "rhyming slang" everything was named by something rhyming with it—a "hit or miss" for a kiss, "plates of meat" for feet, etc. It was so common that it was even reproduced in novels; now it is almost extinct. Perhaps all the words I have mentioned above will have vanished in another twenty years.' But his prediction has proved excessively pessimistic. Quite the reverse has happened. At the beginning of the 21st century new rhyming slang is still being created.

However, the body of British rhymes as they currently exist is not a homogeneous one, analogous to other elements of English vocabulary. It consists of three fairly clearly distinguishable categories. The first might most appropriately be termed 'classic rhyming slang'. This consists of a comparatively limited set of items, many of them dating back to the 19th century, which most British English-speakers are more-or-less vaguely aware of, and which they would almost certainly select from if asked to give an example of rhyming slang, but which are no longer fully 'live' components of people's vocabulary—if they do get used, it's in, so to speak, quotation marks. *Apples and pears* for 'stairs' is the one that generally pops up first when the 'rhyming slang' button is pushed, but it has many fellow usual suspects: *Adam and Eve* 'believe', *dicky dirt* 'shirt', *frog and toad* 'road', *Lucy Locket* 'pocket', *tea leaf* 'thief', *trouble and strife* 'wife', *whistle and flute* 'suit', and so on. These are the museum pieces of 'Cockney' rhyming slang, words that exist on a different plane from the rest of the English lexicon—as objects in themselves rather than as elements in a communication system. And as such they underpin the character of rhyming slang as a whole—as the product not of unconscious evolution but of deliberate creation.

The middle ground of current rhyming slang is occupied by items, of varying degrees of antiquity, which are still plugged into the living language, albeit in a slightly odd and restricted way. In some cases their currency may be due to preservation in a specific environment (for example, the bingo caller's *clickety-click* for 'sixty-six'), or to revival in a particular set of circumstances (as with *currant bun*, a long-standing rhyme for 'sun' which took on a new lease of life with the appearance of the *Sun* newspaper towards the end of the 20th century). But as a generalization, the active users of rhymes such as *boat race* 'face', *Brahms and Liszt* 'pissed', *dog and bone* 'phone', *elephant's trunk* 'drunk', *jam jar* 'car', *la-di-da* 'cigar', *mince pies* 'eyes', *mutt and jeff* 'deaf', and *porky pies* 'lies' are the inheritors of, or see themselves as the inheritors of, the working-class London speech community out of which rhyming slang arose (the linguistic 'dressing down' partly responsible for so-called Estuary English has rhymes in its baggage). However—thanks in large measure to the (often exaggerated or caricatured) use of these and other similar rhymes in television dramas and comedies featuring 'Cockney' life, such as *Minder* and *Only Fools and Horses*, with the occasional support of films such as *The Limey* and *Lock, Stock, and Two Smoking Barrels*—many of these items have become fixtures in at least the passive vocabulary of British English-speakers of all regions and classes. They are unlikely to be used, other than as a deliberate joke, but their meanings are widely understood.

Finally, at the leading edge of rhyming slang are new coinages. It continues to be a genre to which people are eager to make their own contributions, and the final decades of the 20th century showed no slow-down in the birthrate. It's rare to go to the lengths of dreaming up an entirely new sub-system of rhymes:

> What a right Shania Twain in the backside. It's certainly all gone horribly Pete Tong for cockney rhyming slang, which has a new rival—popney rhyming slang.
>
> As *The Sun* reported last week: 'Holidaymakers could fly to Gary Barlow (Monte Carlo) or have a Noel Gallagher (a week in Malaga). And don't forget your Billy Ocean (suntan lotion). After a couple of Britneys (beers) a Jay Kay (takeaway) might be SClub7 (heaven)'.
>
> The new slang, based on the names of pop people, has been devised by Paul Elliott, editor of the music website Music365.com. 'It started as a joke,' he said, 'but now everybody's using it.'
> —*Sunday Times* (2001)

But the impulse remains, apparently, a powerful one. As the above suggests, the favoured current model is a rhyme based on the name of a fashionable or well-known personality. This has always been a popular strategy (see p. xiv below), but in the 1980s and 1990s it swamped all others—whence the profusion of *Tony Blairs, Claire Rayners, Britney Spears, Jeremy Beadles, Leslie Ashes, Camilla Parker Bowles* and the rest. Anyone famous with an easily rhymable name is fair game, and liable to be potted. And anyone can pull the trigger—you need no licence to create a rhyme.

Which brings us to the vexed question of authenticity. Slang in general is resistant to the verification processes and admission procedures which it is the lexicographer's duty to apply to words seeking acceptance into the authorized lexicon of a language. In practice, that acceptance depends on proof that a given lexical innovation has spread widely enough among the speakers of a language to be regarded as a working component rather than its instigator's personal idiosyncrasy. Hitherto, and still to a large extent, 'proof' has meant written (i.e. printed) proof, and that's where slang loses out. Its opportunities to get into print, certainly when it still has the bloom of the newly coined on it, tend to be limited. Lexicographical evidence for it is often restricted to fictional representations (frequently of dubious reliability) and amateur collectors' word-lists (of which the same can be said). These difficulties apply with particular force to rhyming slang, because of its essential artificiality. Anyone can invent a rhyme, and it is a live birth—it does not have to spend months incubating, as is the usual way with new usages. If the inventor is skilful, he (and it usually is he—see below) will ensure that his listeners have enough information to interpret the coinage. But even that is not strictly necessary: by its mere creation this newcomer can claim equal status with all the other rhymes that in the past have been brought into being by the same means.

It is appropriate to ask, therefore, whether it is relevant to require these rigorous proofs of 'genuineness' of rhyming slang. It does not really set out to provide ordinary rank-and-file members of the English lexicon. Some of it survives for a long time, to be sure (albeit often in a mummified condition, as we have seen), some of it never gets beyond its first outing, some of it even, in barely recognizable cut-down form, turns into 'ordinary' English words (see p. xvi below). But it is all really part of a giant ongoing word-game, whose product is much more droll artefact than linguists' lexeme. The rhymes recorded in this collection, therefore, have not had their credentials minutely vetted. If chance has preserved them, whether from the 19th century or from last year, they may be included here. It is entirely possible that the odd rhyme may even be the conscious or unconscious invention of the person who 'recorded' it—but, in this field at least, a lexicographer's inventions are no less authentic than anyone else's.

Who, though, have been the regular players of the game over the decades? Who is your prototypical rhyming slangster? A study of the rhymes themselves quickly makes one thing clear: this has traditionally been a very male-dominated club. Nearly twenty rhyming synonyms for *wife*, for instance, as against just one for *husband*, cannot be entirely a coincidence. And look at the rhymes that have been coined for various types of clothing: wardrobe-fuls for the likes of shirts, trousers, jackets, waistcoats, and ties, but dresses, frocks, and knickers get a very raw deal. This was very much the patois of the market stalls, of the streets in which they were set up, of the pubs that lined the streets, an open-air vocabulary rather than a domestic one, and in the 19th century and for much of the 20th that meant largely a men's vocabulary. It took hold in other male-only environments, such as the army, prison, and, in Australia, sheep-shearing gangs. That restriction has in theory been lifted in these enlightened days, but women have yet to demonstrate an irresisible urge to join in.

So far we have looked at rhyming slang in the context of London speech, but the stereotypical (British) view that it is a strictly 'Cockney' phenomenon is far from being accurate. It is found in other parts of the British Isles, and it has spread around the world to other English-speaking communities. Australia took to it with particular enthusiasm. At first it adopted British usages (their arrival was first reported in 1898), but over the course of the 20th century the denizens of Aussie pubs, shearing sheds, racecourse betting rings, etc. concocted an impressive rhyming vocabulary of their own: *Cobar shower* 'flower', *Dorothy Dix* 'six' (in cricket), *Edgar Britts* 'shits' (i.e. diarrhoea), *Joe Blake* 'snake', *mud and ooze* 'booze', *sausage roll* 'goal', etc. Some of their coinages (e.g. *septic tank* 'Yank') have spread beyond Australia. The fortunes of Australian rhyming slang have broadly mirrored those of British, so that at the beginning of the 21st century, most old-time rhymes are museum pieces, and any new creation is likely to be based on a well-known name (*Barry Crocker* 'shocker', *Stuart Diver* 'survivor'). New Zealand has adopted a few Australian rhymes, but rhyming slang has never been such a big deal there.

Nor is rhyming slang by any means unknown in the USA, although it has never caught on there in a big way. It gained something of a toehold in the early part of the 20th century, along with, in some quarters, the reputation of an import from Australia (an alternative name for it was 'Australian slang'). The occasional writer took to it, to enliven flagging prose (notably the cartoonist and sportswriter T. A. 'Tad' Dorgan (1877–1929), who had a certain partiality to it). A small cache of American rhymes was thus built up, but their range was always extremely restricted and their hold on life tenuous, and at the beginning of the 21st century it is fair to say that very few Americans have even heard of rhyming slang, let alone use it.

It is time to look more closely at the nuts and bolts of rhyming slang. How is it constituted? The prototypical rhyme is a binomial phrase joined by *and*, the second element being a more or less close phonological match with the word rhymed. A good proportion of 'classic' rhyming slang follows this pattern: *apples and pears* 'stairs', *trouble and strife* 'wife', and so on. It continued to be a powerful model throughout most of the 20th century, producing the likes of *bacon and eggs* 'legs', *Brahms and Liszt* 'pissed', *far and near* 'beer', and *mutt and jeff* 'deaf', but in the latter part of the century its popularity went into a decline. Occasionally the initial element of the pair can consist of more than one word: *hop it and scram* 'ham', *old iron and brass* 'grass'.

There are alternative conjunctives to *and*, notably *of*: *field of wheat* 'street', *loaf of bread* 'head', also 'dead', *plates of meat* 'feet', *pot of honey* 'money'. Also sometimes encountered is *on*: *boys on ice* 'lice'.

However, of equal antiquity, and equally influential as a model, is the simple two-part phrase. This may consist of a noun plus noun: *boat race* 'face', *daisy roots* 'boots', *iron hoof* 'poof', *jam jar* 'car', *taxi rank* 'wank'; of a possessive noun plus noun: *butcher's hook* 'look', *elephant's trunk* 'drunk', *housewives' choice* 'voice', *miller's daughter* 'water', *pig's ear* 'beer'; or of an adjective plus noun: *brown bread* 'dead', *charming wife* 'knife', *flowery dell* 'cell', *hollow log* 'dog', *sunny south* 'mouth'. The majority exploit established collocations (*boat race, brown bread, jam jar*, etc.), but new combinations are not ruled out (e.g. *lion's lair* 'chair').

A perennially popular subcategory of the two-part phrase is proper names. They may be geographical names: *Hong Kong* 'pong', *Hyde Park* 'nark' (i.e. an informer), *River Lea* 'tea', also 'sea'; names of firms or institutions: *Barclay's Bank* 'wank', *D'Oyly Carte* 'fart'; names of products: *Mars bar* 'scar', *Maxwell House* 'mouse', *PG Tips* 'lips'; names of cars: *Hillman Hunter* 'punter', *Morris Minor* 'shiner' (i.e. a black eye); names of football clubs: *Bristol Cities* 'titties', *Plymouth Argyll* 'file', *Queens Park Rangers* 'strangers'; and so on and on and on.

They may be relatives: *Auntie Nellie* 'belly', *Uncle Dick* 'sick'; or invented personal names: *Billy Button* 'mutton', *Dicky Lee* 'tea', *Jimmy Riddle* 'piddle'. But overwhelmingly the favourite is the personal names of well-known individuals. The preference goes back to the early days of rhyming slang, when music-hall stars were popular targets: *Gertie Gitana* 'banana', *Harry Lauder* 'warder', *Jenny Hill* 'pill'. As the 20th century progressed, the public appetite moved on to film stars: *Betty Grable* 'table', *Diana Dors* 'drawers', *Errol Flynn* 'chin', *Gregory Peck* 'cheque', also 'neck', *Mae West* 'breast'; variety and radio performers: *Bob Hope* 'dope', *Danny La Rue* 'blue', *Gert and Daisy* 'lazy', *Jimmy Young* 'bung' (i.e. a bribe), also 'tongue'; sporting heroes, mainly boxers, footballers, and jockeys, but with a smattering of other sports represented: *Charlie Smirke* 'berk', *Denis Law* 'saw', *Gene Tunney* 'money', *Len Hutton* 'button'; and popular singing stars: *Marty Wilde* 'mild', *Ruby Murray* 'curry', *Tommy Steele* 'eel', *Vera Lynn* 'chin', also 'gin'. By the end of the century this had become the most widely used resource for creating new rhymes, and names were being grabbed from all areas of popular culture: *Alan Whickers* 'knickers', *Britney Spears* 'beers', *Camilla Parker Bowles* 'Rolls', *Claire Rayners* 'trainers', *Emma Freuds* 'haemorrhoids', *Gary Glitter* 'bitter', also 'shitter' (i.e. anus), *Melvyn Bragg* 'shag', *Selina Scott* 'spot', *Steffi Graf* 'laugh' (note the readiness to add a 'plural' *s* when the rhyme demands it).

Though it is by some way the commonest model, not all rhyming slang follows this two-part pattern. Many rhymes are individual words. Some of these are compounds whose bipartite status is disguised by their being written with a hyphen or as one word: *hearthrug* 'bedbug', also 'mug', *taxicabs* 'crabs' (i.e. body lice) (resourceful rhymesters can make the first element rhyme as well as the second: *jelly-bone* 'telephone'). But there is no shortage of genuinely polysyllabic rhymes, which fit in perfectly well with the stress pattern of multi-word compounds: *cocoa* 'say so', *joanna* 'piano', *paraffin* 'gin', *saveloy* 'boy'. Single-syllable rhymes, on the other hand, are vanishingly rare and of dubious status (see *hot beef* at CRIME AND PUNISHMENT and *kick* at MONEY AND COMMERCE).

Another stratagem occasionally encountered is rhyming on an entire clause, typically only three or four words long. Many of them are well-established idioms or even semi-quotations: *kiss me hardy* 'Bacardi', *sit beside her* 'spider', *stand at ease* 'cheese', also 'fleas', *tickle your fancy* 'nancy' (i.e. homosexual); but arbitrary or ad hoc combinations serve the purpose just as well: *I'm so frisky* 'whisky', *lay me in the gutter* 'butter', *open the door* 'forty-four'.

A notable feature of rhyming-slang usage is that the final element or elements of the rhyme tends to be omitted. Thus *Barry Crocker* 'shocker' becomes *Barry*, *deuce and ace* 'face' becomes *deuce*, *elephant's trunk* 'drunk' becomes *elephant's*, and so on. It is common for such abbreviations to overtake their full forms in frequency: *bristols* 'titties' for *Bristol Cities*, *iron* 'poof' for *iron hoof*, *orchestras* 'balls' for *orchestra stalls*, etc. And for many of them, their origin becomes so obscured over the course of time that probably few of their users realize that they started out as rhymes: *cobblers* 'nonsense', from *cobblers' awls* 'balls'; *dogs* 'feet', from *dogs' meat*; *rammies* 'trousers', from *round the houses*; *tod* (as in *on one's tod* 'alone'), from *Tod Sloan* 'alone', etc. If the curtailed version establishes itself securely enough, it in turn becomes fair game for a rhyme, as with *Lenny the Lion*, rhyming slang for *iron* 'poof'.

The effect of this process is to sever any link with the original rhymed word, but it should not be taken as evidence of a desire to intensify any supposed mystificatory properties of rhyming slang. Most rhymes are comparatively long, and are subject to a similar sort of morphological economizing as produced, for instance, *chimp* from *chimpanzee*, *pram* from *perambulator*, and *regs* from *regulations*. Nor is the procedure by any means uniform. Many rhymes escape curtailment, and the reasons for this are not entirely clear. Avoidance of potential ambiguity may play a part in some cases ('Some of the phrases cannot be cut. For example, there are several that have the same first word, but widely different meanings: it is impossible to say "Uncle" without giving his name, for Uncle Ned is not Uncle Willie', Julian Franklyn, *A Dictionary of Rhyming Slang* (1960)); but that does not explain why *horse and trough* 'cough' can be just *horse* but *horse and trap* 'clap' (i.e. gonorrhoea) cannot.

For a 150-year-old, rhyming slang is in remarkably good health. Its old favourites are still cherished (though few of us go to the lengths of Mike Coles, an East London religious education teacher, who in 2000 produced a rhyming slang version of St Mark's Gospel: 'Jesus took the Uncle Fred (bread) and the Lillian Gish (fish) and fed it to the 5,000'). And new players are constantly taking up the game of inventing fresh rhymes (and posting them on the Internet). It's just an amusing linguistic sideshow these days, but one which promises to run and run for some time yet.

This book is arranged in thematic chapters, not in alphabetical order, to enable readers to get a more coherent picture of the development and range of rhyming slang as it has been applied to various aspects of life. Those wishing to look up a particular rhyme can consult the index at the end of the book.

An enterprise such as this takes an author into several areas of ignorance, and my gratitude is due to many people for their guidance, notably to Bruce Moore of the Australian National Dictionary Centre, Australian National University; to Professor Kate Burridge of La Trobe University, Australia and her listeners on the Evening Show on ABC radio; to Professor Jean Aitchison and Dr Diana Lewis of Worcester College, Oxford; to Iain Cook of Arsenal Football Club; to Harold

Alderman; to the staff of Westminster Reference Library, Surrey University Library, and the library of Cecil Sharp House; and to members of the publishing and editorial staff of Oxford University Press, including Alysoun Owen, Helen Cox, and in particular Elizabeth Knowles, unfailingly resourceful tracker down of lexical solutions. Any lapses remaining are solely the author's responsibility.

People and the Human Condition

Rhyming slangsters have evolved a rich vocabulary for referring to their fellow creatures, but it's in the nature of slang that much of it should reflect the darker side of human nature. There are neutral terms and cosy colloquialisms, to be sure, but it's easier to find rhymes suggestive of unpleasantness (even if they're used playfully), and where women are the subjects, sexual attractiveness is usually on the agenda.

But to begin at the beginning:

Life

fork and knife A late 19th-century rhyme. Mainly used in various idiomatic expressions (e.g. 'not on your fork and knife!').

struggle and strife A heartfelt existentialist encapsulation of its referent. An alternative formulation, equally fatalistic, was **trouble and strife**, but that's been largely taken over by its application to *wife* (see at RELATIVES AND FRIENDS).

In the expression *not on your life* 'not at all', *life* is colloquially replaced by *Nellie*, an abbreviation of rhyming slang *Nellie Duff* 'puff, breath, life' (see *Breath* at THE BODY AND ITS PARTS).

To live

take and give A late 19th-century rhyme, applied especially to two people living together as man and wife. A reversal of the usual homespun formula for a happy marriage, but the message remains the same.

A survivor

Stuart Diver An Australian rhyme immortalizing (no doubt very temporarily) the fortunate 21-year-old ski instructor who survived a landslide at the New South Wales ski resort of Thredbo in 1997, in which eighteen other people were killed:

> Thredbo hero Stuart Diver's name has become rhyming slang for 'survivor'.
> —*Herald Sun* (2001)

People

spire and steeple An Australian rhyme, faintly recalling the verse 'There's the church and there's the steeple, Open the doors and there's the people', recited as an accompaniment to illustrative finger and hand movements.

Women

The word *woman* itself is not an easy rhyme, and anyway it's a little stiff and starchy on its own to attract rhyming slangsters' attention. Only when it turns into *old woman* 'one's wife or mother' do they make the effort—and even then, there's a sense of desperation about the *pudding*-rhymes they've come up with (see *gooseberry pudding* and *old grabbem pudden* at RELATIVES AND FRIENDS).

There are various colloquial alternatives, but—surprise, surprise!—they almost all seem to refer, implicitly or explicitly, to women of an age likely to attract male attention. Rhyming slang is a man's world.

The leading contender is *girl*, which in rhymeland generally connotes someone beyond school age. *Pearl* has sentimental appeal as a rhyming partner, and has produced **ivory pearl** (in use between the 1930s and the 1960s); **mother-of-pearl** (bucking the trend, this slots into *old girl* 'one's wife', so the conventional shortening to **mother** is not as bizarre as it might seem—British working-class men often referring to their wives in the past as 'mother' or 'mum'); and **ocean pearl** (back to nubility—a late 19th-century rhyme which generally related to girlfriends).

In the 19th century *girl* would quite commonly have been pronounced /gal/ (or more likely /gaw/ in 'Cockney' London), which inspired the rhymes **Bob my pal** (alternatively **Rob my pal**), emphasizing the 'girlfriend' aspect, and **pall mall**, after the street in central London.

The winsome **ribbon and curl** is generally reserved for female children, but with the curious **wind do twirl** (dating from the mid 19th century) we're decidedly back with grown-up 'girls'. Undoubtedly the most successful *girl*-rhyme, though, has been **twist and twirl**, first recorded in Australia in 1924 but widely used subsequently in American and British English. It often has a derogatory tinge, perhaps suggested by the 'twists' of female deception, or indeed the idea (as suggested by Ray Puxley in his *Cockney Rabbit* (1992)) of women 'twisting' men round their little fingers. It's often shortened to **twist**:

> I hate to see it happen to a pretty little twist like Fern.
> —Ross Macdonald (1953), in Hillary Waugh *Merchants of Menace* (1969)
> I'm just as good as any of those Pittsburgh twist-and-twirls.
> —Herbert Gold *The man who was not with It* (1956)

A popular colloquial synonym in the mid- to late 20th century was *bird*. **Lemon curd** was tried out for the role but never really caught on, leaving the field to **Richard the Third**. It's universally reduced to **Richard**, first recorded in 1950:

> I was just sleeping at this Richard's place during the day. . . I didn't know she was brassing.
> —G. F. Newman *Sir, You Bastard* (1970)

> I had arranged to meet a richard, but as you're sleeping on the spare bed, which happens to be the sofa, she's not too keen on you clocking the action.
> —Leon Griffith *Minder* (1981)

The Australian version is *sheila*, which is widely rhymed:

Charlie Wheeler Taken from the name of the painter Charles Wheeler (1881–1977), who specialized in female nudes. First recorded in 1942, and generally shortened to **charlie**:

> 'What do you mean by "Charlie"?' 'Your "Charlie",' repeated Max. 'Your canary.' 'Canary?' 'Ay, don't you speak English? Your sheila.'
> —Lawson Glassop *Lucky Palmer* (1949)

> The joint jumps every night, the pubs make a fortune, the charlie-wheelers come in in droves, and the Docs work overtime tryin' to keep the VD rate down.
> —D. O'Grady *A Bottle of Sandwiches* (1968)

> A little charlie from the match factory and her mother.
> —*Kings Cross Whisper* (Sydney) (1973)

potato peeler Almost always unchivalrously shortened to **potato**, first recorded in 1959:

> Even the potater, I'd given her a fiver for herself, and I didn't even want her garters for it.
> —D'Arcy Niland *Pairs and Loners* (1966)

> If I don't make it with a nice broad-minded potato tonight I'll give that quack a knuckle sandwich!!!
> —Barry Humphries *Bazza Pulls it Off* (1971)

two-wheeler The hint of promiscuity in the equation with a bicycle is fairly broad. Never as popular a rhyme as the two previous.

Other synonyms exploited for rhyming purposes include *miss*, which produced **cuddle and kiss** in the 1930s; the Australian *cliner* (probably an Anglicization of German *Kleine* 'little one'), which became **ocean liner**; and 19th-century underworld slang *cherry-ripe* (possibly an allusion to virginity about to be lost), which with minimum imagination was turned into **cherry-pipe**.

If the woman has incurred your displeasure, she'll slot into the category of a *cow* (rhymed as **ruck and row**, neatly suggesting your exchange of opinions with her), or even of a *bitch* (euphemized as **Miss Fitch** in the first half of the 20th century).

Men

Rhymes for *man* itself are as thin on the ground as those for *woman*. There was the vainglorious Australian **heavenly plan**, recorded from the end of the 19th century, but the only other mainstream *man*-rhyme, **pot and pan**, decidedly belongs with 'old man'—i.e. 'husband' or 'father' (see RELATIVES AND FRIENDS).

Once again, though, there's no shortage of colloquial synonyms. *Bloke* is the most frequently rhymed, but always with variations on the rather banal theme of *coke* (this is coke for burning, not for putting up the nose): **bushel of coke** (a bushel is a now disused unit of capacity, equal to eight gallons); **heap of coke** (an ancient rhyme, dating from the mid-19th century (Suppose I want to ask a pal to . . . have a game at cards with some blokes at home with me, I should say . . . 'Will you . . . have a touch of the broads with me and the other heaps of coke at my drum.' Henry Mayhew *London Labour and the London Poor* (1851)), and sometimes contracted to **heapy**); and **lump of coke** (of similar vintage to heap of coke). *Geezer* provides some domestic variety with **ice-cream freezer** and **lemon squeezer** (usually just **lemon**), and if you want to refer to a literal 'old man', there's always *codger*, rhymed unflatteringly with **splodger**, which in the 19th century was also a term for a country bumpkin.

We now come to more acerbic territory. Exasperation breeds unkind names, and rhyming slang follows on every gradation towards the blue end of the spectrum. Its function is at least partly to turn down the volume on these insult words, to make them 'sayable' for people who wouldn't wish to use them, or in situations where their undisguised presence would create more trouble than it was worth. To begin at the (relatively) mild end of the catalogue:

Creep

Uriah Heep The implication of obsequiousness is backed up by the selection of the fawning villain of Charles Dickens's *David Copperfield* (1850).

Snide

A superannuated slang word for 'a despicable person', rhymed in the early 20th century as **Mr Hyde**—no doubt after the evil alter-ego in Robert Louis Stevenson's story 'The Strange Case of Dr Jekyll and Mr Hyde' (1886).

Nark

A largely Australian and New Zealand term for 'an irritating person', rhymed as **Noah's Ark**:

> 'Don't be a Noah's Ark, Corp.,' will go up the cry. 'Pick on someone else, can't y'.'
> —S. W. Keough *Around the Army* (1943)

Ya knows Bill, yer gettin' to be a real Noah's Ark.
—J. Alard *He who Shoots Last* (1968)

Sod

Cod is a handy and obvious rhyme: **fillet of cod** first turns up in the 1970s, but **haddock and cod** (two staples of the fish-and-chip shop) is of greater antiquity and in wide use—almost always shortened to **haddock**. Like *sod* itself, it can be deployed affectionately as well as angrily. Alternatively there's **Tommy Dodd**, also as likely to be friendly as hostile, and usable as a verb (Ray Puxley in his *Cockney Rabbit* (1992) offers the example: 'Tommy Dodd this for a game of mothers and fathers'). It dates from the 19th century, and may be an offshoot of the rhyme Tommy Dodd 'odd' (see *Odd* at GAMBLING).

Prick

There's a wealth of literal *prick*-rhymes (see *The penis* at THE BODY AND ITS PARTS) ready to follow their model in this metaphorical leap, and several have done so. **Hampton Wick** (or plain **Hampton**) and **kiss me quick** have their adherents, but the two clear favourites are **dipstick** (its rhyme status is dubious, but its popularity as an insult was cemented by its frequent use by the David Jason character Del Boy in the BBC TV sitcom *Only Fools and Horses* (1981–)) and the Australian **pogo stick**, now always shortened to **pogo**:

> 'Ready to emplane... Ready to emplane...' 'Jesus, does he think a man's deaf, bloody RAAF pogo.'
> —W. Nagle *The Odd Angry Shout* (1975)

> 'We're on road clearing again...' 'What about bloody 7 section doing it...?' 'Yeah, bloody pogos.'
> —J. J. Coe *Desperate Praise* (1982)

Fucker

The rhymes, like their model, often operate as casual synonyms for *man*, without any undue malice:

feather plucker First recorded in the 1940s. It looks like a variation on pheasant plucker, but the known chronological facts don't support that.

pheasant plucker Not so much a rhyme as a complete (and bitterly ironical) spoonerization of *pleasant fucker*. It emerged in the 1970s, as a self-conscious side-effect of an elaborate tongue-twister involving the plucking of pheasants.

Tommy Tucker A bit of a come-down for the young hero of the nursery rhyme ('Little Tommy Tucker sang for his supper'), but at least the rhyme itself is more convincing.

Twat

dollypot Rhymes for *twat* in its literal sense are based on *pot* (see *The female genitals* at **THE BODY AND ITS PARTS**), and this Australian effort from the 1920s follows suit. Its model was *dolly pot*, a goldminers' term for the receptacle in which gold-bearing quartz is crushed to extract the gold.

Turd

A strong stable of rhymes for the literal sense (see *Turd* at **IN THE LAV**), but of them only one has consistently followed its model over to the metaphorical 'despicable person': **lemon curd**.

Wanker

Casablanca Presumably from the name of the Moroccan city, but perhaps encouraged too by the cult film *Casablanca* (1942), starring Humphrey Bogart.

crown and anchor A ready-made combination, long familiar as, among other things, a pub name and the name of a type of gambling game.

J. Arthur Based on a notional J. Arthur Ranker, derived from J. Arthur Rank 'wank' (see *Masturbation* at **SEX**).

merchant banker A rhyme of the 1980s, aimed particularly at the yuppy-ish City types earning high-profile six-figure salaries.

monkey spanker A 1990s coinage, based on the vivid *spank the monkey* 'to masturbate'.

oil tanker Joined in the late 1980s by the more specific but short-lived **Kuwaiti tanker**.

Cunt

Unlike the above, *cunt* is a unisex insult, but it's included here for convenience. It's liberally rhymed in its original anatomical sense (see *The female genitals* at **THE BODY AND ITS PARTS**), but the only two of these rhymes to have made a significant metaphorical crossover have, in their abbreviated form, become so familiar in their figurative guise that their original application has virtually been forgotten, and in the process their meaning has softened to 'fool' (see *berk* and *Charlie* at **SENSE AND NONSENSE**). As far as can be discerned from the evidence, the other *cunt* insult rhymes were freshly minted for the purpose:

eyes front From the military command, suggesting an origin in the services.

Grannie Grunt Presumably inspired by the earlier, and literal, **grumble and grunt** (see *The female genitals* at **THE BODY AND ITS PARTS**).

National Front From the name of a much despised right-wing extremist organization founded in Britain in 1967.

Sir Anthony Blunt From the name of the British art expert and traitor Anthony Blunt (1907–83), once, as Sir Anthony, surveyor of the Queen's pictures, but stripped of his title after it was revealed that he had been a Russian spy. Generally cropped to **Sir Anthony**.

See also *Joe Hunt* at SENSE AND NONSENSE.

And finally, if the contempt or ridicule arises from someone's outlandish appearance, they can be dismissed as a *sight*—or, in rhyme, a **flash of light**.

Children

In rhymeland, children are *kids*, and the great majority of their rhymes are based on *lids*. **Dustbin lids** and **teapot lids** have had their takers, but there are three clear winners: **saucepan lids**, first recorded in 1961 (The black kids went past with eyes wide. 'Let go Ernesto,' I said. 'You're scaring the saucepan-lids.' John Milne *Alive and Kicking* (1998)), and the Australian **tin lid**, first recorded in 1905 (He's been a bash artist ever since he was a tin lid. S. Gore *Holy Smoke* (1968)), and **billy lid** ('Not much of a holiday for your wife, either. Taking the kids.' 'I thought of that,' he said. 'I suggested I take the billy lids up to Forster, and let her stay home.' J. O'Grady *Survival in the Doghouse* (1973); 'Off you go, billy lids,' he smiled encouragingly. 'Be good at school and don't do anything I wouldn't do.' T. Underwood *In the Middle of Nowhere* (1998)). A popular British alternative is **God forbid**, first recorded in 1909, and often given the genuine 'Cockney' touch with the spelling **Gawd forbid** (You take 'Er Ladyship and the Gawd-ferbid to the party. Margery Allingham *The Beckoning Lady* (1955)): J. Redding Ware identified the rationale behind the rhyme in his *Passing English of the Victorian Era* (1909): '*God-forbids*, kids—a cynical mode of describing children by poor men who dread a long family.' And for particularly obnoxious children, there's *brat*, rhymed with **Jack Sprat**, the fat-hating nursery-rhyme character.

Most *girl*-rhymes actually refer to women (for an exception see *ribbon and curl* at WOMEN), but *boy* is different. The metaphorical application to gang members spawned **san toys** (see *Gang members* at CRIME AND PUNISHMENT), but apart from that the accent is firmly on the parents' pride and joy—which figures strongly in the rhymes:

hipsy hoy A curiosity, perhaps partly inspired by *hobbledehoy*, perhaps simply a nonsense rhyme.

Mark Foy An Australian rhyme, first recorded in the 1940s, and apparently based on the name of a Sydney department store.

mother's joy Another Australian rhyme, from around the turn of the 20th century. Who said Aussies were unsentimental?

pride and joy Current from the 1930s in Britain, the US, and Australia.

Rob Roy From the name of the Scottish outlaw Rob Roy McGregor (1671–1734), brought to a wider audience by Walter Scott's novel *Rob Roy* (1818). A mid-19th-century rhyme which had died out before the Second World War.

saveloy A rhyme based on the name of a type of spicy smoked sausage popular with Londoners. Mainly used literally, but also sometimes applied in the plural to criminal gang members.

Baby

basin of gravy A slightly approximate rhyme, but as it's usually shortened to **basin**, it doesn't really matter.

Names and Titles

A very select handful of forenames (male) have been done the honour of a rhyme: *Bill* transformed into **pitch and fill** (a rhyme from the mid-19th century, when the name was commoner than it later became); *Bob* produced **kettle and hob**, usually reduced to plain **kettle**; and *Sidney* became **steak and kidney**, or **steak** for short.

Patriotic British and Commonwealth rhyming slangsters have seen to it that the royal family are not without their rhymes, either:

King

gold ring Largely in abeyance in Britain in the second half of the 20th century.

Prince

pear and quince An Australian rhyme.

Queen

baked bean A rhyme introduced especially for Queen Elizabeth II.

seldom seen The evidence suggests a 20th-century coinage, although it would certainly have been appropriate for Queen Victoria, notorious for her reluctance to appear in public.

Solitude

On your own

The rhymes, among them some of the most celebrated in the rhyming slang canon, all slot into the *on your* formula, and that's how they're presented here:

on your Darby and Joan From the name of the archetypal old married couple, who first put in an appearance in an 18th-century ballad. Usually just **on your Darby** (perhaps symbolic of the solitude of widowerhood).

on your Jack Jones The (approximate) rhyme with *own* came into use during the First World War. As far as is known, Jack Jones is just a convenient made-up name. The abbreviated **on your jack** is first recorded in 1931:

> Michael went off on his jack an' left me wid de bloody baby.
> —George Orwell *A Clergyman's Daughter* (1935)

> You're on your Jack Jones. Ben's deserted you.
> —Alfred Draper *The Death Penalty* (1972)

on your Pat Malone Originally Australian (it's first recorded in 1908), but it's since spread to other varieties of English. Often shortened to **on your pat**. The variant **on your Jack Malone** is sometimes encountered, perhaps under the influence of the previous rhyme:

> On your pat now, aren't you? When did the old man go away?
> —*Bulletin* (Sydney) (1930)

> First the missus died, then a coupla months later he went, and I was left on me pat malone.
> —Jon Cleary *The Sundowners* (1952)

> Standing there all on his Pat Malone.
> —Colin MacInnes *Absolute Beginners* (1959)

> Pat malone again! Cripes I am cheesed.
> —*Private Eye* (1971)

> And was John Snow the most ferocious bowler he faced?. . . 'I had probably had as much trouble as anyone against him when we lost the Ashes in 1970–71, but I was not on my Pat Malone,' he said.
> —*Australian* (Sydney) (1981)

on your tod An abbreviation which has gone from strength to strength while the rhyme it was originally based on, **on your Tod Sloan**, has virtually disappeared. It commemorates the American jockey Tod Sloan (1874–1933), and is first recorded around the time of his death:

> 'Are you on your tod?' I gathered that she was asking me if I was on my own.
> —Philip Allingham *Cheapjack* (1934)

> Frequent visits to town on your Tod Sloan—no need to account for your doings. Leave her to keep the home fires burning.
> —John Wain *A Travelling Woman* (1959)

> Maybe they don't want your company. . . Never seen you on your tod before.
> —G. Gaunt *Incomer* (1981)

A stranger

Glasgow Ranger From the name of the Scottish football club Glasgow

Rangers. Mainly an underworld rhyme, used by look-outs for street conmen and dodgy traders as a warning when 'strangers' (i.e. police) are approaching.

Queens Park Ranger From the name of the West London football club Queens Park Rangers, and first recorded in the 1960s. A more general rhyme than the above, applied to any unfamiliar person.

The Body and its Parts

If there's one thing above all else that really gets a rhyming slangster rhyming it's his body (most of them are male) or for preference a female body. Rhymes for various parts of the human anatomy far outnumber those in any other area of experience or field of activity.

There's nothing peculiar to rhyming slang about that—our arms and legs, heads and feet, guts and bottoms have always attracted a rich array of slang synonyms of all types. They are intimate and familiar parts of ourselves, and we seem to like to give them comfortable, comforting names that symbolize our attachment to them. And intimacy applies in spades to the genitalia and other naughty bits, where the exigencies of taboo mean that slang has the cover-up role of euphemism to perform. That's a role for which rhyming slang, with its baffling camouflage, its displacement of term from referent, is ideally suited. And so the manic naming-fest feeds off itself: if there are a dozen or more common slang synonyms for *penis* in everyday use, it only needs a few of them to attract a few rhymes for our *penis*-lexicon to expand to at least twice its former size.

The Body

In Britain, the implication of the rhymes is decidedly female and sexually alluring: **hot toddy**, exploiting the name of the comforting bed-time drink, and the more recent **Big Ears and Noddy**, based on the two Toyland characters created by the British children's author Enid Blyton (usually shortened to **Big Ears**, which is a prime example of the power of rhyming slang to disguise with a knowing wink—'Clock the Big Ears on her!'). In America, however, the body is dead, usually as a result of foul play: **Tom Noddy**, recorded in the mid-20th century, is a reworking of an old dialect name for 'a vacant-headed person'.

Bones

sticks and stones The inspiration was presumably the old retort to insults, 'Sticks and stones may break my bones, but words will never hurt me'.

Blood

Roy Hudd Reported on the basis of one sighting by Ray Puxley in his *Cockney*

Rabbit (1992), but apparently correctly interpreted by its hearers on that occasion. A tribute to the English comedian Roy Hudd (1936–).

In the past, and still to some extent in the boxing game, blood has gone under the slang name *claret* (after the colour of red Bordeaux wine). In rhyming slang that becomes **boiled beef and carrot** (from the title of a 'Cockney' comic song popularized by Harry Champion, which also deployed the Derby Kelly rhyme—see THE BELLY below) or **eighteen carat** (a measurement of the purity of gold, also used metaphorically to denote excellence).

Breath

The appropriate if not very imaginative rhyme **life and death** stands in for *breath*, but much more noteworthy is **Nellie Duff**, rhyming with *puff*, a humorous alternative to *breath*. This appears to date from at least the early 1930s, but there's no documented evidence for it. We can only deduce its existence from its later use, in reduced form (first recorded in 1941) in the expression *not on your Nellie* 'not at all', where its base-word *puff* is being used in the metaphorical sense 'life'.

See also *Bad breath* at IN THE LAV.

Muscles

greens and brussels Greens (assorted plants of the cabbage family) and brussels sprouts are founder-members of the London rhymer's stereotypical meat and two veg, and 'eating your greens' is the traditional formula for building up your muscles.

Skin

thick and thin An Australian rhyme—Australians being particularly conscious of the harmful effects of the sun on the skin.

A mole

Nat King Cole Commemorating the African-American popular singer and pianist Nat 'King' Cole (1919–65), and no doubt inspired, in less politically correct times, by the colour of his skin.

Above the Neck

Hair

Far and away the most successful *hair*-rhyme has been **Barnet Fair**, whose shortened form **barnet** has long since cut itself off from its rhyming roots and become an ordinary (if now rather dated) British slang synonym for *hair*:

> As she walked along the street With her little 'plates of meat', And the summer sunshine falling On her golden 'Barnet Fair'.
> —*Referee* (1887)

> They send you to a doss house, so that you can get lice in your barnet.
> —Frank Norman *The Guntz* (1962)

First recorded in the 1850s, it's a reference to a fair for the buying and selling of horses and other livestock which has been held in September in High Barnet, a town on the Great North Road out of London (now a London borough), since the Middle Ages.

The similarly inspired Australian version is **Dublin Fair**. And a distortion of Barnet Fair (logical, but evidently owing to a misunderstanding of the original) was responsible for the American **bonny fair**, recorded in the 1940s.

So 'de-rhymed' and assimilated has barnet become that in the 1970s it began to attract its own rhyme: **Alf Garnett**, after the cantankerously outspoken (and ironically bald) Cockney paterfamilias in Johnny Speight's BBC television sitcom *Till Death Us Do Part*.

Some other *hair*-rhymes:

Fanny Blair Recorded in the mid-19th century, but by the 20th it seems to have largely died out. No known lady of that name is referred to: ostensibly it was a general rhyme, but given the choice of first name, pubic hair may have been specifically in mind.

Fred Astaire From the name of the sleekly coiffeured US dancer and film star Fred Astaire (1899–1987). It refers not to hair in general, but to an individual hair (as found on someone's collar, in the soup, etc.). Often shortened to **Fred**.

here and there An Australian rhyme, first recorded in the 1830s.

The head

The expression *use your loaf*, meaning 'be sensible, think carefully' (first recorded in 1938), has become so ingrained in colloquial English that the majority of its users are probably no longer aware that **loaf** in that context is short for **loaf of bread**, which in turn is rhyming slang for *head*. The rhyme dates back at least to the late 19th century, but over a hundred years on it's become so closely tied to that one expression that it's rare to hear it used independently:

> *Loaf*, head, e.g., 'Duck your loaf–*i.e.*, keep your head below the parapet'.
> —Fraser & Gibbons *Soldier & Sailor Words* (1925)

> Bloody seconds counted in a job like this. You certainly had to use your loaf.
> —James Curtis *They Drive by Night* (1938)

> You want to use your bloody loaf, Stubbs, or we'll never win this war the way you're carrying on.
> —Brian Aldiss *A Soldier Erect* (1971)

In the 19th and early 20th centuries, though, loaf was a sufficiently common literal synonym for *head* that it came to be elaborated to *twopenny loaf*, which was itself then shortened to *twopenny*—a usage current into the 1930s, and a remarkable testimony to the ability of slang to wriggle from one camouflage to another.

Other rhymes based on the *bread* theme have included **crust of bread** (often shortened to **crust** and used metaphorically, like loaf, to denote 'common sense'), **lump of bread**, and **penn'orth of bread**.

A popular alternative to *bread* has been *lead*, with its useful connotations of denseness: **ball of lead** (in use around the the First World War period), **lump of lead**, and **pound of lead** (another soldiers' favourite, frequent enough to be shortened to **pound**: We old hands often used to remark that when we did get hit it would either be a bullet through the pound or stop a five-point-nine all on our own. Frank Richards *Old Soldiers never Die* (1933)).

Head offers yet further opportunities for the rhymester:

alive or dead Reported from the late 19th century and the early part of the 20th, but if it was a question, the answer now lies in the second element.

Judge Dredd A 1990s coinage, featuring the futuristic lawgiver who first saw the light of day in the 1970s in the British sci-fi comic *2000 AD*.

kelly ned An Australian rhyme, based on a transposition of the names of the outlaw Ned Kelly (see *Ned Kelly* at **THE BELLY**).

ruby red A rhyme with some currency in the first quarter of the 20th century.

Uncle Ned A rhyme which enjoyed some success in the middle of the 20th century, but never managed to supplant its original referent, *bed* (see *Bed* at **HOUSEHOLD MATTERS**):

> I have spent an hour fixing the big, loose curls on top of my Uncle Ned.
> —*Listener* (1964)

In colloquial Australian English, the head is the *thinkbox*, occasionally rhymed as **bundle of socks**.

The brain

watch and chain A rhyme dating from the early part of the 20th century, when watches still had chains. Usually used metaphorically, in relation to intelligence, rather than of the physical brain, and shortening to **watch** allows plenty of scope for word-play of the 'His watch is a bit slow' variety.

The face

Since the middle of the 20th century **boat race** has held number one spot in rhyming slangsters' affections when it comes to the face. Calling on the associations of the annual Oxford and Cambridge boat race—London's river, traditional English toffs' pageantry taken to their hearts by the lower orders, and so on—it has established its niche in 'Cockney' patois, more than common enough to be abbreviated to **boat**:

> 'A friend tells you she's going to a Botox [a substance for removing lines from the skin] party. What is she talking about?' 'It's something to do with her boat race.'
> —*Times* (2001)

> I don't want to see your boat, or his, down here again.
> —George Day *Minder* (1981)

Before that, however, the field was held by **Chevy Chase**, an ancient rhyme that goes back at least to the middle of the 19th century. It was originally the name of a place, the site of a skirmish on the Anglo-Scottish border in the 17th century, which became widely known as the subject of a popular ballad:

> After listening for a while her chevy-chase gets serious looks.
> —J. Redding Ware *Passing English of the Victorian Era* (1909)

> You wouldn't have turned up here with that what's-going-on-here look slapped all over your Chevy Chase.
> —*Lock, Stock, and Two Smoking Barrels* (1998)

It was usually shortened to **chevy**, widely pronounced /ˈtʃɪvi/ and accordingly spelt **chivvy** (first recorded in 1889):

> *c.*1886. Music Hall Song. 'Aint he got an artful chevy.'
> —Farmer & Henley *Slang and its Analogues* (1890)

> Just as if the Egyptians had carved your dial in stone, Hawley, just as if your hard chivvy was what it looks like—a stone.
> —J. B. Cooper *Coo-oo-ee* (1916)

> I can't keep this look of modest pride on my chivvy forever.
> —Angus Wilson *The Middle Age of Mrs. Eliot* (1958)

Beyond these two market leaders, there has been a modest demand for 'fish'-rhymes, perhaps subconsciously invoking the insult *fish-face*: **fillet of plaice** and **kipper and plaice** from the sea, with **roach and dace** representing the coarse-fishing contingent.

Some other alternatives:

cherry ace A Second World War rhyme, which had largely died out by the late 1950s.

deuce and ace First recorded in the late 19th century. Generally shortened in use to **deuce**.

glass case First recorded in 1857, but little evidence of post-19th-century use.

Jem Mace Commemorating the name of the bare-knuckle fighter Jem Mace (1831–1910), who rearranged many a face during his career.

Martin Place An Australian rhyme, from the name of a street (now a pedestrianized plaza) in central Sydney, New South Wales.

The eyes

Pies is by far rhyming slangsters' favourite *eyes*-word, and of all the combinations and variations tried out over the decades, the one that has stuck best is **mince pies**. First recorded in 1857, it became widely used in the abbreviated form **minces** (the plurality of *pies* transferred to the theoretically unpluralizable *mince*):

> And I smiled as I closed my two mince-pies.
> —*Sporting Times* (1892)

> He thinks he'll never be able t' shut his mince pies again.
> —E. Dyson *Fact'ry 'Ands* (1906)

> 'I know what's on there' said the boggie looking Solie straight in the minces.
> —Frank Norman *Bang to Rights* (1958)

> She gives me a double glinty butchers out of those sharp minces of hers.
> —*News Chronicle* (1960)

> A general look of dislike in the minces, which tremble a bit in their sockets.
> —Robin Cook *The Crust on its Uppers* (1962)

Sharing the larder with mince pies have been variously **jam pies** (a 1990s coinage, but gastronomically unconvincing); **mud pies** (an Australian contribution); **mutton pies** (a 19th-century rhyme); **pork pies** (usually, as with its more frequent referent *lies*, shortened to **porkies**); **puddings and pies** (first recorded in the 1850s, and no doubt partly inspired by the nursery rhyme 'Georgie Porgie, pudding and pie, Kissed the girls and made them cry'); **sargent's pies** (an Australian rhyme of the 1940s and 1950s, celebrating a popular brand of that Australian gastronomic icon, the meat pie, made in Sydney); and **steak-and-kidney pies**.

And as alternatives to *pies*: **lamb's fries** (an Australian rhyme, graphically suggesting a pair of bloodshot eyes with the cook's euphemism for lamb's testicles) or **Nellie Blighs** (a multi-purpose rhyme, most famously applied in Australian English to meat pies—see *Pie* at FOOD AND DRINK).

The ears

bottle of beers or **glass of beers** The latter goes back to the 19th century. Bottle of beers is more recent, perhaps reflecting the growth of commercial bottled beer in the marketplace.

fusiliers Some sporadic usage, but more commonly encountered in the singular, rhyming with *beer* (see ALCOHOL AND OTHER DRUGS).

King Lears A late 19th-century rhyme, reportedly used mainly in theatrical slang—appropriately enough for the name of a Shakespeare play. Its main modern survival seems to be in the expression *on the King Lear*, a substitution for slang *on the earhole* 'on the cadge'.

Melbourne piers or, in full, **Port Melbourne piers** An Australian rhyme, first recorded in 1942. Commemorating the pier at Port Melbourne, which sticks out into the sea (like sticky-out ears) where the Yarra River flows into Hobsons Bay.

Southend piers The Cockney answer to Melbourne piers—Southend being a traditionally popular seaside resort for Londoners on a spree, and its pier, at one and a half miles, the longest in the world.

And for those who prefer the more colloquial *lug* for 'ear', there's a rhyme to hand in **toby jug**.

The nose

Rose is a popular rhyme for *nose*, no doubt with an eye to the effect of alcohol on the colour of that proboscis: **Irish rose** (apparently a dig at Irish alcohol consumption); **ruby rose** (usually shortened to **ruby**, accentuating the message); and **Tokyo Rose** (from the *nom de guerre* of the Japanese radio propagandist of the Second World War (real name Iva Toguri D'Aquino); usually abbreviated to **Tokyo**). Australian English takes up the theme with **Lionel Rose**, after the Aboriginal boxer (1948–) who held the world bantamweight title between 1966 and 1969:

> I moved my head just in time to avoid a red-bellied snake as thick as a labourer's arm as it stuck its big boofhead out of the undergrowth dead level with my face and about six inches away from my Lionel Rose.
> —*Shimano Yearbook: Fishing Australasia* (1995)

Of the alternatives, **these and those** has enjoyed some success in Australia, and **fireman's hose** (usually reduced to **fireman's**) has a certain pictorial appropriateness, but the front runner has been **I suppose** (sometimes **suppose** for short). First recorded in the 1850s, it survived well into the 20th century:

> Wait till I powder my I-suppose and fix my Barnet Fair.
> —Holmes and Scott *Mr. Lucky* (film) (1943)

There's no shortage of slang synonyms for *nose*, and some of them have their own rhymes: *conk*, rhymed as **glass of plonk**; *hooter* (first recorded in this sense in the 1950s), which becomes **pea-shooter**; *shonker*, a word ultimately of Yiddish origin, fancifully transformed into **beezonker** (probably via a blend with *beezer*, originally US boxing slang for *nose*); *smeller*, a colloquialism from the late 17th century, given new life as **Cinderella**; and *snout*, rhymed as **salmon and trout**.

The cheek

mild and meek An Australian usage. The other rhymes for *cheek* are strictly in its metaphorical sense—see *Audacity* at BEHAVIOUR, ATTITUDES, AND EMOTIONS.

The mouth

Easily the market leader is **north and south**, first recorded in the 1850s and still going strong well into the second half of the 20th century. Sometimes reduced to **north**:

> Dust floating about in the air, which gets in your north and south.
> —Frank Norman *Bang to Rights* (1958)

> Now give your north-and-south a rest.
> —Malcolm Braly *On the Yard* (1966)

> I had one of those emissions last night—a colossal remembrance of the dream that caused it—me copping it in the north with a fortyish tough guy.
> —*The Kenneth Williams Diaries* 21 May 1967 (1993)

> A fat geezer's north opens.
> —*Lock, Stock, and Two Smoking Barrels* (1998)

It received a boost in Britain in 1960 when Tommy Steele recorded the song 'What a Mouth', with its lines 'What a mouth, what a mouth, what a north and south, Blimey what a mouth he's got!'

Variations on the compass theme include **east and south** (similar in vintage to north and south but without the staying power); **Queen of the South** (from the name of a Scottish football club); and **sunny south** (a late Victorian inspiration, perhaps from the epithet applied in the 19th century to the southern states of the US: She'd a Grecian 'I suppose', And of 'Hampstead Heath' two rows In her 'sunny south' that glistened Like two pretty strings of pearls. *Referee* (1887)).

The somewhat unconvincing **salmon and trout**, or **salmon trout**, is recorded in the 1850s, but it did not last long.

The lips

apple pips An early 20th-century rhyme, usually shortened to **apples**.

battleships The shortened form **battle** is used metaphorically in the singular to denote 'insolence' (see *Audacity* at BEHAVIOUR, ATTITUDES, AND EMOTIONS).

fish and chips Also used metaphorically in the singular to denote 'insolence' (see *Audacity* at BEHAVIOUR, ATTITUDES, AND EMOTIONS).

PG Tips From the name of a brand of tea produced by Brooke Bond. Often abbreviated to **PGs**.

The tongue

brewer's bung The tongue's role in imbibing alcohol is celebrated with this rhyme on the cork in a brewer's barrel.

brother bung From an old hyperbolic term for a fellow inn-keeper (the bung being what he used to stop up his barrels).

heart and lung An American rhyme from the 1920s.

JimmyYoung After the pop ballad singer turned radio disc jockey and chat-show host Jimmy Young (1923–), whose BBC Radio 2 *Jimmy Young Programme* (in which he extensively exercised his tongue) became a long-running hit in the latter part of the 20th century. Usually shortened to **Jimmy**.

The teeth

Hampstead Heath, and more particularly its shortened form **Hampsteads**, has established itself beyond the narrow confines of rhyming slang. First recorded in 1887, it comes from the name of the open area of high ground to the north of London:

> The rot had set in something horrible with her hampsteads and scotches [= legs].
> —Robin Cook *The Crust on its Uppers* (1962)

The abbreviation **Hampsteads** is sometimes abbreviated still further, to **hamps**.

It's far from the only heath that's been pressed into rhyming service, though. There are **Bexley Heath** (a late 19th-century rhyme, from the name of a large open heath in Kent, on the London to Dover road near the former village of Bexley, which in the 19th century gave its name to the new township of Bexleyheath—not to be confused with Old Bexley and Sidcup, the former parliamentary constituency of another *teeth*-rhyme, Edward Heath); **Blackheath** (from the district in southeast London, and useful, especially in pre-National Health Service days, for implying rampant dental decay); and **Hounslow Heath** (almost exclusively a 19th-century rhyme, commemorating an area of heathland to the west of London, once the haunt of highwaymen, now long since vanished under the tarmac of Heathrow Airport). There's also a human Heath: **Edward Heath**, or **Ted Heath**, after the British Conservative politician (1916–), Prime Minister from 1970 to 1974, noted for a shoulder-heaving silent chortle which revealed an impressive set of teeth; often shortened to **Edwards** or **Teds**. Some contribution to the rhyme may also have been made by the British bandleader Ted Heath (1900–69), but he was not especially distinguished in the dental department.

Your stereotypical Cockney pronounces *teeth* as /ti:f/, but that can be accommodated in rhyme too: **roast beef**.

In Australian and New Zealand slang, 'teeth' are *tats* (the word originally denoted 'dice'). The rhyme which grew out of that was **cricket bats**.

From time to time it may be necessary to refer to a single tooth, and rhyming slang has that covered as well: choose between **Auntie Ruth** and **General Booth** (after William Booth (1829–1912), founder and first General of the Salvation Army).

The gums

breadcrumbs Apparently a one-off coinage, recorded by Ray Puxley in his *Cockney Rabbit* (1992).

currants and plums A recycling of a now obsolete rhyme for *threepence* (see MONEY AND COMMERCE), generally shortened to **currants**.

The throat

nanny goat Usually abbreviated to **nanny**.

The chin

Andy McGinn A rhyme current from the 1930s to the 1950s. Its precise inspiration is unknown, but given the context, the original Andy McGinn may well have been a boxer.

Errol Flynn A rhyme dating from the 1940s, featuring the finely chiselled and subtly dimpled chin of the Hollywood film star and rake Errol Flynn (1909–59).

Gunga Din From the name of the regimental water-carrier who is the eponymous hero of Rudyard Kipling's poem 'Gunga Din' (1892): 'Though I've belted you and flayed you, By the livin' Gawd that made you, You're a better man than I am, Gunga Din!'

thick and thin A 20th-century rhyme, recorded in American usage.

Vera Lynn An Australian rhyme from the 1940s, from the name of the popular British singer Vera Lynn (1917–), whose rendition of morale-boosting sentimental ballads helped the Allies to take it on the chin during the Second World War.

The jaw

jackdaw An ancient rhyme, first recorded in the 1850s.

A beard

Charley Sheard First recorded in the 1970s. Not based on any identifiable individual, so perhaps an ironical comment on the need for a beard to be shorn.

just as I feared Inspired by one of the best known of Edward Lear's nonsense limericks: 'There was an Old Man with a beard, Who said, "It is just as I feared!—Two Owls and a Hen, four Larks and a Wren, Have all built their nests in my beard!"'. An unwieldy rhyme, usually curtailed to **just as**.

strangely weird A reflection of the suspicion in which beards are held in some quarters. Usually shortened to **strangely**.

A moustache

Both of the standard rhymes, **dot and dash** and **whip and lash** (usually abbreviated to **whip**), are probably based on the colloquial short form *tash*, rather than on *moustache* itself.

The neck

Peck is all that rhyming slangsters have come up with for *neck*. Its use for a measure of capacity (equal to about 9 litres) is now such ancient history that the rhymes based on that—**bushel and peck** and **three-quarters of a peck**—have long vanished from everyday usage. But the Hollywood film star Gregory Peck (1916–) is still familiar enough for **Gregory Peck**—or just plain **Gregory**—to remain in business.

From Shoulders to Waist

The shoulder

burn and smoulder Perhaps coined in the wake of a touch of the sun.

granite boulder A late 19th-century coinage, suggesting shoulders that are intimidatingly broad.

rock and boulder Another late 19th-century rhyme, almost always used in the plural—rocks and boulders.

An arm

Chalk Farm A common London rhyme in the late 19th century, and generally shortened to (in the plural) **chalks**. Inspired by the area of northwest London known as Chalk Farm, just to the east of Primrose Hill.

false alarm Originally an army rhyme, from the First World War period, but it enjoyed some civilian use thereafter.

fire alarm Another military rhyme, almost always used in the plural (in which context it can mean 'weapons' as well as 'upper limbs').

Warwick Farm An Australian usage, current around the middle of the 20th century. Warwick Farm is a racecourse in Sydney, New South Wales.

The wrist

oliver An Australian usage, dating from the late 19th century. In Britain, the rhyme is used for *fist* (see below).

A hand

Band has always been a popular *hand*-rhyme: there's **brass band**, in use since the early 20th century; **German band**, a relic of the days, in the 19th and early 20th centuries, when groups of strolling musicians, known as 'German bands', used to play in the streets of London and other cities (Then 'e said to the geezer, 'Stretch out your German band (hand)'. He stretched it out and blinky blonky blimey it was made well. Mike Coles *St Mark's Gospel in Rhyming Slang* (2000)); and (of completely different inspiration, and always in the plural) **Darby bands**, from the old expression *Father Darby's* (or *Derby's*) *bands*, perhaps based on the name of an unknown 16th-century usurer, and denoting the tight grip in which a money-lender held his clients.

The sands of seaside resorts popular with Londoners provide plural opportunities: **Margate Sands** and **Ramsgate Sands**, both Kentish holiday destinations. And for something rather more uplifting, in the latter part of the 19th century there was **Martin-le-Grand** (or in full **Saint Martin-le-Grand**), from the name of a street, *St Martin's le Grand*, in the City of London, to the north of St Paul's Cathedral, which itself took its name from a medieval monastery and college once on that site.

In the busy life of rhyming slangsters the *d* at the end of *hand* is sometimes forgotten, and this is catered for too, with **frying pan** (in use in the first half of the 20th century) and **Mary Ann** (applied mainly to the fists, but never widespread).

An old slang synonym for *hand*, dating back to the 18th century, is *fin*. This got the rhyming treatment as **Lincoln's Inn**, from the name of one of the London inns of court. But the begetter of a far more vigorous progeny was *forks*, 19th-century slang for 'hands', especially as used for surreptitious extractions from other people's pockets. It was rhymed as **Duke of Yorks**, which has been widely touted as the origin of *duke* 'a hand, and especially a fist used aggressively' (although a more cautious derivation might be from Romany). First recorded in the 1850s, this enjoyed a lengthy career, especially in American slang, where it is still in use, as a verb as well as as a noun (to *duke it out* is to fight with the fists). In the 19th century it was often spelt *dook*, no doubt reflecting a pronunciation /duːk/:

> 'E could 'andle 'is dooks, an' no error: the way 'e set abaht Bill was a fair treat.
> —J. D. Brayshaw *Slum Silhouettes* (1898)

> The funeral men are always ready with dukes up to go to the offensive.
> —Jessica Mitford *The American Way of Death* (1963)

> A street punk dukes it out with Doyle.
> —*TV Guide* (1986)

A fist

oliver Short for *Oliver Twist*, from the name of the eponymous hero of the novel (1838) by Charles Dickens. In Australian English, the rhyme is applied to the wrist (see above).

The fingers

Linger is an obvious choice for *finger*, and on it comes with **lean and linger**, **long and linger**, and **wait and linger** (the latter two usually pluralized as longs and lingers and waits and lingers).

Beyond that, it gets a little difficult. **Bell ringer** doesn't quite rhyme (/ˈrɪŋə/ versus /ˈfɪŋɡə/). The curious **bees winger** (a 1960s coinage) appears to be a nonsense combination put together merely for the sake of the rhyme (again an imperfect one), which is comparatively rare in rhyming slang (it seems unlikely it was based on *beeswing* 'a filmy crust that forms on old port'). And then there's the startling Australian **onkaparinga** (usually **onka** for short), based on the brand-name of a type of woollen blanket.

The thumb

Jamaica rum Often used in the context of thumbing lifts.

Fingernails

worms and snails Usually shortened to **worms**, which is scarcely more appetizing (especially as it's often used in the context of 'biting your nails').

The back

Cilla Black Some limited late 20th-century use, based on the name of the popular Liverpudlian singer and TV dating-show hostess Cilla Black (1943–) (real name Priscilla White).

    hammer and tack Apparently a coinage of the 1950s.

    haystack Used for the rear part of anything, not just the human back.

    Penny Black From the name of the first British postage stamp, originally issued on 6 May 1840. Commonly shortened to **penny**, which allows for some mildly humorous word-play when discussing bad backs.

    Union Jack From the familiar name of the flag of the United Kingdom. Commonly abbreviated to **union**, again often in the context of a painful or injured back.

The chest

There are chests and chests. The safest, most neutral rhyming choice is **east and west**. Of the alternatives, **bird's nest** definitely suggests hairy masculinity (He flicks a flaming match into his bird's nest, and the geezer's lit up like a leaking gas pipe. *Lock, Stock, and Two Smoking Barrels* (1998)), while **Mae West** leaves little or nothing to the imagination. Celebrating the name of the provocatively bosomed American film actress Mae West (1892–1980), famed for her racy one-liners, it invites and often receives the interpretation 'breast' rather than 'chest' (but at the level of euphemism the two are interchangeable). Which brings us to. . .

Breasts

Frankly, the average rhyming slangster has little time for *breasts*. Apart from contextual interpretations of Mae West (see above), the only established rhyme extracted from the word has been **cabman's rests**. In use in the late 19th century, it comes from the term applied to the various small locations around London where cab-drivers can take a break, have a simple meal, etc.—but manages surreptitiously to suggest an alternative location where a cabbie might lay his head.

In the world of rhyming slang, a woman's breasts are usually *tits* or *titties*, and the rhymes certainly reflect this. A favourite strategy for the latter is to rhyme on the plural of *city*. Some of the results are less than inspired— **capital cities**, **towns and cities**—but a more specific approach pays better dividends. American English in the 1950s and 1960s had **Jersey Cities**, after Jersey City, New Jersey. British English, laddishly, homes in on football clubs that have *City* as part of their name: **Bradford Cities**, **Manchester Cities**, and, most famously and successfully of all, **Bristol Cities**. A product apparently of the 1950s, its shortened form **bristols** has cut itself free from its rhyming origins and become a general British slang synonym for *breasts*:

> These slag birds used to go trotting upstairs . . . , arses wagging and bristols going.
> —Robin Cook *The Crust on its Uppers* (1962)

> She was in her early twenties, with a wonderful pair of bristols; I could see their outline, firm and round, against her dress.
> —James Leasor *They don't make them like that any More* (1969)

> The main point (or should it be points?) of this programme is Miss Barbara Windsor's bristols which are . . . well-developed.
> —*Observer* (1969)

Some alternative options for *titties*:

cats and kitties A rather winsome effort in fashion between the 1930s and the 1950s.

Lewis and Witties An Australian rhyme of the post-Second World War period, based on the name of a well-known Melbourne department store, Lewis and Witty.

Tale of Two Cities From the name of the novel (1859) by Charles Dickens, set in London and Paris at the time of the French Revolution. First recorded in the 1950s, it has maintained a modest vogue. Its shortened form **tale o' twos** has a certain flamboyance, and it offers an opportunity for spoonerization that is apparently hard to resist (*sale of two titties*).

thousand pities A late 19th-century rhyme, which didn't survive long into the 20th.

Although it can't quite match *titties*, *tits* puts on a good rhyming show too:

brace and bits A 20th-century rhyme in use in both America (first recorded in 1928) and Britain. Based on the name of a type of manual drill, it also incorporates a pun on *brace* = 'pair'. Often shortened to **braces**.

Brad Pitts From the name of the Hollywood film star Brad Pitt (1964–). The usual form in which it's used is actually **bradleys**, blending the formality of his full first name with the familiar lopping-off of the rhyming element.

Eartha Kitts Probably not how the seductive US cabaret singer Eartha Kitt (1928–) would have chosen to be remembered, but at least it beats rhyming with *shits* (see under *Diarrhoea* at ILLNESS):

> She [Martine McCutcheon] is hugely popular with young women (she was voted 'best female body' by 3,000 25-year-olds) and men could hardly avoid noticing those well constructed Eartha Kitts.
> —*Sunday Times* (2001)

fainting fits A rhyme dating from the Second World War period.

first-aid kits Generally shortened to **first aids**, and no doubt containing an underlying reference to the psychologically reviving effect of breasts on the male rhyming slangster.

threepenny bits A creation of pre-decimal days, when such three-pence coins existed in Britain, but it continued in use after their demise. It partook in its time of the various colloquial erosions of *threepence*, including **fruppence** and **thrups**, and Australian English used its own version, **trey-bits** (*trey* 'three' ultimately from Italian *tre*), as a rhyme for *tits*. See also *Diarrhoea* at ILLNESS.

And, replacing *tits* with *teats*, **racks of meat**, usually abbreviated to **racks**.

That more or less exhausts the rhymesters' *breast*-repertoire, although *knockers* has inspired **mods and rockers** (after the antagonistic British youth-clans of the early 1960s, and usually shortened to **mods**) and the florid *melons* (implying a Z-cup) has been rhymed as **Mary Ellens**. And some have suggested that slang *charlies* for 'breasts', which dates back at least to the 1870s, may be a shortened form of Australian rhyming slang Charlie Wheeler for *sheila* 'woman'. It would be an interesting example of metonymy in reverse (*tail* or *skirt* for 'women' are metaphors of more conventional directionality), but unfortunately for the theory, the real Charles Wheeler on whom the rhyme seems to have been based wasn't born until 1881 (see *Women* at PEOPLE AND THE HUMAN CONDITION).

Nipples

raspberry ripples A rhyme which is first recorded in the 1970s, not long after the raspberry ripple appeared on the scene—a commercial confection consisting of vanilla ice-cream with bands of raspberry-flavoured syrup running through it. Usually shortened to **raspberries**, which fits in well with other *nipple*-metaphors based on small firm red fruits—notably *berries* and *cherries*.

The heart

Tart is the rhyming slangster's preference for *heart*, with *cart* a not very strong second. The former has inspired **gooseberry tart** (the earliest of these rhymes, first recorded in the 1850s, but largely obsolete by the 1930s); **jam tart** (some anatomical usage, but largely confined to the playing-card suit—see *The Four Suits* at **GAMBLING**); **raspberry tart** (a late 19th-century creation, but it's been put into the shade by the alternative rhyme with *fart*—see *Fart* at **IN THE LAV**); and **strawberry tart** (first recorded in the 1960s—the shortened form **strawberry** reinforces the visual appropriateness of the metaphor).

Cart has produced the Australian **grocer's cart** and the inevitable **horse and cart** (a late 19th-century coinage, later muscled in on by *fart*—see *Fart* at **IN THE LAV**). Phonetically of the same family is **D'Oyly Carte**, which according to Ray Puxley in *Cockney Rabbit* (1992) is often rationalized by non-operetta-loving rhyming slangsters as de [i.e. the] oily cart. Based on the name of the English opera company specializing in Gilbert and Sullivan, it too has been encroached on by *fart* (see *Fart* at **IN THE LAV**).

An alternative to all these is the alarming **stop and start**, while the colloquial *pump* has inspired **skip and jump**—also suggestive of a certain irregularity.

The liver

bow and quiver *Quiver* here in the sense 'a container for arrows'. Often used in metaphorical contexts which link the liver with irritability.

cheerful giver An ironic reference to the irritability produced by an upset liver, inspired by 'God loveth a cheerful giver' (2 Corinthians 9:7). In use among Covent Garden porters in the middle years of the 20th century.

Swanee River Can refer to an animal's liver used for food as well as to the human liver. From the name of the Swanee River in Georgia and Florida, USA, popularly associated with the culture of the Deep South.

The belly

Quite apart from the intractability of *abdomen* and *stomach* from a rhyming point of view, they're not really in the rhyming slangster's starting vocabulary. The comfortable colloquiality of *belly* serves for both, particularly in their role as receivers of nosh. Names are favoured for the rhyme, and the one that's had the longest and most successful track record in Britain is

Darby Kelly (or **Derby Kelly**). First recorded in the late 19th century, it can be shortened to **Darby** or (more unusually) **Kelly**, but its most familiar abbreviation is **Darby Kel**, popularized in the Harry Champion music-hall song (1910; words by Charles Collins): 'Boiled beef and carrots, boiled beef and carrots, That's the stuff for your Darby Kel, makes you fat and keeps you well.'

> Er cold, proud man tumbles on his Darby Kel in ther dirt.
> —Edward Dyson *Fact'ry 'Ands* (1906)

> Just that ride home. Cor, I still feel it down in the old darby kel.
> —Terence Rattigan *Flare Path* (1942)

> The only places now making boiled beef available to your darby kellies, or bellies, are the Jewish salt-beef bars.
> —Len Deighton *London Dossier* (1967)

> My old kelly was rumbling and I fancied a pie and chips.
> —Alfred Draper *Swansong for a Rare Bird* (1970)

The Australian equivalent is **Ned Kelly**, after the celebrated Australian bush-ranger and outlaw Ned Kelly (1857–80). First recorded in the 1920s, it continued in use throughout the 20th century:

> If I don't get a drop of hard stuff up me old Ned Kelly there's a good chance I might chunder in the channel.
> —Barry Humphries *Bazza Pulls it Off* (1970)

Another member of the convenient Kelly family is the doubly rhyming **Nellie Kelly** (also from the Australian branch)—maybe the same person as **Auntie Nellie** (a long-established rhyme, often used in the context of stomach upsets). A more recent addition to the canon is **George Melly**, perhaps inspired by the noble *embonpoint* of the jazz singer and journalist George Melly (1926–).

New Delhi, from the capital city of India, inevitably recalls the gastro-intestinal affliction nicknamed 'Delhi belly'.

The guts

comic cuts An Australian rhyme, first recorded in 1945 and often reduced to **comics**. In Britain, it's applied to *nuts* (see TESTICLES below):

> 'Never drink this well water,' he said. 'It makes you crook in the comics.'
> —F. B. Vickers *Mirage* (1958)

> I got a bit crook in the comic cuts and had to run for the latrine about ten times a day.
> —F. A. Reeder *Diary of a Rat* (1977)

Limehouse Cut Standing for the singular, *gut*, and usually referring to the size of someone's paunch. Limehouse Cut is a London waterway which links the Regent's Canal with the River Lee Navigation; it joins the former at Limehouse, in East London's Dockland.

Newington Butts Commonly shortened to **newingtons**, and used in the context of stomach ache (although it can also stand for *guts* in the sense 'courage'). Newington Butts is a road in Newington, in the southeast London borough of Southwark, said to be on the site of a former archery practice range, or 'butt' (although another explanation of the name is that it comes from a family called Butts who owned land nearby).

A kidney

Australians have the perfect rhyme to hand, and they exploit it to the full, if without a great deal of imagination: a kidney is either a **North Sydney** or a **South Sydney**, after the capital city of New South Wales.

Below the Waist

The crutch

The rhymes for this sensitive part of the body (in practice usually the male genitalia in verbal disguise) predate the late 20th-century reimportation into British English (perhaps partly for euphemizing reasons) of the American *crotch* (hitherto largely restricted in Britain to tailoring usage):

Lord Sutch From the nickname of the British pop singer turned politician 'Screaming Lord' Sutch (real name David Sutch) (1940–99), who as leader of the 'Monster Raving Loony Party' enlivened many a bye-election campaign in the last quarter of the 20th century.

Mister Mutch An Australian rhyme of the 20th century.

rabbit hutch A charming image of a shy inoffensive creature lurking at the back of its cage.

The penis

In the world of rhyming slang, penises are usually *cocks* or *pricks*, but the fortuitous (approximate) rhyme with the Roman goddess of love means that *penis* itself does get a couple of outings: as the **good ship Venus** (inspired by the words of a scabrous rugby song) and as **Mars and Venus** (the veneer of classical allusion is quickly dispelled by the frequent conversion of the first element into *Mars bar*, after the popular chocolate-and-toffee bar).

The favourite target for rhyming slangsters is *prick*, a slang synonym for *penis* which dates back to the 16th century (phonetically, the rhyme might just as plausibly be based on *dick*, another *penis* synonym, but that's more recent and much less pervasive than *prick*). The mother of all *prick*-rhymes is **Hampton Wick**, a late 19th-century coinage based on the name of a locality in southwest London, between Hampton Court and Kingston-upon-Thames. The full form has long gone out of use, but the abbreviated **hampton** is still very much in evidence (sufficiently to form the basis of the name-pun *Hugh Jampton*). More controversially, it has been suggested that the second element is represented in *dip one's wick* (of a man) 'to have sex' and *get on one's wick* 'to annoy one'. This seems perfectly plausible, especially in the former case, but it's unusual to isolate the second element of such a rhyme, and a more likely explanation is that these usages are based on a metaphorical use of the (etymologically unrelated) *wick* 'burning cord in a candle or lamp', with perhaps a *post hoc* glance at the rhyme.

As often happens when the detached non-rhyming part of a rhyme establishes itself in the language, **hampton** has been the object of further word-play—not, in this case, in the guise of a new rhyme, but extended to **Lionel Hampton**, after the American jazz musician (1909–2002) of that name. By a further reduction, **Lionel** has become a slang synonym of *penis*.

An occasionally heard alternative to Hampton Wick is **Hackney Wick**, after a locality in the London borough of Hackney which is far more nearly within earshot of Bow Bells than is Hampton Wick.

The sittingest target for a *prick*-rhyme is *stick*, and rhyming slangsters would appear to have been eager to oblige, with **dipstick** (first recorded in the 1960s and, like *prick* itself, widely used as an insult word for inadequate males—it was popularized in that role by the David Jason character Del Boy in the BBC TV sitcom *Only Fools and Horses* (1981–)); **giggle stick** (an American usage, presumably similarly motivated to joystick); **joystick** (originally American, and first recorded in 1916: I haven't seen a joystick on a guy that size before in my life. *Chippie Wagon* (1941)); **pogo stick** (an Australian rhyme, but surviving only in the shortened form **pogo** and in the metaphorical sense 'stupid or irritating man'—see *Men* at **PEOPLE AND THE HUMAN CONDITION**); and **sugar stick** (a coinage of the late 18th century). There must be serious doubt, though, whether these are genuinely rhyming slang. They undoubtedly rhyme with *prick*, but their metaphorical relationship with their referent is far too obvious—not just in the *stick* element, but also in the innuendo of its combinations: 'dipping' into the vagina, a source of 'joy' to the owner or recipient, and so on. Rhyming slang typically has no surface semantic connection with its referent. It seems far more likely that they started out as figurative extensions of existing compounds (a *joystick*, for instance, was originally an aeroplane's control column).

Some other, perhaps more genuine *prick*-rhymes:

Bob and Dick First recorded in the 1970s, and very unlikely to be a rhyme on *dick* 'penis'.

kiss me quick Presumably based on that traditional prop of British seaside ribaldry, the hat with the plea 'Kiss me quick!' fixed to it (or possibly even on the earlier, 19th-century *kiss-me-quick*, which was a woman's small hat, worn on the back of the head), but inevitably interpreted as an invitation to fellation.

mad mick An Australian rhyme, characterizing the penis as something with a deranged mind of its own.

Moby Dick Based on the name of the huge white whale which is the eponymous villain of Herman Melville's novel *Moby-Dick* (1850)—so one may well sense an undercurrent of exaggeration in the application of the rhyme.

Pat and Mick First recorded in the late 19th century, and reputedly Anglo-Irish.

stormy dick An American rhyme, first recorded in 1944.

Uncle Dick An early 20th-century coinage, and perhaps the brother of Uncle Bob (see below).

The backslang version of *prick* is *kcirp* (pronounced /kə:p/ and often written *curp*). It has its own rhyming slang equivalent in **Wyatt Earp**, from the name of the US Wild West lawman (1848–1929) familiar to rhyming slangsters from pulp fiction, films, and TV series.

Cock conveniently rhymes with *rock*, and rhyming slangsters have not been slow to pick up on the punning possibilities of that pink phallic seaside confection, the stick of rock. And so we have **Blackpool rock** (from the mecca of Northern English holidaymakers, and no doubt partly inspired by the heavy *double entendre* of George Formby's song 'With my Little Stick of Blackpool Rock' (1937)); **Brighton rock** (from the archetypal English South Coast seaside resort, with perhaps a nod to Graham Greene's 1938 novel of that name, made into a popular film in 1947); and **stick of rock**—all of them with strong innuendos of oral sex. Perhaps with something of the same in mind is **almond rock**, a 19th-century rhyme inspired by a now long-forgotten sweetmeat made from almonds; its abbreviation **almond** still had enough life in it at the end of the 20th century to be included in *Viz* magazine's 'Roger's Profanisaurus' (1997). Of less certain inspiration is the late 19th-century rhyme **Hampton rock**; perhaps it was an arbitrary alteration of Hampton Wick.

The other strand of *cock*-rhymes relates to clocks. **Grandfather clock** has largely given way to its shortened form **grandfather**, which recalls such *penis*-synonyms as *old fellow* and *old man*. **Dickory dock** comes from the nursery rhyme 'Hickory dickory dock, The mouse ran up the clock'—no doubt with acknowledgements to *dick* 'penis'.

After *prick* and *cock*, the most frequently rhymed *penis*-substitute is *corie*, which comes from the Romany word *kori* 'a thorn', and was in use mainly in the 1940s, 1950s, and 1960s. Rhyming slangsters responded to it with the rather off-putting **gruesome and gory** (nearly always shortened to **gruesome**, and Ray Puxley in *Cockney Rabbit* (1992) suggests that it was inspired by the old chestnut 'She touched it again and it gruesome more');

Jolson Story (after the 1946 film biography of the popular American singer Al Jolson (who himself featured in the first 'talkie', *The Jazz Singer*, in 1927), starring Larry Parks); and **morning glory** (referring to the gratifying discovery of an erection on waking, and based on the name of a plant of the convolvulus family).

For the rest, there's *chopper*, rhymed as **gobstopper** (the fellatious overtones are all too obvious); *knob*, avuncularly disguised as **Uncle Bob**; and *tadger*, rhymed in the 1990s as **fox and badger**.

For rhymes relating to the erect penis, see *Erection* at SEX.

Testicles

The two commonest colloquialisms for *testicles*, *balls* and *bollocks*, are probably used more often figuratively, to mean 'nonsense', than they are literally; and much the same goes for the rhymes based on them.

The supreme example is **cobblers**. Starting off in the 19th century as the now obsolete **cobblers' awls** (rhyming with *balls*; an awl is a pointed tool for making small holes) or **cobblers' stalls** (a less common variant), it's never entirely lost its original literal meaning (Well, they got us by the cobblers. James Curtis *The Gilt Kid* (1936)), but by the middle of the 20th century **cobblers** was being widely used for 'nonsense', in many cases no doubt by people unaware of its rhyming origins:

> Oh, that's all cobblers.
> —Peter Wildeblood *Against the Law* (1955)

> Geno Washington says Grapefruit's recent attack on the Maryland Club, Glasgow, was 'a load of cobblers'. They are one of the best audiences in Britain, says Geno.
> —*Melody Maker* (1968)

English offers several other convenient rhymes for *balls*: *halls*, for instance. That can be exploited in its literal sense: **marble halls** has enjoyed some success (inspired by the well-known lines 'I dreamed that I dwelt in marble halls With vassals and serfs at my side', from Alfred Bunn's libretto to Balfe's opera *The Bohemian Girl* (1843)); *marbles* for 'testicles' looks like a classic curtailed rhyme, but it's on record far earlier than the full form, and it may be that originally (in the mid-19th century) it was a non-rhyming metaphor inspired by spherical glass marbles.

It has blossomed most, though, as a family name: **Nobby Halls**, inspired by the monotesticular hero of an old music-hall song; **Sammy Halls**— perhaps Nobby's brother, his condition similarly immortalized in song; and, probably the most widely used in its time, **Henry Halls**, after the British bandleader Henry Hall (1898–1989), who had a considerable following on the radio in the middle years of the 20th century.

Waterfalls have provided sturdy models, too. **Niagara Falls** (**Niagaras** for short) has been in use since the 1950s, mainly in the literal sense 'testicles'.

An Australian alternative is **Wentworth Falls**, after a waterfall near Katoomba in the Blue Mountains of New South Wales.

Other rhymes include **coffee stalls** (generally shortened to **coffees**) and **Max Walls** (after the lugubrious-faced English comedian Max Wall (1908–90), and abbreviated if need be to **Maxies**). But probably the most popular of all at the end of the 20th century was **orchestra stalls** (literally, 'a theatre seat near the orchestra and stage'). Almost always shortened to **orchestras** (which can be further shrunk to **orcs** or **orks**), it refers strictly to testicles:

> His orks are about the only bits of him you can't see. 'Orks?' 'Yeah, orks. You know—orchestra stalls.'
> —*Campaign* (1994)

Orchestras is an example of a rhyme that's only ever used literally, but virtually all *bollocks*-rhymes do double duty for 'nonsense'. There's a family rather unimaginatively named the 'Rollocks' (*rollocks* itself is a frequent euphemistic substitution for *bollocks*): **Jimmy Rollocks**, **Johnny Rollocks**, and (probably the senior member; first recorded in the late 19th century) **Tommy Rollocks** (abbreviated at need—to **Tommies** in the literal sense, **Tommy** in the metaphorical). Those with classical leanings may have a preference for **Castor and Pollux**, more familiar to horoscope-readers as Gemini the heavenly twins, while the younger generation of movie-goers plump for **Sandra Bullocks**, a decidedly dodgy rhyme based on the name of the Hollywood film star Sandra Bullock (1966–). Perhaps the most widely used of all, though, is **fun and frolics**, with its occasional substitute **flowers and frolics**—both characterized by Julian Franklyn in his *Dictionary of Rhyming Slang* (1960) as Irish in origin.

The 1990s coinage *betty swallocks* is more a case of spoonerization than rhyming slang—swapping over the initial letters of *sweaty bollocks*.

Knackers has produced **Christmas crackers** (first recorded in the 1970s); **cream crackers** (a 1990s rhyme, after a type of crisp, non-sweet biscuit); and **Kerry Packers** (after the Australian media mogul Kerry Packer (1937–), who became well known in the 1970s for his efforts to corner the television cricket market with World Series Cricket). *Nuts* is rhymed as **comic cuts**, or **comics** for short (based on the name of a once popular children's comic, *Comic Cuts*, which first appeared in 1890; in Australia it denotes 'guts'—see THE GUTS above), or as **General Smuts** (an inglorious memorial for General Jan Christiaan Smuts (1870–1950), South African war leader and statesman; often reduced to the anonymity of **generals**). *Goolies*, a term apparently picked up in India in the 1930s, found its rhyme in the 1950s when the Kingston Trio popularized the traditional ballad *Tom Dooley* ('Hang down your head, Tom Dooley, Hang down your head and cry, You killed poor Laurie Foster and you know you're bound to die')—hence, **Tom Doolies**. *Cods* is a much more ancient synonym for *testicles*, dating back at least to the early 16th century, but it can't escape a rhyme: **Ken Dodds**, after the zany

Liverpudlian comedian Ken Dodd (1931–) (abbreviated at need to **Kennys**). And finally *pills*, rhymed by courtesy of the old sea dog Barnacle Bill— **Barnacle Bills**, or **barnacles** for short.

The female genitals

When it comes to female genitalia, the rhyming slangster is fairly single-minded. A smattering of other synonyms get desultory attention, but overwhelmingly it's *cunt* that's the focus of the rhymes. It has a wider range of application than the purely physiological, of course, and that's a factor that has particularly affected its most famous set of rhymes, based on *hunt*.

The best known of these is probably **Berkeley Hunt**, after a celebrated fox-hunt in Gloucestershire. Its inception, probably in the late 19th or early 20th century, was probably anatomical, but by the time it appears in the written record, in the 1930s, the metaphorical application to 'a despicable person' is already well to the fore, and the literal meaning seems to be in the process of being lost. A few traces of it remain from before the Second World War (including the whimsical **Sir Berkeley**, used here metonymically for 'sexual intercourse': She gives me plenty of the old Sir Berkeley, but she knows how to look after herself, I guess. James Curtis *There ain't no Justice* (1937)), but by the end of the 1940s its shortened form **berk** was in such wide use for 'a fool' that both its original form and its original meaning were fading from memory. The Gloucestershire place-name is standardly pronounced /ˈbɑːkli/, but the non-standard variant /ˈbəːkli/ has fed through into the abbreviation berk, resulting in the alternative spellings *burk(e)* and *birk*; see *Fools* at SENSE AND NONSENSE.

The synonymous **Berkshire Hunt** (after the English county) is not recorded in print before 1960, and probably originated as a variation on *Berkeley*. Similarly but more punningly inspired is **Birchington Hunt**, with its suggestion of the *vice anglais*.

If knowledge of the link between *berk* and *cunt* is still reasonably widely known, most people would probably be surprised to learn that *charlie* 'a fool' had similar origins. But there is a theory that Charlie started out as **Charlie Hunt**, rhyming with *cunt*—along with his close relative **Joe Hunt**; see *Charlie* at SENSE AND NONSENSE.

With all these *hunt*-rhymes straying off into metaphorical territory, the literal field has been left open to the *grunt*-clan—a numerous family, probably inspired by sounds associated with vigorous love-making. First recorded in the 1930s, the most widely used is **grumble and grunt** (commonly reduced to **grumble**), but there are also **gasp and grunt**, **groan and grunt** and **growl and grunt** (transformed in the 1990s into **growler**). Here too, though, meaning is slippery, and the rhymes have been widely used to designate sexual intercourse, or as collective terms for women as sexual objects:

> There's this copper . . . and he puts away a local tea-leaf. And this tea-leaf's old woman's a fair bit of grumble.
> —E. Brock *Little White God* (1962)

> American visitors are invariably delighted by references to birds, scrubbers, grumble.
> —*Melody Maker* (1966)

(The personified **Grannie Grunt** shares the rhyme, but seems never to have been used literally; see *Cunt* at PEOPLE AND THE HUMAN CONDITION.)

Of the remaining rhymes for *cunt*, the only one used anatomically is **sharp and blunt**—although that too can be extended to cover 'sexual intercouse' (as in *have a bit of sharp and blunt*).

Given this flight to metaphor, it's been necessary to recruit some synonyms to replenish the source of rhymes. The British *fanny* produced in the late 20th century **Jack and Danny** (but growing British familiarity with American English *fanny* 'buttocks' seems to be resulting in ambiguity—see below at THE BOTTOM). The euphemistic *hole* found a 19th-century rhyme in **South Pole** (it's now more usually used for 'anus'—see below). The equally ancient *pit* was rhymed as **bob and hit**, and the even more venerable *gash* (dating from the 18th century) has found a new rhyme in **Leslie Ash** (after the popular British television actress Leslie Ash (1960–); almost always shortened to **Leslie**, which is in close proximity to various colloquial abbreviations of *lesbian*). *Twat* inevitably attracts *pot*-rhymes: **gluepot**, the more complimentary **honey pot**, and **mustard pot** (perhaps partly inspired by 19th-century slang *mustard-and-cress* for 'pubic hair'). See also *dollypot* at PEOPLE AND THE HUMAN CONDITION.

Beaver, denoting especially the vulva and associated pubic hair, is **Sigourney Weaver**, providing a dubious tribute to the American film star Sigourney Weaver (1949–).

The bottom

Arse might be the rhymer's stereotypical choice of target, but in fact it's the comfortable colloquial *bum* that has gathered more rhymes over the years. *Drum* works well: **big bass drum** (or just **big bass**) implies prominent buttocks; **fife and drum** (dating from the 1940s) exploits two key instruments of the military band; and **pipe and drum** inevitably gravitates towards the anus. Alternative formulations are **deaf and dumb**; **kingdom come** (first recorded in the 1970s); and **Tom Thumb** (**tom** for even shorter).

But *arse* exercises an irresistible attraction for rhyming slangsters. Top of the league since the latter part of the 20th century has been **Khyber Pass** (usually reduced to **Khyber**), from the name of the chief pass in the Hindu Kush mountains between Afghanistan and northwest Pakistan:

> Not knowin' wevver they wz on their 'eads or their Kybers [sic].
> —Michael Harrison *Reported Safe Arrival* (1943)

> If we sit on our Khybers, we will miss out on all the things that make our lives the richer.
> —*Crescendo* (1968)

As alternatives there are **bypass**; **looking glass** (an American rhyme); and **bottle and glass**. This last has been the starting point for a more than usually bizarre trail of further rhymes. Its shortened form **bottle** (widely touted as the origin of *bottle* 'courage'; see *Courage and its Lack* at BEHAVIOUR, ATTITUDES, AND EMOTIONS) attracted to itself the 19th-century rhyme for a literal *bottle*, **Aristotle** (after the 4th-century BC Greek philosopher). This was itself soon shortened to **arris**, which became a widely used London slang synonym for *buttocks* (its fortuitous resemblance to *arse* probably enabled it to play something of a euphemistic role). Then, later in the 20th century, yet a third layer of rhyme came to be added: **April in Paris**.

The rather more polite synonym *tail* attracted the rhyme **Daily Mail**, after the British middle-market newspaper of that name (first recorded in the 1930s). Often shortened to **daily**, and used metaphorically (a car following too closely could be described as *up your daily*).

Jack and Danny started off as a rhyme for *fanny* in the British sense 'vagina' (see above), but American English *fanny* 'buttocks' is now well enough known in Britain to start muscling in on the two lads:

> I'm gonna put my rocket up his Jack and Danny.
> —*Lock, Stock. . .* Channel 4 (2000)

The anus

Too high-falutin to attract its own rhymes, but there are plenty of more down-to-earth synonyms to do that job. *Arsehole*, for one: **North Pole** and the rather more appropriate **South Pole** probably represent that, as does the jolly **merry old soul** (traditional characterization of Old King Cole)—though all three could simply be rhymed on *hole*. More watertight *arsehole*-rhymes, reflecting a reduced pronunciation /ˈɑːsl/, are **Elephant and Castle** (**elephant** for short), from the area of that name in South London, **Windsor Castle**, a cheeky application for the name of the royal residence in Berkshire, and **Roy Castle**, from the name of the British singer, trumpeter, comedian, and all-round entertainer Roy Castle (1932–94).

Ring in the sense 'anus' has been rhymed with that quintessential Cockney character the **Pearly King**, and the venerable slang synonym *jacksie* has been transformed into **London taxi**.

In the 1990s, *shitter* attracted the uncomfortable **council gritter**, and also **Gary Glitter**, from the stage-name of the flamboyant British pop singer Paul Gadd (1940–), who was convicted of a paedophilia-related offence in 1999. Its alternative form *shiter* is behind **Ronson lighter** (from the type of cigarette lighter manufactured by Ronson), generally shortened to **ronson**.

The legs

Pegs has always been a popular rhyme for *legs*, perhaps because *pegleg* 'a wooden leg' is already stored in the mental lexicon (and indeed *peg* itself has been used humorously for the human leg). **Scotch pegs** is probably the oldest rhyme (it's first recorded in 1857), and it persisted in its shortened form **scotches** well into the 20th century:

> If he had occasion to allude to his leg he would probably have called it 'Scotch peg'.
> —Ward Muir *Observations of an Orderly* (1917)

> Down to wearing my head in its proper place and not between my scotches like a sporran.
> —Robin Cook *The Crust on its Uppers* (1962)

But there have been numerous other *peg*-rhymes: **clothes pegs**, **cribbage pegs** (after the small pegs used for keeping score in the game of cribbage; recorded in the 1920s), **Dutch pegs**, **mumbly pegs** (after a knife-throwing game called *mumble-the-peg*, or *mumblety-peg*; it had some limited currency, in American as well as British English, in the middle decades of the 20th century), and **wooden pegs**. Australian English has stretched the rules to include **gregory pegs**, a punning rhyme based on the name of the US film star Gregory Peck (1916–).

The other consistent theme is *eggs*, which come in a variety of combinations: **bacon and eggs** (originally Australian), **fried eggs** (another Australian rhyme), **ham and eggs** (also originally Australian), **Scotch eggs** (dating from the mid-19th century), and **scrambled eggs**.

Those two strands exhaust rhyming slangsters' imagination as far as legs go, although *gams*, an old slang synonym for *legs*, did sometimes go by the rhyme **trams** in the early part of the 20th century.

The knees

birds and bees Usually curtailed to **birds**.

biscuits and cheese First recorded in the 1940s.

Robert E. Lees After the American Confederate general Robert E. Lee (1807–70). Almost always shortened to **Robert E.'s**.

The feet

There aren't many rhymes for *feet*, but most of them have made a mark in the language. **Dogs** is one of those synonyms that became such an everyday part of English slang (I feel more like goin' to bed and sleeping for a week than prancing round the ballroom on me poor dogs. Monica Dickens *One Pair of Hands* (1939)) that its rhyming origins were forgotten—it's short for **dog's meat** (first recorded in the 1920s).

Almost as naturalized are **plates** and **platters** (the preferred form in US slang), shortened from **plates of meat** (first recorded in 1857) and **platters of meat** (first recorded in 1923):

> But his plates of meat stuck across the street, so the Lord Mayor drove across them.
> —R. P. Weston & F. J. Barnes *The Hobnailed Boots that Farver Wore* (1907) (as recorded by John Foreman in 1966; the original text had unrhymed 'feet')

> To get your 'plates of meat' frostbitten wasn't such a 'cushy wound' as it was cracked up to be.
> —Ward Muir *Observations of an Orderly* (1917)

> He . . . took off his shoes. 'Heaven!' he sighed. 'My plates have been quite, quite killing me.'
> —P. Branch *The Lion in the Cellar* (1951)

In this case, though, users are usually aware of the original full form, even if they don't use it.

The singular *foot* has been rhymed as **chimney and soot**, and taking a different tack *trotters*, sometimes used as a facetious synonym of *feet*, has yielded the rhyme **Gillie Potters**, after the English comedian Gillie Potter (1887–1975).

The toes

buttons and bows An Australian rhyme, recalling the words of the 1948 song 'Buttons and Bows'.

old black joes Another Australianism, suggesting perhaps the toes of an Aborigine.

Seb Coes After the British middle-distance runner and Olympic gold medallist Sebastian Coe (1956–), and almost always used (in the reduced form **Sebs**) not of literal toes, but in the slang expression *have it on your Sebs* 'to make a quick getaway'.

stop and goes Sometimes shortened to **stops**.

these and those Always in full—never chopped down to *these*.

A bunion

See *Spanish onion* at ILLNESS.

A tail

alderman's nail A venerable rhyme, usually shortened to **alderman**.

Jonah's whale A 19th-century rhyme which didn't survive more than a decade or so into the 20th century.

See also *Daily Mail* at THE BOTTOM, and *hammer and nail* at CRIME AND PUNISHMENT.

The Senses

Vision and Observation

A look

Since the late 19th century, taking a look at something has been rhymed as having a **butcher's hook** (from the double-ended hook used by butchers for hanging up sides and joints of meat). The full form is still passively familiar, but it's the curtailed **butcher's** (first recorded in the 1930s) that has established itself in colloquial British English beyond the bounds of rhyming slang:

> And while he's there he takes a butchers.
> —James Curtis *The Gilt Kid* (1936)

> Have a butcher's at the *News of the World*.
> —Kingsley Amis *Take a Girl like You* (1960)

> 'I'm gonna have a butcher's round the house.' 'Who you gonna butcher?' 'Butcher's hook? Look?'
> —*The Limey* (1999)

Australian rhymers, on the other hand, have gone with **Captain Cook** (also first recorded in the 1930s), after Captain James Cook (1728–79), the Yorkshire-born navigator and explorer who claimed the east coast of Australia for Britain:

> Take a captain cook at love's young dream.
> —L. Mann *Flesh in Armour* (1932)

> Got a Captain Cook at your dossier—it's thicker than your frickin' head.
> —D. O'Grady *Deschooling Kevin Carew* (1974)

Give a cook or *take a cook* for 'have a look' is recorded in use in British slang, but this seems to be an adaptation of Yiddish *guck* 'a look' rather than a rhyme on *cook*. British English has had its own *cook*-rhyme, though: **Charlie Cooke**, after the Chelsea and Scotland footballer of that name (1942–).

In the middle of the 19th century to 'observe' something or 'inspect' it was to *pipe* it, which got the rhyming treatment as **Tommy Tripe**—usually **tommy** for short.

Glasses

The straightforward British rhymes are **mountain passes** and **working classes**. Rather more problematical from a phonological point of view are

Hackney Marshes (not a convincing rhyme, but it originated in the singular form, for *glass* 'a receptacle'—see *Glass* at HOUSEHOLD MATTERS); **Irish lasses** (a US usage, where the rhyme with /las/ works smoothly); and **Lancashire lasses** (hardly consistent with Southern British English /ˈglɑːsɪz/ for *glasses*, but again it's an adaptation of the singular form—see *Glass* at HOUSEHOLD MATTERS).

But there's more to glasses than *glasses*. The popular colloquialism *specs* is transmogrified into **Gregory Pecks**, after the Hollywood actor Gregory Peck (1916–), a favourite with rhyming slangsters—see *The neck* at THE BODY AND ITS PARTS and *A cheque* at MONEY AND COMMERCE. The more recent *bins*, short for *binoculars* but usually used for 'spectacles', has been rhymed as **Errol Flynns**, after the decidedly non-four-eyed Hollywood film star Errol Flynn (1909–59). And for trendies who refer to their sunglasses as *shades*, there's a rhyme available in **jack of spades**—commonly shortened to **jacks**.

Blind

all behind An inconsequential-sounding rhyme, perhaps loosely based on such expressions as *all behind like the cow's tail* 'late'.

Golden Hind From the name of the ship in which Sir Francis Drake circumnavigated the globe in 1577–80—long an icon of English folklore.

Colour

Black

coalman's sack Used generally with connotations of dirtiness.

jumping jack Occasionally applied to the black ball in snooker, but mainly this designates black people (see *Blacks* at ETHNIC AND NATIONAL GROUPS).

Blue

Danny La Rue A tribute to the Irish-born drag artiste Danny La Rue (1928– ; real name Daniel Patrick Carroll).

Irish stew Used metaphorically, to connote melancholy, as well as literally.

Brown

half-a-crown From a former British coin worth two shillings and sixpence. Applied to the brown ball in snooker.

up and down A general rhyme, but often attracted to brown ale.

Grey

night and day Usually used with reference to hair.

Pink

rinky dink A particular application is to the pink ball in snooker. Also substituted in the figurative phrase *in the pink*.

Red

bald head Applied to the red ball in snooker.

Yellow

Cinderella After the fairy-tale character who finally did go to the ball. Applied coincidentally to the yellow ball in snooker.

Sound

Noise

box of toys A late 19th-century rhyme which had largely died out by the Second World War. Perhaps inspired by the cacophany which often accompanies the use of toys.

  girls and boys A tribute to the disproportionate volume produced by tinies.

  Theydon Bois From the name of a village in southwest Essex, beyond Debden on the Central Line. According to Ray Puxley in *Cockney Rabbit* (1992) it was the frequent venue for children's outings from the East End of London in former times, so the connection in these rhymes between children and noise is maintained.

Deaf

Mutt and Jeff One of the most widely used of all rhymes, first recorded in the 1930s. It was based on the name of two characters, *Mutt* and *Jeff*, one tall and the other short, in a popular cartoon series by the American cartoonist H. C. Fisher (1884–1954):

> They don't hear the cry 'Feet!' sometimes on account of being a bit 'Mutt and Jeff'.
> —*Bowlers' World* (1992)

> Volume Control: Depending on how Mutt and Jeff you are, you'll want to adjust the volume of incoming calls.
> —*Stuff* (1997)

Smell

In the world of rhyming slang, *smell* almost always equals a bad smell. That's certainly the case with the two *smell*-rhymes, **heaven and hell** and **William Tell** (after the legendary 14th-century Swiss hero—who as portrayed on television by Conrad Phillips in the 1950s wore a possibly evil-smelling sheepskin coat)—both of which are probably more often used as verbs than as nouns.

Other rhymed 'smell'-words leave no room for doubt. *Pong* has yielded **Anna May Wong** (after the no doubt fragrant film star Anna May Wong (1907–61)) and **Hong Kong** (from the port and former British colony on the Chinese coast, which has not always lived up to the literal meaning of its Cantonese name: 'fragrant harbour'). A *stench* is a **Judi Dench**, from the name of the British actress Dame Judi Dench (1934–) (first recorded in the 1990s). *Stink* (verb as well as noun) has appeared as **food and drink** and as **kitchen sink** (an often odoriferous fitting), but its most famous and widely used rhyme is **pen and ink**, first recorded in 1859 and given a boost in the late 20th century in the television series *Minder*. Often shortened to **pen**:

> 'I don't mind, provided he takes a bath.' 'Yeah, he does pen a bit.'
> —G. F. Newman *You Nice Bastard* (1972)

> That old cigar don't half pen and ink, don't it?
> —Barry Purchese *Minder* (1983)

> I don't half pen and ink, and apparently her indoors made Arthur sleep in the car.
> —Andrew Payne *Minder* (1984)

In the Lav

Bodily effluvia allow rhyming slang to exploit to the full its special talent for euphemism. Items not fit to be displayed in public, or at any rate not in mixed company (*turd*, *slash*, *piddle*, and the like), can be draped in the curious translucent veil of rhyme and made instantly, and often whimsically, acceptable. The innocence of **tomtit**, **Jimmy Riddle**, and **my word**, the humour of **Kermit**, **Zorba**, and **Pat Cash**, the sheer impenetrability of **Mrs Chant's**, all neutralize embarrassment with a light touch of knowingness.

Urination

The whole colloquial spectrum of urination comes in for the rhyming treatment, from the ancient and forthright *piss*, though the no-nonsense *slash*, to the dainty *tinkle*:

Leak

Leak as a verbal euphemism for 'to urinate' goes back at least to the late 16th century, but its more familiar modern role as a noun (as in *take a leak*) is not recorded before the 1910s. It is the noun usage that is represented in the Australian rhyme **bubble and squeak**, a coinage probably of the second half of the 20th century, but **Zorba the Greek** (or more usually **Zorba**) maintains a dual function. It comes from the title of an earthy novel (1946; later made into a successful film) by the Greek author Nikos Kazantzakis.

Pee

Originally itself a late 18th-century euphemism (covering up *piss* by using just its first letter), by the 20th century it was in need of its own wrappings. (All the rhymes can equally well, of course, stand for *wee*):

   cup of tea A confusing, if not downright surreal intermerging of cause and effect.

   fiddlededee A survival of a fairly ancient exclamation of disbelief or disagreement. The first element has the advantage (for the incurable word-player) of rhyming with *piddle*. Standardly shortened to **fiddley**, although Ray Puxley's suggestion (*Cockney Rabbit* (1992)) that this may have something to do with uncooperative fly buttons is probably more *ben trovato* than *vero*.

fiddlers three Inspired by the violin trio summoned by Old King Cole in the nursery rhyme (perhaps originally as a variation on **fiddlededee**). Usually abbreviated to **fiddlers**.

Jerry Lee A post-Second World War creation, based on the name of US rock-'n'-roll singer and pianist Jerry Lee Lewis (1935–).

lemon tea A more refined version of **cup of tea**. In practice usually truncated to just **lemon**.

Peters and Lee From the name of a British singing duo of the 1970s (see *Tea* at **FOOD AND DRINK**).

riddle-me-ree Another choice from the locker of Olde Englishe whose first element (like **fiddlededee**'s) rhymes with *piddle*. This, and no doubt the resemblance to **Jimmy Riddle** (see at **PIDDLE** below), discourages any abbreviation. *Riddle-me-ree* was originally (from the 17th century) an incantatory phrase meaning 'expound my riddle aright'.

Robert E An undignified memorial for the US Confederate general Robert E. Lee (1807–70). Sometimes shortened still further to **Robert**.

Southend-on-Sea From the name of the Essex seaside resort, traditionally a favourite destination for London's East End day-trippers, whose excursions were no doubt the occasion for much urination.

sweet pea Mainly a long-standing rhyme for *tea*—*pea*/*pee* is fairly feeble.

you and me Suggesting a shared experience.

Piddle

The word that most catches rhymers' attention when it comes to *piddle* is *riddle*, and they love nothing better than to turn it into a name: **Jerry Riddle** dates back to the 19th century; Australians have their variant **Gerry Riddle**; the unfortunate US composer/arranger **Nelson Riddle** (1921–85) found himself bang in Australian rhyming slangsters' sights (often abbreviated to **Nelson**); but undoubtedly the most popular member of this incontinent family is **Jimmy Riddle**. First recorded in the 1930s, the rhyme probably dates back further than that, and its shortened form **Jimmy** has established a niche for itself in the language beyond rhyming slang:

> I must do a Jimmy Riddle before I go.
> —Julian Symons *The End of Solomon Grundy* (1964)

> Mrs D. was in there having a jimmy.
> —Douglas Clark *Sick to Death* (1971)

> You're going straight down there and straight back, stopping only for a Jimmy.
> —Andrew Payne *Minder* (1984)

Other *piddle*-rhymes:

dicky diddle Used both as a noun, meaning 'urine', and as a verb, 'to urinate'.

hey-diddle-diddle or **hi-diddle-diddle** From the opening lines of the nursery rhyme, 'Hey diddle diddle, the cat and the fiddle, the cow jumped over the moon'. First recorded in the 1950s.

pig in the middle From the name of the game in which two people throw a ball to each other and a third person standing between them tries to catch it. Commonly shortened to **pig**.

Piss

A complicating factor in the rhymes for *piss* is that many of them do not only denote 'urine' or 'urination' but also stand in for *piss* in *take the piss* 'to make fun of someone', and the evidence is often conflicting as to which rhyme can refer to what. For convenience both strands of meaning are treated here.

The most popular rhyming word is *kiss*. It forms the basis of **angel's kiss** (a 20th-century Australian rhyme), **cuddle and kiss** (often shortened to **cuddle**, but when used metaphorically (see above) only the full form is employed), **French kiss**, **goodnight kiss**, **gypsy's kiss** (usually curtailed to **gypsy's**), and **ta-ta kiss** (reportedly mainly in *take the ta-ta*).

There is a small family tree of *Blisses* too. The distinguished British composer and Master of the Queen's Musick, Sir Arthur Bliss (1891–1975) would have been disconcerted to find himself hanging from it as **Arthur Bliss**, alongside his Australian cousin **Johnny Bliss**. But much the best known and most successful of the clan is **Micky Bliss** (sometimes also known as **Mike Bliss**). The metaphorical role of its shortened form is very likely the source of the expression *take the micky*, which appears to date from the 1930s.

Further *piss*-rhymes:

boo and hiss If you are going *on the boo and hiss*, you are going on a drunken spree; but the rhyme is also used metaphorically (as in *take the boo and hiss*).

comical Chris A usage commemorating a character (played by Bill Stephens) in the 1940s BBC radio comedy programme *ITMA*, but not recorded until the 1970s and 1980s.

cousin sis A coinage showing a distinct lack of family feeling.

hit and miss or **hit or miss** Also usable in the 'drunken spree' sense—*on the hit and miss*. The *or* form dates from the late 19th century, but the *and* form does not seem to have been recorded before the 1960s.

rattle and hiss As with the other *hiss*-rhymes, there could well be some underlying onomatopoeic motivation.

snake's hiss Used in both British and Australian English, and generally shortened to **snakes**.

that and this A serviceable 20th-century coinage, if not exactly the height of imagination.

Slash

A metaphor which came on the scene in the middle of the 20th century and quickly gained a firm foothold, as the number of rhymes based on suggest. It, and they, are used mainly with reference to males:

eyelash A product of the very late 20th century:

> I'm desperate for an eyelash.
> —Bernard Dempsey & Kevin McNally *Lock, Stock and Two Sips* (Channel 4) (2000)

Frazer-Nash A piece of middle-class boys' nostalgia, recorded in the 1970s. It comes from the name of a type of pre-Second World War British sports car.

J. Carroll Naish Another 1970s coinage, commemorating the US actor (1900–73) best remembered for his television portrayal of Charlie Chan. Generally shortened to **J. Carroll**.

Johnny Cash First recorded in the 1960s, and based on the name of the US country-and-western singer (1932–).

Leslie Ash A late-20th-century rhyme based on the name of a British actress (1960–) best known for her role in the BBC television sitcom *Men Behaving Badly*. Usually shortened to **Leslie**.

Mark Ramprakash A 1990s coinage, from the name of the Middlesex, Surrey and England batsman (1969–).

Pat Cash Another sporting rhyme, immortalizing the Australian tennis player (1965–), Wimbledon men's singles champion in 1987.

pie and mash First recorded in the 1970s, and probably the most widely used of all the *slash*-rhymes. Appropriately 'Cockney', as pie and mash is a traditional London dish.

Tinkle

A winsome echoic euphemism probably dating from the 1960s—but the rhyme may also conceal the more up-front *sprinkle*:

Rip van Winkle Used as a verb—*to Rip van Winkle*. After the character invented in the early 19th century by US author Washington Irving, who went to sleep for twenty years.

Defecation

Crap

The rhymes apply to *crap* in the sense 'an act of defecation', not 'excrement':

Andy Capp From the name of the strip-cartoon character, a put-upon, virulently politically incorrect, flat-cap-wearing working man, invented by Reg Smythe in 1956 and featuring regularly thereafter in the *Daily Mirror*.

game of nap Based on a type of card game popular in the late 19th and early 20th centuries (*nap* was originally an abbreviation of *Napoleon*). Also used as a rhyme for *cap* (see under *Headgear* at **CLOTHING**).

horse and trap An alternative formulation to pony and trap (see next), and apparently sharing its pattern of usage.

pony and trap Dating from the late 19th century, and firmly established in its shortened form **pony**. Widely used in the metaphorical sense 'nonsense, rubbish' (as in 'He's talking a load of old pony!').

Shit

The most popular and versatile rhyming-word is *hit*: **hard hit** is an act of defecating (as in 'go for a hard hit'); **bob and hit** is a 1990s rhyme for 'excrement'; and **big hit**, an Australianism dating back to the 1920s, can be either of these, and also a verb—'to defecate'.

Many of the rhymes which started out in the singular have gone on to greater plural things, denoting 'diarrhoea'—notably **Eartha Kitt**, **Edgar Britt**, and **two-bob bit** (see under *Tummy upsets* at ILLNESS). Australian English has favoured this role for **tomtit** too, but in British rhyming slang it continues to major in its original literal senses (first recorded as a noun in the 1940s, but apparently in use as a verb since the late 19th century), with the usual metaphorical extensions and a sideline in the plural for 'the willies':

> 'You're always doing it, you shower of tom tit, you.'
> —Richard Llewellyn *None but the Lonely Heart* (1943)

> 'Break it down,' said the corporal. 'You'll give these blokes the tomtits before they get their first lot of C.B.'
> —Lawson Glassop *We were the Rats* (1944)

> You can cut the Tom Tit, sergeant.
> —John Gardner *Madrigal* (1967)

> Perhaps 'e stopped for a tomtit.
> —Christopher Wood *'Terrible Hard'*, *Says Alice* (1970)

> I was just sitting there, trousers round me ankles. . . If I hadn't been doing it already, he'd 've given me the tom-tits.
> —Liza Cody *Bad Company* (1982)

And finally, an honourable mention for **Brad Pitt**, from the name of the Hollywood film star (1964–), raised to this exalted company in the 1990s.

Turd

Turd rhymes very conveniently with *third*, which has led to a rash of royal rhymes: **George the Third**, **Henry the Third** (first recorded in the 1950s), **Richard the Third** (the oldest, dating from the late 19th century, and probably the most widely used), and **William the Third** (a loyal Australian contribution).

Outside the royal circle, the stayer in the field is **my word**, first recorded in the early 20th century, which is often claimed as an exclamation (commendably restrained) on treading in dog excrement on the pavement. **Lemon curd** (or just plain **lemon**) has had its adherents, for its metaphorical sense ('despicable person') as well as its literal. And at the end of the 20th century the Conservative politician **Douglas Hurd** (1930–) achieved a certain transitory fame in this role.

Lavatorial Venues

English overflows with colloquialisms and euphemisms for 'lavatory', and this is reflected in the number of different targets selected by rhyming slangsters. Probably the most bizarre result is **Mrs Chant's**—in the 1920s, 'to visit Mrs Chant's' was a way of avoiding saying 'go to the lavatory'. The explanatory trail leads back via the coy euphemism *my aunt's* for 'the lavatory' to a rhyme based on the resounding name of Mrs Ormiston Chant (1848–1923), a noted moralist of the time who would no doubt have been suitably outraged by the link.

Another, rather more down-to-earth avoidance word is *throne* (for the receptacle itself; first recorded in 1922), and this has been rhymed as **rag and bone**.

In more up-front territory, *bog* has an ancestry stretching back at least to the late 18th century. **Cat and dog** is its favoured rhyme, joined in the latter part of the 20th century by **Kermit the Frog** (generally **Kermit** for short), after a puppet frog character in the 1970s US television programme *The Muppet Show*.

In colloquial Australian English the loo is the *dunny*, which translates in rhyming slang into **don't be funny**. Also Australian is **snake's house**, or just plain **snakes**, which, although not strictly a rhyme itself, appears to have been based on snake's hiss 'piss' (see under URINATION above).

At the franker end of the spectrum are *shitter*, which has inspired **light and bitter** (after two types of beer) and **Tex Ritter** (from the name of a star of early US westerns (1905–74)), and *pisshole*, yielding **savoury rissole** (also applied by extension to anywhere which might be described as a 'dump').

Then there is **lemon and dash** (i.e. a 'dash' of something stronger added to a lemon drink), which is applied specifically to a public lavatory or washroom. The usually suggested rhyme with *wash* fails to carry conviction, but *slash* 'act of urinating' is a more promising candidate. The term (generally shortened to **lemon**) was once common among the pickpocketing fraternity, for whom the expression 'the lemon lark' denoted stealing from coats left hanging in public washrooms, changing rooms, etc. Compare *Bob Squash* at HOUSEHOLD MATTERS.

The *chain* pulled at the completion of business may be the **Frankie Laine**, in memory of the American singer Frankie Laine (1913–) who became popular in Britain in the 1950s with hits such as 'I Believe', 'Running Wild', and 'Rawhide'. People still 'pull the **Frankie**', even though actual chains have largely been replaced by handles and buttons.

And finally, if the lavatory is too far away in the middle of the night, it may have to be the *potty*—or for rhyming slangers the **mazawattee** (from the name of a brand of tea once popular in Britain).

Miscellaneous Effluvia and Eructions

Fart

By far the most pervasive and influential *fart*-rhyme is **raspberry tart**, but it seldom gets due credit for this, since its shortened form **raspberry** is in such common use in the extended sense 'fart-like derisive sound made with the lips' that its rhyming origins have been covered up. The full form is not recorded before 1959, but since **raspberry** was well established in this usage by 1890, it must have been in circulation in the 19th century. Out of the same basket comes the Australian **apple tart**, which is also used as a verb.

Other *fart*-rhymes:
Billy Smart From the name of the British circus proprietor (1893–1966).
bullock's heart A late-19th-century coinage, which did not survive long in the 20th century.
D'Oyly Carte A rhyme popular in the 1970s and 1980s, and based on the name of the English opera company specializing in Gilbert and Sullivan. Generally abbreviated to **D'Oyly**.
heart and dart Another 19th-century rhyme, now obsolete, based on the name of a type of moth (it comes from the patterning on its wings, an alternative take on which is its Latin name *Agrotis exclamationis*).
horse and cart A coinage of the 1970s, used as both a noun and a verb.

Wind

Jenny Lind From the name of the Swedish soprano (1820–87) who was immensely popular in the 19th century, and was known as the 'Swedish nightingale'.

Belch

Raquel Welch From the name of the glamorous US film actress (1940–), not otherwise associated with breaking wind.

Burp

Wyatt Earp From the name of the US Wild West lawman (1848–1929) familiar to rhyming slangsters from pulp fiction, films, and TV series.

Bad breath

king death Appropriate-sounding, but Julian Franklyn (*Dictionary of Rhyming Slang* (1960)) casts doubt on its authenticity.

Bogie

Jimmy Logie An uncomplimentary memorial to the Arsenal footballer (1919–84).

Illness

The types of indisposition that get particularly picked on for the rhyming slang treatment offer a persuasive insight into the underlying motivation of rhyming. Which come at the top of the list? Sexually transmitted diseases, by some distance. Which is the best of the rest? Haemorrhoids. The common factor is easy to spot: embarrassment. We are here in the territory of strong taboo: the sorts of illness, connected with the sexual and excretory organs, that defy ordinary discourse. If you need to talk about them, you either have to resort to medical euphemisms or circumlocutions, or else go for the comic disguise which subverts the threat. The pox goes by a number of colloquialisms which simultaneously belittle it and cover it up—*clap*, *dose*, *jack*, *syph* and so on. An even bigger put-down, and a deeper disguise, can be achieved with rhyming slang.

Ill

The main 'ill'-adjective to have attracted the attention of rhyming slangers is *sick*—which is unfortunate since, particularly in British English, it also means 'nauseous' or 'vomiting'. The ambiguity often crosses over into the rhyming slang, but cannot be assumed in every case.

There are several *sick*-rhymes to choose from, and easily the most favoured is *dick/Dick*. Names go down well in rhyming slang, and there is a *Dick* lurking in the Everyman triumvirate *Tom, Dick, and Harry*. Minimal ingenuity transposes this into rhyming slang **Harry, Tom, and Dick** (often pared down to **Tom and Dick**: DEL: Well, alright, we'll say he's ill. CASSANDRA: Oh what, more lies? DEL: No. When Rodney finds out, he's bound to be a bit Tom and Dick anyway. John Sullivan *Only Fools and Horses* (1989)) or **Tom, Harry, and Dick**. If *Tom* fails to please, you can bring on a substitute: **Bob, Harry, and Dick**, or simply **Bob and Dick**.

Taking a more adventurous tack, there is **Moby Dick**, the great white whale and eponymous villain of the 1851 novel by Herman Melville. This enjoys a subsidiary role in reference to sick leave—if you are *on the Moby Dick*, you are off work because of illness. And moving away somewhat from the 'name' association—indeed, skirting close to the more risqué connotations of *dick*—is **spotted dick**, from the colloquial name for a suet pudding dotted with raisins.

Undoubtedly the most successful of the *dick*-rhymes, though, is **Uncle**

Dick ('I'm feeling a bit Uncle Dick—I'd better sit down'). It has been claimed that this might be the origin of *dicky* 'in poor health' (as in 'a dicky heart'), but it seems unlikely: the chronology is against it (*dicky* dates back to the late 19th century, but Uncle Dick is not recorded until the early 20th century), and it is usually the first, not the second element of a rhyme that goes on to a solo career:

> 'Hot sweet tea! Hot sweet tea!' 'You look a bit uncle to me.'
> —Leon Griffith *Minder* (1979)

Other *sick*-rhymes are **old mick** (first recorded in the late 19th century) and the American **half-a-lick**.

Challenging the supremacy of *sick* are *lousy* (which started to be used for 'ill' in the early 20th century) and *queer* (which dates back in this sense to the 18th century, but waned as *queer* 'homosexual' first spread and then fell into disrepute in the 20th century). For the former there was **housey-housey**, from the name that emerged in the 1930s for the game known previously as *lotto* and latterly as *bingo*; for the latter, **Brighton pier**, which subsequently followed *queer* into gay territory. Then there is *rough*, which finds a rhyme in **Micky Duff**, from the name of the British boxing agent and promoter (1929–). Or perhaps you may just be feeling a little **currant-cakey** (a rhyme on *shaky* current in the first half of the 20th century).

In Australian English, *crook* is 'ill'—hence **butcher's hook**, first recorded in 1967, which, as with its British incarnation (= 'look'), is regularly shortened to **butcher's** (Still feeling butcher's after your op, are ya? Barry Humphries (1981)); and **Captain Cook**.

Pain

The main British rhyming strategy with *pain* is to link it with a road named 'Lane'; hence:

Hanger Lane More usually a metaphorical pain (as in 'a pain in the neck') than a literal one. The association is apt, since the traffic-clogged junction between Hanger Lane and the A40 in West London is certainly a pain in the neck to drivers.

Kennington Lane From a road in Southeast London, leading off Vauxhall Bridge, and just to the north of the Oval cricket ground.

Petticoat Lane From the name still attaching (although the road was officially renamed Middlesex Street in about 1830) to a famous street market in East London, near Liverpool Street Station. Literal or figurative (= 'nuisance').

Then there is **Michael Caine**, from the name (stage name—he was originally Maurice Micklewhite) of the British film actor (1933–). It is fitting that the man whose voice probably typifies 'Cockney' to cinema audiences around the world should be immortalized in rhyming slang, but given the choice he might have preferred a more elevated memorial than (in its shortened form) 'a **Michael** in the Khyber'.

Venereal Diseases

In the days before Aids, 'sexually transmitted diseases' meant VD. Under this banner marched syphilis, gonorrhoea, and various assorted odds and ends. The vocabulary of this embarrassing subject is more about concealment than enlightenment, and its slang is a murky mixture whose most salient characteristic is imprecision. *The pox*, for instance, can often be interpreted as 'VD' in general, although it is often specifically 'syphilis'; *clap* is generally 'gonorrhoea', but is also open to a broader interpretation. Rhymes based on them share their ambiguity.

Syphilis

The ostensibly most specific rhyming slang is based on the abbreviation *syph*, which dates from the early 20th century—but in practice, most of it can be used for 'VD' in general:

bang and biff An Americanism from the first half of the 20th century, whose components recall the metaphors applied to sexual intercourse.

fighting fifth Presumably in imitation of the stirring nicknames given to army regiments.

lover's tiff Such as may ensue when one of the partners discovers the other has the disease.

Wills Whiff From the name of a brand of small cigars available in Britain in the middle years of the 20th century.

In the main, though, it is *pox* that has attracted the rhymes. There are several obvious candidates, and some have been heavily exploited. The most popular is *docks*, which might seem to reflect subliminal associations with the activities of sailors ashore. Most have London links: **East India Docks** (usually *the* **East Indias**), from the docks in Blackwall originally owned by the East India Company, which were the first of London's inland docks to close down, in 1967; **Royal Docks**, from the collective name of the Royal Albert Docks, the Royal Victoria Docks, and the King George V Docks, to the east of the Isle of Dogs; **Surrey Docks**, from the complex of docks in Rotherhithe on the south bank of the Thames, closed in 1970; and **Tilbury Docks**, from the docks on the north bank of the Thames in Essex, which by the end of the 20th century were London's main port (also used as a rhyme for *socks*; see **socks**). Broadening the geographical scope is **Whitehaven Docks**, first recorded in the 1970s, from the large and important port at Whitehaven, Cumbria.

A more diverse set of options is presented by *box*. The oldest is **coachman**

on the box, dating back to the days of coach and horses (when *box* was a term for the driver's seat), and generally shortened to **coachman's**. **Jack-in-the-box** invariably becomes simply **jack**, first recorded in 1954 and especially favoured in Australian English: Got malaria, beri-beri, malnutrition and probably a dose of jack N Medcalf (1985). American English has the jaunty **band in the box**, first recorded in 1944. And most recently there have been **cardboard box**, which seems to date from the 1970s, and **Dairy Box**, from the brand name of a chocolate assortment produced by Cadburys, and rich in ironic potential—could a liaison which began with the gift of a box of chocolates end with one partner giving the other *the* **dairy**?

Rhymes on the name *Knox* have been timebound, disappearing as their originals have faded from memory. **Nervo and Knox** is based on the names of Jimmy Nervo (1890–1975) and Teddy Knox (1896–1974), one of a number of pairings who made up the Crazy Gang, a British variety combo of the middle years of the 20th century (it is also used as a rhyme for *socks* and *box* (= television); another Crazy Gang pair, Naughton and Gold, rhymes with *cold* (see **A COLD**)). **Reverend Ronald Knox** commemorates the priest and detective-story writer (1888–1957) who was the fashionable face of Roman Catholicism in England in the first half of the 20th century. The unwieldy three-parter was often shortened to **Reverend Ronald**, or even amended to **right reverend** (inappropriately, as Knox was never a bishop). The man behind **Collie Knox** was a radio critic, author, and broadcaster well known in the 1930s and 1940s.

And finally, the homely **shoes and socks**, generally abbreviated to **shoes**.

Gonorrhoea

Gonorrhoea is colloquially *the clap* (the word comes from Old French *clapoir* 'venereal bubo'), which is somewhat more amenable to rhyming than *gonorrhoea*. The classic formulation is **horse and trap**, which appears to date from the first half of the 20th century, but there is some use also of the not inappropriate **handicap**. In practice both are applied to undifferentiated VD as well as specifically to gonorrhoea.

Aids

Since the term came on the scene in the early 1980s, **shovels and spades** seems to have been the only rhyme coined from it. The gallows humour is presumably intentional: Aids—death—the digging of graves . . .

Thrush

Not strictly a venereal disease, but it strikes in the same general area. Paired with **Basil Brush**, a puppet fox who appeared on British television from the late 1960s and whose catch phrase was 'Boom boom!'—somewhat incongruously paired, until you remember that *brush* can be a slang term for the female pubic hair.

Haemorrhoids

The squirm factor is high with haemorrhoids, both literally and figuratively, and unhappy sufferers are accustomed to having their condition made light of and even laughed at by others. It is hard not to see an element of ridicule in some of the outlandish rhyming slang in this area, but victims seem content enough to use it themselves as a euphemistic disguise. *Piles* (used in this sense since at least the 14th century) being rather easier to rhyme than *haemorrhoids*, it gets the lion's share:

Chalfont St Giles From the name of the village in Buckinghamshire, most respectable in every way. Popular in theatrical circles, usually in the abbreviated form **Chalfonts**.

Farmer Giles From the mildly humorous generic name for a farmer, dating back to at least the late 18th century. Probably the most widely used *piles*-rhyme, and commonly contracted to **farmers**:

> I've got bumps all over the head, a tongue that is numb, earache, the farmers, backache, neckache & I'll never risk this sort of thing ever again.
> —*The Kenneth Williams Diaries* 20 December 1978 (1993).

A more up-to-date variant is **Johnny Giles**, from the name of the Leeds United and Republic of Ireland footballer (1940–).

laughs and smiles Decidedly not the sufferer's, but a common reaction among unsympathetic friends. A 20th-century Australianism.

Michael Miles Commemorating the New Zealand-born TV quizmaster (1919–71) who hosted *Take Your Pick* on ITV in the 1950s and 1960s.

nautical miles From the marine measure, roughly equivalent to 1.2 land miles. Late 20th century (popularized particularly by *Viz* magazine, which has a great fascination with piles), and usually abbreviated to **nauticals**.

Nobby Stiles From the name of the Manchester United and England midfield player (1942–) who was in the 1966 World Cup-winning England team. He was a combative player who was as bothersome in his way to opposing forwards as haemorrhoids no doubt are to their sufferers, and the application gains further point in the abbreviated form **Nobbies** (*Nobby* is actually short for *Norbert*), which might be interpreted as descriptive.

Nuremberg trials From the proceedings held at Nuremberg, south Germany, 1945–6, in which leading Nazis were tried for war crimes and crimes against humanity. Mainly used in the form **Nurembergs**.

Rockford Files Commemorating a US television series of that name

(1974–80) centred on the adventures of private detective Jim Rockford, played by James Garner:

> I'm having a bit of trouble with my Rockford Files. You don't fancy rubbing a bit more of that cream, do you?
> —Caroline Aherne & Craig Cash *The Royle Family* (2000)

Seven Dials There is more than one seven-way road junction in England known as 'Seven Dials' (there is one in Brighton, for instance), but the original, and no doubt the one rhyming slangsters have in mind, is in the Covent Garden area of London. It was first built in the late 17th century, and took its name from a column in the centre which had a clock with seven dials that looked down each of the roads. The surrounding streets became a notorious haunt of criminals in the 18th and 19th centuries.

Valentine Dyalls From the English actor (1908–85) whose deep dark voice suited him perfectly to roles of mystery and menace. He made his reputation as 'The Man in Black' on radio during the Second World War. Generally shortened to **Valentines**.

X Files From the name of a US television series (first shown in 1993) about two FBI agents who investigate paranormal and supernatural happenings.

Anyone wishing to rhyme *haemorrhoids* itself seems to be irresistibly drawn to the name *Freud*. Probably the most frequent donator of the family name is the British journalist Emma (1961–), daughter of Sir Clement and great-granddaughter of Sigmund. **Emma Freuds** (or **Emmas**) was popularized by the British comic magazine *Viz* (Congratulations, Mr Piles! Your Emma Freuds are almost completely gone. *Viz* (1998)). It might be imagined that Sigmund himself (1856–1939), the Austrian psychoanalyst, got in first, but in fact **Sigmund Freuds** (or **Sigmunds**) seems to be no earlier than the 1990s.

Skin afflictions

Spots

Randolph Scotts From the name of the actor Randolph Scott (1903–87) who starred in many Hollywood westerns in the 1940s and 1950s. Such timebound references often fade away when their original leaves the scene, but **Randolphs** were kept in the public mind by the BBC sitcom *Only Fools and Horses* (first broadcast in 1981).

Selina Scotts A more contemporary note struck in the 1980s: from the name of the television presenter Selina Scott, who first made her mark on BBC breakfast TV.

Boil

can of oil A 20th-century coinage; usually shortened to **can of**.

Conan Doyle Arthur Conan Doyle (1859–1930) sprang to fame for his 'Sherlock Holmes' stories in the early 1890s, and his somewhat undignified rhyming-slang role presumably postdates that.

Jack Doyle A now largely superseded alternative to **Conan Doyle**; from the name of an Irish boxer (1913–78) whose gimmick was to sing in the ring.

Blister

ugly sister From the two Ugly Sisters, persecutors of Cinderella in the fairy tale and pantomime of that name.

Corns

Cape Horns From the cape at the southern extremity of South America, so some anatomical/geographical appropriateness. But one rhyme is a surprisingly low score for an affliction so frequently and so feelingly complained about.

Splinter

Harold Pinter From the British playwright (1930–), whose works are famous for their elusive, pause-filled dialogue and an atmosphere of menace. Usually shortened to **Harold**, but the likelihood of confusion with harolds 'trousers' (see BAGS) seems slim.

Scar

Mars Bar Apparently in use since the 1970s, mainly in the context of facial scars caused by a knife or razor attack. From the proprietary name of a chocolate-covered bar with a toffee-like filling, registered in 1932.

Black eye

It is the slang synonym *shiner* (first recorded in 1904) which gets the rhyming treatment: originally probably with **ocean liner**, generally abbreviated to **ocean**; and subsequently with **Morris Minor**, from the best-selling small car first produced by Morris Motors in 1948.

Itch

Little Titch From 'Little Tich', the stage-name of the diminutive English music-hall comedian Harry Relph (1867–1928), who was given the nickname as a child because of a resemblance to the so-called 'Tichborne claimant' (Arthur Orton (1834–98), who claimed to be the long-lost Roger Tichborne, heir to an English baronetcy). **Little Titchy** has reportedly been used for *itchy* (*titchy* 'small' itself is not recorded before 1950).

Colds and related ailments

A cold

There is a clear demarcation between these rhymes for acute rhinitis and rhymes for the adjective *cold* (compare *Cold* at TIME AND TIDE).

Naughton and Gold From Charlie Naughton (1887–1976) and Jimmy Gold (1886–1967), a pair of British comedians who formed part of the Crazy Gang, a wacky ensemble popular in music hall and variety in the middle years of the 20th century (for a less innocent contribution of theirs to the rhyming slang of illness, see Nervo and Knox at SYPHILIS).

soldier bold Dating back to the 19th century, and usually shortened to **soldier** (as in 'You'll catch a soldier if you go out in this weather'). An occasional variant was **warrior bold**. (The parallel adjectival forms are pluralized—see *Cold* at TIME AND TIDE.)

A chill

frock and frill Current in the late 19th and early 20th centuries, when *frock* was the most usual term for a woman's dress.

Flu

It is of course *flu* (first recorded in the 1830s), not the more high-falutin *influenza*, which gets the rhyme. Three of them are on record, all probably reflecting how the flu sufferer feels or looks. **Inky blue**, dating from the 1970s, is perhaps based on *blue* 'sad, miserable'. The somewhat earlier **lousy Lou** relies on *lousy* 'wretchedly unwell', although it is not clear whether *Lou* is intended to be male or female. The variant **scraggy Lou** vividly pictures the ravages of the disease.

In colloquial Australian English, *wog* is a term applied to an insect, and hence by metaphorical extension (like *bug*) to a germ, to an illness, and ultimately specifically to flu. In this last guise it is rhymed as **chocolate frog**.

Fever

Robinson and Cleaver From the name of an originally Belfast-based firm of linen drapers which opened a large store in Regent Street, London in 1894. In its early days apparently often applied specifically to typhoid fever, in the 20th century the rhyme more often stood in for scarlet fever.

Cough

Darren Gough A recent coinage, based on the name of the Yorkshire and England fast bowler Darren Gough (1970–).

　horse and trough Evocative of the days when urban transport was fuelled not from petrol stations but from water troughs strategically placed in the streets. Usually shortened to **horse**, which appositely conjures up *hoarse*.

Sneeze

bread and cheese Functioning as both a noun and a verb. First recorded in the late 19th century, and always used in full.

Tummy upsets

Diarrhoea

If any rhymes on *diarrhoea* have been attempted, they do not survive. It is more colloquial alternatives that get the treatment, especially *the shits* (most of the rhymes are adaptations of singular forms already used for *shit* (see **IN THE LAV**)); and many of the rhymes are more often used metaphorically (*give someone the jimmies/threepennies/toms*, etc. = get on someone's nerves) than literally:

　Eartha Kitts An unflattering application for the US cabaret singer (1928–) with the seductive voice and a penchant for old-fashioned millionaires. See also *Breasts* at **THE BODY AND PARTS**.

　Edgar Britts An Australianism, first recorded in 1969 and presumably modelled on the earlier Jimmy Britts. Edgar Britt (1913–) was a well-known Australian jockey.

> 'Jeez,' said Wooffer. 'You give me the Edgar Britts, sometimes.'
> —B. Dawe, *Over here, Harv!* (1983)

Jimmy Britts or **Jimmy Brits** Australian, from the name of the American-born boxer Jimmy Britt (1879–1940). First recorded in the Second World War period, it has gone on to widespread use, especially in its abbreviated form **jimmys** or **jimmies**:

> Malaria and the jimmy britz [*sic*] have sucked him dry.
> —Jon Cleary, *Climate of Courage* (1954)

> Men was growlin' crook tucker, gettin' the jimmies, an' all that, they said.
> —D'Arcy Niland, *The Shiralee* (1955)

nicker bits A fairly precisely datable piece of rhyming slang, based as it is on a colloquial term for pound coins, which were introduced in Britain in

1983 (one nicker = £1). Modelled presumably on **threepenny bits** or **two bob bits**, which by then were obsolescent.

threepenny bits Dating from the 19th century, and based on the colloquial term for a British coin worth three old pence—originally a small silver coin, latterly (1937–70) a twelve-sided nickel-brass one. Generally shortened to **threepennies**. An analogous rhyme in Australian and New Zealand English is **trey-bits**, which originally denoted literally 'threepenny bits'. See also *Breasts* at **THE BODY AND ITS PARTS**.

two bob bits Inflationary pressures push the amount up to two shillings—colloquially 'two bob'. A two-shilling coin, often called a 'florin', was in circulation in Britain between 1849 and 1971.

tomtits In British usage much commoner in the singular form, meaning 'excrement' or 'defecation', but Australian English has enthusiastically adopted the plural for 'diarrhoea', and also uses the abbreviated **toms**:

> What's the matter, got the tom tits?
> —Patsy Adam Smith *The Barcoo Salute* (1973)

Zazu Pitts Another ungallant rhyme, from the name of the Hollywood actress Zazu Pitts (1898–1963)

The shits does not get it all its own way, though; there is also *the runs*, producing **Tommy guns** (from the colloquial name for a Thompson sub-machine-gun) and **Radio Ones** (from the BBC's pop music station, which began broadcasting in 1967); and *the trots*, whence **red hots** (perhaps with a subliminal reference to the effects of overspiced curry) and **Zachary Scotts** (from a Hollywood actor (1914–65) noted for his 'cad' roles, often shortened to **Zacharys**).

Vomiting

The key word in this area, *sick*, also means more generally 'unwell', and rhymes based on it tend to share in its ambiguity (see **ILL**). *Vomit* itself has been rhymed as **Wallace and Gromit**, after a pair of plasticine characters, human and canine, in a series of award-winning animated films by Nick Park. There is one very specialized 'vomiting' colloquialism, though, and it belongs to Australian English—not altogether inappropriately, as vomiting sometimes seems to be an Australian national pastime, and the language contains a number of colourful synonyms for it:

Chunder itself is probably an eroded rhyme: it appears to come from **Chunder Loo**, rhyming slang for *spew*, which in turn was based on *Chunder Loo of Akin Foo*, a cartoon character originally drawn by Norman Lindsay (1879–1969) and appearing in advertisements for Cobra boot polish in the Sydney *Bulletin* between 1909 and 1920. From *chunder* comes **up and under**, also, like *chunder*, a verb. Dating apparently from the 1950s, it originated (probably in Australia) as a rugby term, denoting a kick high enough for the kicker and his team-mates to run forward and try to catch the ball as it lands.

Trouble with joints, muscles, and the like

Gout

salmon and trout Recorded since the 1930s, but dismissed by Julian Franklyn in *A Dictionary of Rhyming Slang* (1960) as spurious on the grounds that the sort of people who use rhyming slang do not suffer from gout, and even if they did, they would not talk about it. In fact, gout is by no means the preserve of the stereotypical port-drinking classes, and strikes high and low alike, so the rhyme might be genuine; and even if it is not, **salmon and trout** has plenty of other rhyming slang jobs to do—with *snout*, *stout*, and *tout*, among others.

Bunion

Spanish onion The rhyme was irresistible, given the line 'I'll raise a bunion on his Spanish onion if I catch him bending tonight', from the 1911 Billy Merson song 'The Spaniard that Blighted my Life'. But the bunion seems to be largely a 19th- and 20th-century concept, and there is vanishly little use for the rhyme.

Cramp

rising damp 20th century, and perhaps drawing a parallel between damp creeping up a wall and cramp attacking the legs.

Delirium tremens

For rhyming slang purposes this is *the shakes*, and translates into **rattlesnakes** (**rattles** for short, and no doubt with a side-glance at 19th- and 20th-century slang *rattled* 'drunk'), **currant cakes** (early 20th century, and complemented by the adjectival **currant-cakey** 'shaky'), and **Joe Blakes** (Australian, and better known as rhyming slang for 'snakes'—which one no doubt sees when one has the DTs).

And if the trouble is severe, you could end up a *cripple*—in the 21st century a word too non-PC for use, even perhaps in rhyming-slang disguise, but in the 1970s you could get away with **raspberry ripple** and **strawberry ripple** (often abbreviated to **raspberry** and **strawberry** respectively), from varieties of ice cream recently introduced in Britain.

Cancer

The rhyme with *dancer* confirms a non-British origin: **Jack the dancer** and **Jimmy dancer** are both Australian:

And your Dad had a dose of Jack the Dancer when he died.
—L. Stevens **(ed.)** *Pub Fiction* (1997)

Medical treatment

Pills

There is more to pills than medicine—mind-bending drugs come in pills, and the word is also slang for 'testicles'—and the rhyming versions reflect the diversity:

Fanny Hills Applied mainly to the contraceptive pill, whose introduction in the early 1960s coincided with the controversial reissuing of the erotic novel *The Memoirs of Fanny Hill* (1749) by John Cleland.

jack and jills Chiefly drug-users' slang, and applied in the main to pills of heroin (**jack**, presumably a shortening of **jack and jills**, has been used since the 1950s for a tablet of prescribed heroin (or a substitute such as methadone), or more generally for a single dose of a narcotic). The original inspiration was the celebrated nursery rhyme ('Jack and Jill went up the hill to fetch a pail of water'), but the specific application was no doubt reinforced by slang *jack up* 'to inject (oneself) with heroin or another drug'. Since the 1980s some usage, too, for 'contraceptive pill', and in the 1990s for the virility pill 'Viagra':

> He did a lot of booze and jack and jills in a nightclub, stepped out into the cold night air, and pow!
> —*The Bill* (2001)

> *Lock, Stock and a Fistful of Jack and Jills.* Jamie, Lee, Bacon, and Moon undertake deliveries on behalf of the Dutchies in return for some 'sex' pills
> —*Radio Times* (2000)

Jenny Hills From the British music-hall artiste Jenny Hill (1851–96). Reputedly originally applied to medicinal pills, but more recently transferred to 'testicles'.

Jimmy Hills Referring to legitimate medicine or illicit drugs and commemorating Jimmy Hill (1928–), Fulham footballer and latterly ubiquitous TV soccer pundit.

William Hills Apparently a coinage of the 1990s, and named after a British chain of bookmakers, the William Hill Organisation Ltd.

Crutches

rabbit hutch Its main role is as a rhyme for *crotch* (see THE BODY AND ITS PARTS), but apparently some residual application also to the leg substitutes.

Doctors

king's proctor Latterly seldom used, and a reminder of a time, up to the reform of the divorce laws in 1969, when divorce was the stuff of high-profile court cases in England, and widely reported in the tabloid press: the King's (or Queen's) Proctor is an official of the Probate, Divorce, and Admiralty Division of the High Court of Justice, who has the right to intervene in probate, divorce, and nullity cases, when collusion between the parties or suppression of material facts is alleged—in other words, if dodgy evidence has been cooked up in a divorce case, he can stop a decree nisi being made absolute. No known connection with doctors, apart from the rhyme; a subliminal link with *proctologist* 'specialist in afflictions of the anus' is perhaps too far-fetched.

Medical practice

In Britain, the official list of doctors in a district who accepted patients under the terms of the National Health Insurance Act of 1913 was known as the *panel*. A patient under the care of a 'panel doctor' was said to be *on the panel*. The scope of this expression was extended to denote 'off work because of sickness', and it was mainly in this context that rhyming slang **English Channel** and **soap and flannel** came into use. The panel disappeared with the advent of the National Health Service in 1946, but the rhymes continued to be used by those off sick.

And if medication fails. . .

Dead

brown bread The best-established British rhyme for *dead* in the early 21st century, but not in fact recorded before 1973. Perhaps a healthier variation on the earlier loaf of bread.

gone to bed 20th century, and overtly euphemistic to an extent that is unusual for rhyming slang; it taps into the well mined vein of 'asleep, resting' = 'dead' circumlocutions.

loaf of bread Dating from the 1930s, and later largely supplanted by brown bread:

> O how I cried when Alice died The day we were to have wed! We never had our Roasted Duck And now now she's a Loaf of Bread,
> —Auden & Isherwood (1935).

In Australian English, the metaphorical use of *hors de combat* for 'dead' (*combat* pronounced *à l'Anglaise*) has given rise to the rather surreal rhyme

wombat (from the stocky bearlike Australian marsupial).

Send for the:

Undertaker

overcoat maker A not very subtle reference to *wooden overcoat*, a slang term for 'coffin'.

Ethnic and National Groups

A glance at the rhyming epithets attached to various races and nationalities over the past one hundred and fifty years does not leave a very attractive impression: bigotry and xenophobia are probably the two characteristics which leap most obviously from the page. The people most rhymed against are by a very long distance the Jews—well over twenty different rhymes, and the underlying motivation of most of them, if not openly expressed, seems to be hostility. Next on the list come blacks, with rhymes based on terms (*nigger*, *spade*, *coon*, etc.) that by the end of the 20th century had become firmly taboo. And in fact the majority of these rhymes have this in common: that they are directed against a (usually minority) racial group that are disliked or feared among the language community they find themselves in.

But there is nothing particularly characteristic of rhyming slang about this. It is a common feature of slang, rhyming or not. Slang is what we turn to to do our linguistic dirty work. Perhaps part of the original intention of the rhymes was to mitigate the ugliness of the likes of *yid* and *wog*. But as with all euphemism, what is underneath shows through sooner or later.

Jews

Rhymes in this category are based either on *Jew* (the great majority) or the much more overtly offensive *Yid*. Most of them date from the late 19th century or the beginning of the 20th; by the last third of the 20th century powerful taboos were in place which progressively drove existing rhymes out (or underground) and prevented the emergence of new ones.

Jew

Although *Jew* is a neutral term, the effect of rhyming it (taken as belittling or condescending or indicative of contempt) is no less offensive than that of rhyming the derogatory *Yid* (yet the rhymes are not intrinsically offensive— none alludes, for example, to the stereotypical sharpness of Jews in business dealings).

The fact that *Jew* rhymes with *two* is the starting point for most of these synonyms: *two* is paired with other numbers in patterns suggesting a clock time or racing odds (or both) or a measurement. Probably the best-established is **four by two**, first recorded as late as 1936, which was inspired by the term employed in the British Army for a piece of cloth, four inches by two, used to clean the inside of a rifle barrel. Still encountered at the end of the 20th century:

> That's all right so long as it's not ham. . . I'm a four-be two, you see.
> —James Curtis *The Gilt Kid* (1936)

> It was like the rhyming slang 'four-by-twos' for 'Jews', used . . . perhaps with an undertone of lurking contempt.
> —Leila Berg *Risinghill* (1968)

> 'This Marx, was he a four by two?' demanded Quimple. 'Pardon?' 'A Jew, sir, a Jew.'
> —Edmund McGirr *Death Pays Wages* (1970)

In abbreviated form it is **forby**, which is probably as close as any of these items come to inoffensiveness.

This is fairly closely followed by **five to two**, which represents racing odds rather than time and was hence reputedly particularly popular amongst bookies and other members of the racing fraternity. First recorded in 1914, it was still recognizable in context in its shortened form **five**:

> Fancy going off . . . with that big-mouthed five-to-two.
> —Compton Mackenzie *Sinister Street* (1914)

> They respect us. Your five-to-two is a judge of quality.
> —Evelyn Waugh *The Loved One* (1948)

A variation on this sometimes encountered is **five by two**, probably the result of blending with four by two.

The 'time' metaphor is represented by **half past two**, **quarter past two**, **quarter to two**, and **ten to two**, all apparently coinages of the early years of the 20th century.

US English in the 1940s produced **fifteen-two**, or **fifteen and two**, inspired by the scoring system of the game of cribbage. And another exploitation of *two* is **tea for two**, inspired no doubt by the 1925 song of that name (lyrics by Irving Caesar), and frequent enough to be truncated to **teafer**.

Other *Jew*-rhymes:

box of glue A US rhyme, dating from the 1920s:

> We took it on the heel and toe down to the old box of glue on the corner, and got a fin for the lay-out.
> —R. J. Tasker *Grimhaven* (1928)

buckle my shoe A late 19th-century rhyme which enjoyed some popularity in the services during the First World War. Inspired by the old nursery rhyme 'One, Two, Buckle my Shoe'.

kangaroo First recorded in the 1940s, and apparently used especially among the racing fraternity, particularly with reference to Jewish on-course bookmakers.

pot of glue Another variant on the *glue* theme, somewhat less common than box of glue. The shortened version has been represented orthographically as **potter**.

Sarah Soo First recorded in the 1920s.

Yid (originally a back-formation from *Yiddish*) first appeared in English around two-thirds of the way through the 19th century. Originally it seems to have been a neutral term, but there is clear evidence that by the 20th century it was being used abusively. Rhymes based on it are generally in the same vein:

four-wheel skid Dating from the 1930s. Similarly inspired are **front-wheel skid** and **three-wheel skid**.

God forbid or **Gawd forbid** First recorded in 1960, and reflecting a self-exculpatory expression supposedly often on the lips of Jewish traders and others.

non-skid Reportedly a coinage of the 1920s.

saucepan lid Probably the most widespread of the *lid*-rhymes—others are **teapot lid** and **tin lid** (reputedly often applied to the supporters of Tottenham Hotspur, which is said to attract many Jewish fans).

An older uncomplimentary term for *Jew* is *ikey-mo* (coined from abbreviated forms of the names *Isaac* and *Moses*). US English has rhymed this as **eskimo**.

Gentiles

Shikse

Shikse is a generally uncomplimentary term used by Jews to refer to a non-Jewish woman. In rhyming slang it becomes **flour mixer**.

Blacks

Jumping jack occasionally does rhyming duty for *black*, but that apart, rhyming slang in this area draws resolutely on three contemptuous terms that by the end of the 20th century had been consigned to PC outer darkness (and allows the taboo to be circumvented):

Coon

Short for *racoon*, and in use in this sense since at least the 1830s:

cameroon Reportedly coined in the wake of the good showing put up by Cameroon in the 1990 football World Cup.

egg and spoon Dating from the 1960s. The collocation first came together in *egg-and-spoon race*, denoting a race typically run by parents or small children at school sports days and involving carrying an egg in a spoon without dropping it—first recorded in the 1890s.

macaroon It and its abbreviated version **macker** had some currency in London in the early 1990s.

silvery moon Possibly inspired by the 1909 song 'By the light of the silvery moon', though the sentiment was already a cliché by then. Generally shortened to **silvery**. From the same stable comes **harvest moon**.

Nigger

gravedigger It's no coincidence that before it was put to rhyming use, *gravedigger* was a slang term for the spades suit in cards. *Spade* being also a casual insult word for 'black' (see below), the underlying double entendre is not hard to spot.

mechanical digger Probably based on the model of **gravedigger**, and generally reduced to **mechanical**. Possibly fuelled by racist associations of blacks with manual labour.

square rigger A 20th-century coinage that has as much of euphemism in it as of hostility. Perhaps originally a sailors' or dockers' rhyme.

Spade

A patronizing synonym first recorded in the 1920s, inspired by the colour of the playing-card suit (and possibly specifically by the simile *as black as the ace of spades*, first recorded—with reference to black people—in the 1880s):

lemonade A variation on the theme established by **Lucozade**.

Lucozade From the name of a British energy-giving carbonated drink, registered as a trademark in 1930. In abbreviated form it is transformed to **Luke**.

razor blade A coinage of the 1960s, when the racial climate in Britain was conducive to such dismissive epithets. Often shortened to **razor**.

Europeans

English

The English have not rhymed themselves. They have left that task to the Australians, who have happily complied with a rhyme on *Pom*:

to and from First recorded in 1946, and like *Pom* often applied specifically to English immigrants in Australia. The implication of a short stay before a return to the old country has often been borne out:

The to-and-froms speak in a most peculiar way.
—*Daily Telegraph* (Sydney) (1978)

As a 'To-and-From', one of the things that baffled me in the Australian leisure lifestyle when I first arrived here many years ago was the esky routine.
—*Weekend Australian Magazine* (1982)

French

jiggle and jog A 1970s rhyme based on that perennial pejorative *Frog*.

muddy trench A product of comradely encounters during the First World War. Ray Puxley in *Cockney Rabbit* (1992) suggests that the phrase represents in full *bloody French*.

German

Rhyming slang usually being racially uncomplimentary, the rhymed word here is not surprisingly *kraut*. This has yielded **holler and shout**, a mild enough imputation of boisterousness, followed in the 1990s by **lager lout**.

Greek

bubble and squeak In use since before the First World War and current throughout the 20th century, often in its shortened form **bubble**. Based on the name of the traditional British (and decidedly non-Greek) dish which consists of mainly fried cabbage and potatoes:

All the best Anglo-Saxon grafters come from mine [*sc.* my school], and the Bubbles and the Indians from the other.
—Robin Cook *The Crust on its Uppers* (1962)

It also stands in metonymically for a Greek meal or restaurant:

'That was fantastic for a bubble,' said the Bloke as we left the restaurant . . .
'Bubble, as in bubble and squeak. It's rhyming slang for Greek.'
—*Sunday Times* (1999)

werris An Australian coinage of the 1960s, short for *Werris Creek*, the name of a town in New South Wales.

Irish

goodie and baddie A 20th-century rhyme based on *Paddy*, perennial nickname and epithet for the Irish. Usually reduced to **goodie**.

shovel and pick Rhyming with another (and rather less complimentary) Irish cognomen, *Mick*, and picking up on the stereotype of the Irishman as building labourer.

Italian

bottle of pop A rhyme based on the insult word *wop* (first recorded at the beginning of the 20th century). Its shortened form **bottler** coincides with slang *bottler* 'coward' (i.e. someone who has lost his 'bottle'), and probable reflects the reputation of Italian soldiers in Britain during the Second World War and after.

  grocer's shop A coinage apparently of the 1970s, also based on *wop*. Possibly a reference to Italian delis.

  sky An Australian coinage of the 1920s, rhyming with *Eyetie*, a contemptuous shortening of *Italian*.

Liverpudlian

Mickey Mouse A late 20th-century application for the diminutive Disney rodent, rhyming with *Scouse* 'Liverpudlian', and used mainly as a taunt by London football supporters against Liverpool fans, relying heavily on the metaphorical *Mickey Mouse* 'second-rate'.

Pole

For Londoners in the early and middle years of the 20th century, *Pole* was often a vague cover term for any Eastern European:

  sausage roll A coinage of the 1940s, possibly originally applied to Poles who came to fight in the RAF and other British armed forces during the Second World War. It reportedly enjoyed a revival in the mid 1960s, when gangs of Polish thieves operated in London, taking away the aggrieved locals' business.

Portuguese

pork and beans A British services' coinage of the First World War period, when tinned pork and beans (mainly beans) was often on the menu. The similarity of the first elements makes up slightly for the fact that the last scarcely rhyme.

Scot

sweaty sock Rhyming with *Jock* 'Scot', and popular as a taunt among English football supporters.

Spaniard

oil slick Based on the insulting *spick* 'Spaniard, Latin American' (ultimately short for *no spika de English*, supposedly the Spanish immigrant's reply to questions in English), and picking up on stereotypical associations with oiliness—olive oil in the food, hair oil in the hair, etc.

Welsh

riff-raff A highly uncomplimentary rhyme based on *Taff* 'Welsh person'.

Asians

Chinese

With instinctive non-PCness, rhyming slangsters reach for *Chink* (a patronizing insult of Australian origin, dating from the late 19th century). Rhymes based on it are **kitchen sink**, **tiddlywink** (the most widely used, and first recorded in the 1970s) and **widow's wink** (also apparently a 1970s coinage).

Japanese

mousetrap Rhyming with *Jap*. An occasionally encountered alternative to rat-trap:

> If it hadn't been for the Mousetraps (equals Japs in rhyming slang) I wouldn't have met Biggs at all.
> —Lynn Barber *Sunday Express* (1984)

microchip A late 20th-century coinage reflecting Japanese dominance in microelectronics. But the word rhymed is the good old-fashioned insult *Nip*. The shortened form **micro** fits neatly into the stereotype of Japanese stature.

orange pip Another *Nip*-rhyme, generally shortened to the off-colour **orange**.

rat-trap Rhyming somewhat more respectably with *Jap*, but the shortened form **rat** reveals the motivation of this Second World War coinage.

Pakistani

For rhyming purposes, *Pakistani* becomes *Paki* (first recorded in the 1960s):

flunky and lackey Insulting either in its full form or abbreviated to **flunky**.

ounce of baccy No doubt reflecting the stereotype of Bangladeshi-owned corner shops in Britain (Bangladesh was formerly East Pakistan), where tobacco (among other things) is sold. The shortened form is represented as **ouncer**. A less generous variation on the same theme is **half an ounce of baccy**.

Americans

USA

In the world of rhyming slang, US citizens are *Yankees* or *Yanks*:

ham shank Originally used in Naval circles during the Second World War. It seems to have died out by the end of the 1960s.

septic tank An Australian coinage, first recorded in 1967 and widely used (not just in Australia) ever since, generally in the shortened form **septic** (sometimes amended further still with the Aussie suffix -*o* to *seppo*). The literal meaning of the term, 'tank in which sewage is treated', gives a clue to the connotations of the rhyme:

> We've got too many poms and septic tanks floodin' the box, and it's about time we had our own accent heard for a change.
> —*Australasian Post* (1972)

> Jesus, lover of my soul, if it isn't the Goddams, the Septics themselves! . . . Stick around long enough, I told myself, and . . . you'll see some real live Yanks.
> —D. Stuart *I Think I'll Live* (1981)

> Some compliment, eh, comin' from a Septic Tank on Fifth Avenue?
> —Clem Gorman *A Night in the Arms of Raeleen* (1983)

> From then on Keith and I were known as 'Foxtrot Lima 1' and 'Foxtrot Lima 2' while Jon was christened 'Septic', from the cockney [sic] rhyming slang Septic Tank—Yank!
> —*Today's Pilot* (2001)

> I [Guy Ritchie] got her [Madonna] to admit she is a septic.
> —*Daily Star* (2001)

Sherman tank Coined in the 1940s, when most people were familiar with the main US battle tank of the Second World War, named after US General W. T. Sherman (1820–91). Usually used in the shortened form **sherman**, but its currency waned as the rhyme came more and more to be attached to *wank* (see under *Masturbation* at **SEX**).

Widow Twankey Commemorating the comical dame character from the pantomime *Aladdin*. Usually shortened to **widow**.

wooden plank Often specifically denoting US tourists in England. A variation on the theme is **board and plank**.

Foreigners

Wog

Current since the 1920s, *wog* has been used as a general insult word for any foreigner, but usually the specific reference is to a member of a dark-skinned race. In rhyming slang it becomes **hedgehog**.

Immigrant

Jimmy Grant An Australian and New Zealand rhyme, also with some currency in South Africa. First recorded in 1845, it had largely disappeared as a live usage by the 1920s. Common in the run-together form **jimmygrant**, and also abbreviated to **jimmy**:

> Most of the 'Jimmy Grants' arrived so far look like Dukes in disguise.
> —*Truth* (Sydney) (1907)

> The 500 home-bolting 'Jimmies' (as he calls them) who were pining for the bacon and bread or slice of suet pudding which was all they knew of meat.
> —*Truth* (Sydney) (1915)

Relatives and Friends

A glance at the rhyming slang for 'spouses' leaves us in little doubt as to where the rhymes are coming from. Nearly twenty synonyms for *wife*, a mere one for *husband*. Admittedly *husband* itself is virtually impossible to find a satisfactory rhyme for, but even making allowances for that, the conclusion is inescapable: it is mainly men who make up the rhymes. Other female relations (mothers, sisters, daughters, aunts) do rather better than their male counterparts, too, suggesting perhaps that (surprise, surprise) men tend to talk more about women than about men.

Spouses

Wife

Three or four key themes can be teased out in the rhyming treatment of *wife*, all with their own particular angle. The one with the highest profile is probably *strife*, with its subtle suggestion of marital disharmony and the shrewishness of wives. Its rhyming partner reinforces the implication, as in **struggle and strife**, **war and strife**, **worry and strife**, and—probably the original version, and model for the rest—**trouble and strife**. First recorded in print in 1929, it has become the archetypal 'wife'-rhyme, familiar to those not versed in the lingo:

> 'Thanks for looking after my old trouble and strife' said Bruce.
> —Angus Wilson *The Wrong Set* (1949)

> It is a long time since I heard a peer mention his wife in terms other than 'trouble and strife'.
> —Christopher Sykes 'What U-Future?' [written humorously from the perspective of 2055], in *Noblesse Oblige*, edited by Nancy Mitford (1956)

> My posh trouble-and-strife, I'll be hers.
> —John Osborne *The World of Paul Slickey* (1959)

Rather more positive opportunities are offered by *life*, which prompts the romantic-sounding **light of my life** (although alas for our illusions, this is said to be used mainly ironically, of rolling-pin-wielding battleaxes) and **kiss of life** (but that may just come from the term for mouth-to-mouth resuscitation, which dates from the early 1960s). The exclamatory **pon my life** came in and went out in the late 19th century (*pon* being an archaic abbreviation of *upon*). It might be tempting to make some link between

sporting life and the mainly US slang term for the 'good life', but in truth it was probably inspired by the long-established racing newspaper of that name, favoured daily reading of many a rhyming slangster.

Knife, we must assume, is a nod to domesticity, rather than a subliminal glimpse of marital hostility. Certainly **fork and knife** belongs firmly in the kitchen and dining room, but there is something uncomfortably cutting about **carving knife**, especially in its abbreviated form **carving**—'That was no lady, that was the carving!'

Colloquially, the wife is the *missis*, which brings the impeccably uxorious *kisses* into play. Combinations include:

cheese and kisses A curious pairing dating from the late 19th century. It has long since disappeared, but it lives on in its shortened form **cheese**. Australian English has used *cheese* for 'girlfriend', and it has been suggested that US slang *cheese* '(sexy) young woman or women' (Gap teeth and bare snatch are surefire signs. This cheese wants to get planked John Lahr *Hot to Trot* (1974)) may come from the same source (although *cheesecake* '(photos of) attractive young women' seems a more likely inspiration).

cows and kisses If anything an even more bizarre combination, first recorded in the 1850s but unsurprisingly not a long-term survivor. No man seems to have had the temerity to abbreviate it.

hugs and kisses A well-established 20th-century example, generally shortened to **hugs** (/ʌgz/ for Cockneys, unflatteringly).

love and kisses What can one say but 'Aaaah!'

plates and dishes A somewhat approximate rhyme, usually shortened to *the plates*.

Your wife can also be your *old woman*, which calls into play the strange 19th-century coinage **old grabem pudden**. A distinctly approximate rhyme, it pictures women as sweet-toothed creatures who cannot resist grabbing the pudding. (It also applies to *old woman* 'mother'.) Its 20th-century continuation is **gooseberry pudding**, usually curtailed to **gooseberry** (a man's 'old gooseberry' is his wife).

Returning to *wife*, one of the most venerable of rhymes is **Duchess of Fife**, which dates from the mid-19th century. It is generally abbreviated (and remodelled) to **Dutch**:

> I detected a coster . . . with some one to act as his Dutch.
> —R. C. Lehmann Anni Fugaces (1901)

In practice this usually appears as **old Dutch** (first recorded in 1889), popularized in Albert Chevalier's 1893 song 'My Old Dutch' and thereafter associated particularly with a partner in a long and happy marriage:

> There ain't a lady livin' in the land As I'd 'swop' for my dear old Dutch!

Husband

Husband has understandably defeated rhymers, so they have had to have recourse to the colloquial *old man*. In rhyming slang this becomes **old pot and pan**, a 19th-century coinage which maintained its currency in the 20th century:

> How's yer ole pot-'n'-pan, Tutsie?
> —Edward Dyson *Fact'ry 'Ands* (1906)

It also does duty for *father*.

Blood Relations

Mother

God love her Every good Cockney boy loves his mum, so this 1970s rhyme is particularly appropriate.

one and t'other Like its variant **one and another**, this late 19th-century coinage also means 'brother'.

strangle and smother An Australian offering that betrays more than a hint of unresolved conflicts.

Mum

finger and thumb Around since the late 19th century, but only comparatively recently applied to *mum* (see also FRIENDS). Commonly shortened to **finger**.

Father

The only straight rhyme for *father* to have gained any currency is the late 19th-century **soap and lather**—shades of dad's early-morning shave. A much more popular strategy is to rhyme the colloquial *old man*: **old pot and pan**. This goes back to the 19th century too, and has always been somewhat more common than its other application, to 'husband'. The abbreviated form **old pot** is favoured particularly in Australian and New Zealand English:

> 'What about Mr. Pilgrim?' 'Aw, he's different . . . I get on with him good-oh, even if his old pot is one of these lords. Him and me's cobbers.'
> —Ngaio Marsh *Artists in Crime* (1938)

Sister

The key rhyming-word when it comes to *sisters* is *blister*—not a very flattering reflection on the warmth of the brother–sister relationship. The best-established combination is **skin and blister**, first recorded in the 1920s:

I saw your skin and blister last night.
—George Ingram *Cockney Cavalcade* (1935)

Alternative formulations are **bubble and blister** and the Australian **blood blister** and **kid blister**.

It is possible to avoid the skin blemishes, but only at the expense of deploying the bizarre **black man kissed her**. This seems to have emerged in the early years of the 20th century, but despite some fluctuations in usage it had died out before the end.

Brother

manhole cover Rhymed with /ˈbrʌvə/, for that authentic Cockney touch. Generally shortened to **manhole**.

one and t'other and **one another** Alternative uses for rhymes that are more commonly applied to *mother*.

Daughter

Largely a *water*-theme for *daughter*. Probably the longest established combination is **soap and water** (first recorded in 1925, and redolent of cleanliness, or possibly household chores), but it was soon joined by **bottle of water** and **holy water**. For something a little stronger, try a stout **bottle of porter**.

The stolid-sounding, uncomplimentary **bricks and mortar** is another 20th-century coinage.

Son

Economizing on effort, and with little fear of confusion, rhymers tend to use the same formulations for *son* as they do for its homophone *sun* (see *The sun* at TIME AND TIDE), most of them based on *bun*. They comprise **Bath bun**, **currant bun** (The story of Jesus begins with the Angel Gabriel informing Mary she is going to give birth to a currant bun (son). *Sunday Times* (2000), reporting a new translation of the Bible into Cockney rhyming slang), **hot cross bun**, **penny bun**, and **sticky bun** (the only one not used for *sun*—but apt for *son* because of its juvenile connotations).

Non-*bun* offerings are limited to **pie and one** (which is also used for *sun*!). It comes from a familiar order in a caff or pie shop—'one' being a single portion of mashed potato.

Aunt

garden plant A 20th-century creation, usually reduced to **garden**.
See also *Mrs Chant's* at IN THE LAV.

Cousin

baker's dozen A late-19th-century rhyme, exploiting an ancient expression for 'thirteen'. When used, generally abbreviated to **baker's**.

Head of the family

daily bread A late 19th-century rhyme which survived into the mid-20th century. Based on the words of the Lord's Prayer ('Give us this day our daily bread'), it suggests the paterfamilias as bread-winner.

Friends

Friend

Friend itself has inspired only one rhyme, **mile end**—but the geography is appropriate, Mile End being an area of East London, to the north of Stepney (the name comes from its originally having been the hamlet at the end of the first mile on the road east from the City of London).

Considerably more favoured is the matily colloquial *mate*, which has found a constant companion in *plate*:

china plate Now little used, as the abbreviated form **china** has broken free from its rhyming-slang roots and become an established Cockneyism for 'friend' (often, if fictional accounts of Cockney life are to be believed, in 'my old china')—although even that was fading out towards the end of the 20th century.

> 'Remember that China of his?' 'What, the bloke with the hair?'
> —*Penguin New Writing* (1945)

> I have my hands full with his china who is a big geezer of about 14 stone.
> —*New Statesman* (1965)

> 'Eddie? Yeah—he's my new china.' 'What?' 'China plate—mate.'
> —*The Limey* (1999)

China plate itself is first recorded in the 1880s, in the language of building labourers.

Dutch plate A usage that had some currency in the 1960s and 1970s, mainly in its shortened form **Dutch**—which no doubt occasionally caused confusion with Dutch 'wife'.

tin plate A more downmarket article than a china plate, and much less favoured for rhymes.

Also rhyming with *mate* is **garden gate**—but in this case not the friend, but the naval person. A British Merchant Navy usage of the first part of the 20th century.

The homely *chum* can be rhymed as **finger and thumb**, which also stands for *mum*—but then a girl's best friend . . . And the uncompromisingly Australian *cobber* yields the not very friendly **thief and robber**.

Neighbour

hard labour An uncomplimentary rhyme suggestive of a certain lack of harmony over the garden fence.

Marriage

Married

The earliest rhyme to establish itself was probably **cut and carried**; the metaphor is an agricultural one, based on the idea of cutting corn and carrying it away to your barn, and the application is usually to the female spouse (often in the context of unavailability for extramarital sexual dalliance). **Carried** can be used on its own in the same sense, and other spin-offs are **dot and carried** (based on the old expression *dot and carry one* 'to walk with a wooden leg, limp', and implying the hobbling effect of marriage; not much used after the early 20th century) and **cash and carried** (from the retailing strategy pioneered in the US in the early years of the 20th century), which produced the further derivatives **cash and carriage** 'marriage' and the verb **cash and carry** 'to marry'.

Bride

fat and wide A maximally unflattering quotation from those cruel childhood lyrics to the 'Bridal Chorus' from Act III of Wagner's *Lohengrin*, 'Here comes the bride,/Short, fat, and wide'.

mother's pride Appropriate enough for the apple of proud mother's eye, but not very complimentary if the packaged sliced bread was at the back of the coiner's mind.

Not forgetting:

Love

heavens above A suitably ethereal reference. The expression is not recorded as an exclamation of surprise or horror until the 1890s.

Behaviour, Attitudes, and Emotions

Among the multifarious facets of human personality and behaviour, there are some in particular that seem to call forth rhymes—but most of them, sad to say, are decidedly negative ones. Slang does tend to be language produced under pressure, and it shows. There are rhymes in plenty for anger and its consequences; cowardice and decampment are abundantly covered, but courage gets scarcely a look in (unless it's of the cheeky, up-yours variety); and lying and deception claim, alas, a large chunk of the rhyming lexicon. To begin, however, on a more positive note:

Amusement

Laugh

cow and calf A long-established rhyme, dating from at least the 1850s. It can be used as both a verb and a noun (often in the sense 'an amusing or convivial occasion'). Sometimes shortened to **cow**.

    Steffi Graf A rhyme of the 1990s, based on the name of the German tennis player Steffi Graf (1969–), five times winner of the Wimbledon Ladies' Singles. A noun only, and often substituted (in the abbreviated form **Steffi**) in the expression *you're having a laugh* 'you must be joking'.

A smile

crocodile An iffy rhyme, given the outlook when a crocodile shows you its teeth.

    penny-a-mile Originally applied to 'a hat' (see *Hat* at CLOTHING), but in later usage it came to mean 'a (presumably not very sincere) smile'.

    River Nile An appropriate pairing with **crocodile**.

Joke

oak An unusual instance of a piece of rhyming slang shorter than what it rhymes with. First recorded in 1909, and used as both a noun and a verb (in the sense 'to lark about').

To tease

In rhymeland, to *tease* is usually to *kid*, which has scored two hits with **saucepan lid** and **teapot lid**, both dating from the late 19th century. They're generally shortened for convenience to **saucepan** and **teapot**.

Easily the most widely used rhyme in this area, though, lies concealed in *take the micky* 'to tease someone', first recorded in 1935. *Micky* is almost certainly short for **Micky Bliss**, rhyming with *piss* (see *Piss* at **IN THE LAV**). *Take the piss* 'to tease' is not actually recorded in print before 1945, but it's perfectly plausible that it could have been around in the 1930s to form the model for *take the micky*.

Courage and its Lack

Courage is a rather high-falutin word, and concept, for rhyming slang. Think stoicism or bravado, facing down an opponent or coping with a tricky situation, or even chirpy effrontery, rather than selfless heroism on the battlefield. The more down-to-earth metaphors are targets: *guts* becomes **Newington Butts**, after a street in Southwark (the rhyme was originally a literal one—see *The guts* at **THE BODY AND ITS PARTS**); and *spunk* yields **Maria Monk** (also used literally—see *Semen* at **SEX**).

Metaphors don't get much more unheroic than **bottle**, which has been used for 'courage' in British slang since at least the 1950s, and came to a wider public (mainly via television crime dramas) in the mid-1970s. Its origins are still in dispute, but one school of thought makes it a reduction of **bottle and glass**, rhyming slang for *arse* (see *The bottom* at **THE BODY AND ITS PARTS**). Proponents of this theory point to the metaphorical use of *bottom* for 'firmness of character' or 'staying power' since the late 18th century.

Bravery shades off into audacity, which colloquially, if you're on the receiving end of it, means *cheek*. Rhyming slangsters' take on that is either **hide and seek**, from the childrens' game (*hide* is used solo for 'effrontery' or 'nerve', but that appears to be a metaphorical extension of *hide* '(thick) skin' rather than an abbreviation of hide and seek), or **once a week**, often shortened to **oncer**. Alternative synonyms include *sauce*, rhymed as **rocking horse**; *front*, represented by both **James Hunt** (from the British racing driver James Hunt (1947–93), Formula One world champion in 1976 and possessor of a fair amount of front himself) and **National Hunt** (from the term applied in Britain to horse-racing over jumps); and *style*, a term of unashamed approval, which becomes **Tate and Lyle** (after the firm of sugar refiners which was a prominent presence in London's dockland). If the effrontery takes a verbal form, it can be described as *lip*, which translates rhymingly into **battleship** (usually shortened to **battle**), **fish and chip**, and **slippery dip** (an Australian rhyme).

Regrettably, however, if the number of metaphors for running away is anything to go by, spunk is a commodity sadly lacking in the world of rhyme. If you don't want to simply **Botany Bay** (a—surprise, surprise—Australian rhyme, dating from the 1940s, and based on *run away*), you can **Brighton pier** (a 1990s rhyme, from *disappear*) or even do a **Harold Holt** (from *bolt*, and based on the name of the Australian prime minister Harold Holt (1908–67), who disappeared in mysterious circumstances while swimming in the sea). If you prefer the straightforwardness of *go*, there are rhymes available in **Scapa Flow** (first recorded in the First World War period, and apparently a folk-etymological rationalization of the rather older *scarper* (which dates from at least the 1840s and probably came ultimately from Italian *scappare* 'to escape') on the basis of *Scapa Flow*, the name of a British port and naval base in the Orkneys) and **swiftly flow** (a 19th-century Australian rhyme which didn't survive long into the 20th). The same idea can be expressed as a noun with **read and write**, a 19th-century rhyme on *flight*. Anyone not disposed to make their own departure plans can be sent packing with **Edna!** (short for **Edna May**, the name of an American musical-comedy star popular in Edwardian London, rhyming with *on your way*).

It begins to seem that rhyming slangsters inhabit a world of *cowards* (**Charlie Howards**, a rhyme from the 1930s, not apparently based on any particular person, or **Frankie Howerds**, after the nervous English comedian Frankie Howerd (1917–92)), who are perpetually *yellow* (**Cinderella**, from the fairy-tale character). But it's not necessarily a question of being *terrified* (**bona fide**—an Australian rhyme, its second element resolutely Anglicized to /fʌɪd/). They might just be getting a little agitated. In its mild form, this condition could be described as 'a *state*', which has prompted some long-lived rhymes: **Harry Tate** (from the stage-name of the English music-hall comedian R. M. Hutchison (1872–1940), and first recorded in 1932) and **two and eight** (first recorded in 1938 and lasting well into the second half of the 20th century: Poor old Clinker! Bet she's in a proper two-and-eight! M. Cecil *Something in Common* (1960); After yesterday's turn-out she'll be in a right two and eight, won't she. Tony Hoare *Minder* (1984)). A parallel formation to the latter, less often heard, is **six and eight**, first recorded in the 1960s. Roughly similar in severity is 'a *stew*'. This has been claimed as the progenitor-by-rhyme of *how-d'ye-do* 'a confused or embarrassing situation', but although that's chronologically plausible (both emerged in the first half of the 19th century), the semantics don't really fit too well: a *stew* involves internal psychological perturbation, whereas a *how-d'ye-do* is an external state of affairs. Turning up the fear factor brings us to 'the *shivers*', which has inspired two Australian rhymes: **Hawkesbury Rivers**, first recorded in 1941 and based on the name of a river in New South Wales (Danny would have been the first to admit that he was as game as

Ned Kelly in most things, but girls gave him the Hawkesbury Rivers D. McLean *The World turned upside Down* (1962)), and **Swanee Rivers**, from the name of the Swanee River in Georgia and Florida, USA, generally shortened to **Swanees**. An uncontrollable nervous shaking of the bowing arm experienced by some violinists, violists, etc. is known as 'the **pearlies**' (first recorded in 1974), which may be a shortened version of an unrecorded **pearly whites**, rhyming on *frights*. The more advanced stages of terror qualify as 'the *shits*'. Most of the rhymes applied to diarrhoea have from time to time been employed in this metaphorical sense (see *Diarrhoea* at **ILLNESS**), but one in particular has made its mark: **Jimmy Britts**. It appears in various combinations in Australian English, including *have the Britts up* and *get the jimmies*: A bloke who's got the jimmies bad is very quick on the draw. F. B. Vickers *Mirage* (1958).

Laziness

Lazy

Gert and Daisy Based on the names of the two personae in a BBC radio comedy double act created in the 1930s by Elsie (*c*.1895–1990) and Doris (*c*.1904–78) Waters. The pair of Cockney gossips were a rhyme waiting to happen.

Anger and After

If someone gets on your **West Hams** (in full **West Ham reserves**, rhyming with *nerves*—from the second team of the East London football league club) or gives you 'the **Jeremy Beadle**' (*needle*, from the name of the British television entertainer Jeremy Beadle, who has been known to get on some people's nerves), you may well become **milkman's horse** (*cross*—a late 19th-century rhyme reflecting the now largely defunct 'Cockney' pronunciation /krɔːs/), or **Uncle Bertie** (*shirty*—an extension of Uncle Bert for *shirt*), or **Punch and Judy** (*moody*, from the traditional puppet-show characters). You might even be inclined to exclaim **mop and bucket!** (*fuck it!*).

Some commentators would place *get on one's wick* 'to annoy one' among this group of 'anger'-rhymes, too, on the grounds that *wick* is short for Hampton Wick, rhyming with *prick*—but serious doubts remain about the validity of this derivation (see *The penis* at **THE BODY AND ITS PARTS**).

All too often, an angry confrontation can end up with *trouble*: **Barney Rubble** (from the name of Fred Flintstone's sidekick in the Hanna-Barbera animated cartoon series *The Flintstones* (1960–6); often shortened to **Barney**, and no doubt influenced by the much longer-standing *barney* 'a row or fight'); **froth and bubble** (an Australian rhyme dating from the 1960s); or **nap and double** (a 1930s rhyme based on betting terminology: a *nap* is a tip for the winner of a race, and a *double* is a cumulative bet on two events).

There could be a *row*: **bull and cow**, an ancient rhyme, first recorded in 1859 and still very much alive in the latter part of the 20th century (The murder might have been the result of a private bull-and-cow. Anthony Gilbert *No Dust in the Attic* (1962); There's been a right bull and cow over here. I'm standing in what's left of a pub. Barry Purchese *Minder* (1983)). You might even get into a *fight*: **dynamite**, usually abbreviated to **dyna**; **left and right**, appropriating the image of a succession of punches with the left and right hands (or kicks with the left and right feet); or **read and write**, a rhyme dating from the 1850s, and commonly used as a verb. You might get caught with a **fourpenny bit** (a *hit*, an ancient rhyme from the days when fourpenny coins existed, later substituted by the now more familiar *fourpenny one*) or a **Rotten Row** (a *blow*, after the fashionable riding track around Hyde Park known as *Rotten Row*). In Australian English, you could be **fancy sashed** (a verb based on *bash*) or **pat and micked** (*licked*, no doubt invoking the stereotype of the fighting Irish).

Lying and Deception

A lie

collar and tie An early 20th-century rhyme which later lost out to pork pie.

Nellie Bligh A further role for the versatile Nellie (see *Pie* at **FOOD AND DRINK**).

pork pie Probably well established by the middle of the 20th century, but it wasn't until the late 1970s that exposure in the media propelled it into general usage (the earliest recorded example is from 1984). Mainly used in the somewhat softened forms **porky pie** and **porkie**:

> I think you'll be finding that William's been telling porky-pies again. Recorded, secretary, London 1986; quoted in Tony Thorne *Dictionary of Contemporary Slang* (1997)

> The word 'porkie' was deemed unparliamentary last week, and thus no longer a proper word to be used in the Commons.
> —*Observer* (1992)

> 'I don't want the family to find out I told a porkie,' Francis parroted. 'Well there's no proof it is a porkie, Ted,' said Archer.
> —*Observer* (2001)

Lie is rather blunt, though. Various euphemisms are used to deflect its full force, and rhymes can add a further layer of padding. *Story*, for instance, becomes **Jackanory**, an apparently arbitrary formation originally applied to a literal story (whence its use as the title of a long-running series of stories for children on BBC television, first broadcast in 1965), but later extended to cover the euphemistic sense 'lie' (He's had a good few hours in the cell. Enough time to dream up some Jackanory. Jason Sutton *The Bill* (1998)). Australians have the (on the face of it) less child-friendly **grim and gory**. Then there's the mysterious verb *spruce*, originally military slang, meaning 'to lie or deceive' or 'to malinger', which in the post-First World War period begat the exotic noun rhyme **Madame de Luce** 'deceptive talk, bullshit'. It's possible that that's the origin of the slang expression *madam*, used in much the same sense ('I was getting a hundred quid for this job . . . and I couldn't turn him down.' 'The usual "madam"!' sneered the inspector. 'It's not "madam", Mr. Brown,' said Jerry earnestly, 'though I admit it sounds as likely as cream in skilly; but it's true.' Edgar Wallace *The Feathered Serpent* (1927); It was not the sort of place conducive to putting over a spot of old madam. The normally glib flannel tended to stick in his throat and the guff and eye-wash hadn't enough elbow-room to . . . sound . . . feasible. John Wainwright *A Touch of Malice* (1973)). The chronology is plausible, but there are other candidates as its source: the fawning addresses of shopkeepers to female customers, and simple animosity to foreign women. *Hanky-panky* in the now largely obsolete sense 'deceit or verbal trickery' produced in the 1930s the rhyme **Moody and Sankey**, in honour of the US evangelists and hymnists Dwight Lyman Moody (1837–99) and Ira David Sankey (1840–1908). This was soon cut down to **moody** (Emmie was always giving me a lot of old moody about you having some money stashed. Allan Prior *The Operators* (1966)), and its rhyming origins have largely been forgotten. It's even been turned into a verb, meaning 'to bluff or deceive by flattery, bullshit, etc.' (Trying to moody through to the royal enclosure on the knock. Robin Cook *The Crust on its Uppers* (1962)). And in its turn, it's been rhymed: to **Punch and Judy**, after the puppet-show characters. Also fairly euphemistic, after its pruning from *bullshit*, is *bull*, which in Australian English received the rhyme **three bags full** (from the fourth line of the nursery rhyme 'Baa baa, black sheep, Have you any wool? Yes sir, yes sir, Three bags full', which has come to be symbolic of subservience).

Easily the most productive euphemism, though, is:

Tale

Binnie Hale Applied to the sort of tale used by conmen to fleece their targets. Its vintage matches that of its source, British actress Binnie Hale (1899–1984), one of the brightest stars of musical comedy and revue on the London stage in the period between the two world wars.

Daily Mail A rhyme dating from the 1930s, quite possibly containing a comment on the believability of that British national daily newspaper.

hill and dale First recorded in the 1940s, and referring to confidence trickery.

Newgate Gaol Applied particularly to a hard-luck story, of the sort that might be told by an ex-con. After the infamous gaol which stood on the site of what is now the Central Criminal Court, Old Bailey, London.

post and rail An Australian rhyme, first recorded in 1945, and said to be based on *fairy tale*. *Post and rail* is a term for a type of fence.

weep and wail Current from the late 19th century to the middle of the 20th, and applied particularly to a beggar's tale of woe.

A liar

Dunlop tyre From the name of a brand of tyre, and usually shortened to **Dunlop**. There may be a subliminal suggestion of the type of rubber cheques often issued by liars and conmen (in Australian slang, such documents have been termed *Dunlop cheques*).

holy friar A long-standing and successful rhyme, with its suggestion of sanctimoniousness and hypocricy. Its advocates insist, though, that it's only used of frivolous or light-hearted fibbers, not serious and harmful liars.

town crier Reflecting a certain scepticism about the reliability of that official.

Carney

A 19th- and early 20th-century slang adjective meaning 'sly' or 'two-faced', transmogrified by rhyming slangsters into **lakes of Killarney**—phonetically more successful than its original application to *barmy* (see *barmy* at SENSE AND NONSENSE). Usually reduced to **lakes** or **lakey**.

To cheat

daisy beat A rhyme dating from the late 19th century.

Bounce connoting financial deception (as in 'to bounce a cheque') has produced the rhyme **half-ounce**, applied particularly to giving someone short change. And a cheat's dupe has colloquially been '*done*', which in rhymeland becomes **hit and run**.

A poser (or *poseur*)

bulldozer A recent rhyme, replacing the now superannuated Carl Rosa.

Carl Rosa From the name of the Carl Rosa Opera Company, a touring group which brought opera to many parts of Britain between 1875 and 1958.

For deception of the criminal variety see *Fraud* at CRIME AND PUNISHMENT.

(The other side of the scales is not entirely empty: the *truth* is **dog's tooth** (possibly representing *God's truth*, since *dog* is backslang for *God*) and **maud**

and ruth (first recorded in the 1970s); and *true* is rhymed as **eyes of blue**
and **Irish stew**. Both of these figure mainly in the expression *too true*—the
first punningly transformed to **two eyes of blue** (first recorded in the
1920s) and the second usually shortened to **Irish**: 'Too Irish, my old mate,
too Irish!')

Belief

Here belongs one of the sturdiest chestnuts of rhyming slang, **Adam and
Eve** for *believe*. Although not recorded before the 1920s, it was probably
around in the late 19th century, and it continues in use in the 21st. Its usual
context is now surprise and humorously feigned disbelief:

> A *baby*! Would you Adam-and-Eve it!
> —Anthony Thorne *The Baby and the Battleship* (1956)

> Would you Adam and Eve it? Last week a woman was tipped to head the armed
> forces and a think tank was set up to help men become more emotionally literate.
> —*Life* (*Observer Magazine*) (2001)

Which brings us conveniently to matters of religion:

God

Tommy Dodd A 19th-century euphemism liable to turn up in stock
expressions such as 'Tommy Dodd knows!' (For the origins of this much-used
rhyme see *Odd* at GAMBLING.)

A church

Lurch is the favoured rhyme here. The ancient **lean and lurch**, which dates
from the mid-19th century, suggests the shakiness of a venerable
foundation, as does the Australian version **rock and lurch**. Still more
appropriate is the 19th-century **left in the lurch**, conjuring up brides
abandoned at altars. As an alternative there's the cheeky late 19th-century
chicken perch, generally shortened to **chicken**.

A vicar

half a nicker In London slang, the equivalent originally of ten shillings, now
of 50p. The abbreviated version generally comes out as the 'Cockney' form
of *Arthur*.

   pie and liquor Inspired by a traditional Cockney dish available at pie and
mash shops: meat pie and gravy. In practice, the local vicar is generally 'the
old pie'.

A Catholic

cattle tick An Australian contribution, but as much a playful alteration of the original as a rhyme on it.

A Mormon

Jerry O'Gorman A scarcely appropriate attribution of Irishness.

A Quaker

muffin baker A rhyme which dates back to the mid-19th century, when specialist muffin bakers still existed.

Hymns

hers and hims A fairly feeble Australian effort, barely worthy of the name 'rhyme'.

A ghost

pillar and post Exploiting a long-standing alliterative partnership which was based on a metaphor drawn from real tennis (although the original formulation, in the Middle Ages, was actually *from post to pillar*).

  slice of toast In the often mirror-image world of rhyming slang, almost the reverse of holy ghost for *toast* (see *Toast* at **FOOD AND DRINK**).

Sense and Nonsense

The higher mental faculties are stony ground for rhyme. Native wit and common sense manage a few rhyming synonyms, but, as with slang in general, this is in the main the territory of inadequate understanding and foolishness. Mugs and simpletons attract a wider range of insults than most, and several of them have been turned into rhymes in their time.

Understanding

To understand

With the exception of **dry land?**, a mid-19th-century rhyming question, equivalent to 'Do you understand?', the word *understand* itself hasn't attracted the attention of rhyming slangsters. But there's been no shortage of more suitable colloquial substitutes. *Tumble* was paired in the mid-19th century with **Oliver Cromwell**, reflecting the contemporary pronunciation /ˈkrʌməl/, which has long since been replaced with one more closely reflecting the spelling. Commemorating the former Lord Protector of England (1599–1658), it was almost always reduced to **oliver** (as in *Do you oliver?* 'Do you understand?'). A more recent Australian alternative has been **violet crumble**. In Britain the preference has latterly been for *twig*, rhymed as **earwig**.

Sense

Queries as to someone's common sense, or lack of it, have a convenient financial rhyme to hand in *pence*. The earliest, **shillings and pence** (usually reduced to **shillings**) and **eighteen pence**, betray their pre-decimal origins. More recent economic realities are faced up to in **pounds and pence**.

Clever

now and never A late 19th-century rhyme.

For someone whose cleverness is of the sharp, street-wise variety the slang term from the late 19th century to the mid-20th was *wide* (as in 'wide boy'), which Irish rhyming slangsters converted into **cowhide**.

Fools

A fool

lump of school A curious late 19th-century rhyme apparently based on the rhyming classes' view of education as deleterious to native wit.

   sharper's tool A rhymers' adoption of a term used in the plural since the late 18th century for 'dice' (a *sharper* being a confidence trickster).

   two-foot rule A mid-19th-century rhyme, later joined by the equally pre-metric **twelve-inch rule**.

A mug

The chief rhyming options are *jug* and *tug*. The latter produced **Tom Tug** in the 19th century, later replaced by **steam tug**, usually shortened to **steamer**:

> If you think I'm going to make a steamer of myself and let you hang about half a dozen more charges on me, you're mistaken.
> —James Curtis *The Gilt Kid* (1936)

> The third player at the table was a 'steamer', a bad gambler who chased losing bets.
> —Mario Puzo *Fools Die* (1978)

Jug has produced **milk jug** (an Australian rhyme dating from the 1920s), **stone jug** (another 1920s rhyme), and **toby jug** (from a type of jug in the shape of a man dressed in a frock-coat and three-cornered hat, popular in the 19th and early 20th centuries).

   And if none of these please, there's **hearthrug**, in use in the first half of the 20th century.

Muggins

Harry Huggins Used, like *muggins*, self-referentially—'It was Harry Huggins here who got the blame!'

A chump

lump and bump A late 19th-century rhyme which survived into the 1930s.

A prat

top hat Ray Puxley in *Cockney Rabbit* (1992) speculates that the rhyme may be a dig by the lower orders at the idiocy of their betters, as displayed annually at Ascot.

   trilby hat Generally reduced to **trilby**.

A goon

egg and spoon An Australian rhyme from the 1970s.

A loon

The rhymes take us etymologically back full circle to *moon*, since *loon* 'a fool', although its antecedents are not entirely clear, was probably strongly influenced at the very least by *lunatic*, which derives ultimately from Latin *luna* 'moon'. The fairly obvious choices have been **full moon** and **man in the moon**, and, going off on a different tack altogether, **Keith Moon**, from the name of the former drummer of The Who (1947–78).

A loony

Mickey Rooney From the name of the diminutive American film star Mickey Rooney (1920–).

A muff

A superannuated term for an incompetent person, rhymed as **beery buff**.

A nutter

brandy butter A recent addition to the canon:

> 'Brandy butter' is, I'm told, rhyming slang for 'complete nutter'.
> —*Independent* (2000)

A dill

An Australianism for 'fool', rhymed as:

   Beecham's pill After the celebrated proprietary tablets introduced in Britain by Thomas Beecham in 1850. First recorded in the 1950s.

   jack and jill After the boy and girl in the nursery rhyme who went up the hill. Usually reduced to plain **jack**.

A gay

An early to mid-20th-century Australian slang term for a 'sucker', apparently based on *galah* with the same meaning. It was rhymed as **thirty-first of May**.

In Caribbean English the rhyme **Billy Button** had some currency in the 20th century for a 'sucker', especially one who takes on a job of work without first making sure he'll get paid for it. For such improvidence he *gets nothing* (/ˈnʌtn/).

And finally, some account must be given of two rhymes which didn't arrive in this semantic area until their rhyming origins had effectively been forgotten. Their starting point was *cunt*, and in metaphorical use they would have inherited much of its invective (see *Cunt* at **PEOPLE AND THE HUMAN CONDITION**), but over the decades their second, rhyming, element dropped out of sight, and their meaning softened to simply 'fool':

berk A shortened version of Berkeley Hunt (see *The female genitals* at **THE BODY AND ITS PARTS**), first recorded in 1936, and now so cut off from its original that it's frequently spelt as **burk** or **burke**, and sometimes as **birk**. As long ago as the early 1960s it was sufficiently denatured to appear in a family Sunday newspaper:

> 'Stick the burke in a taxi,' he said.
> —Walter Greenwood *Only Mugs Work* (1938)

> The Tories were burglars, berks and bloodlusters.
> —John Osborne *The World of Paul Slickey* (1959)

> You mutt. . . You birk!
> —Harold Pinter *Dumb Waiter* (1960)

> All my mates thought I was a burk to try to break away: now they know they were the burks.
> —*Sunday Express* (1963)

As quite often happens in such circumstances, the de-rhymed berk itself went on to attract a rhyme: **Charlie Smirke**. Not recorded until the 1970s, it commemorates the celebrated English jockey Charlie Smirke (1906–93), who enjoyed a long and highly successful career in the saddle. The choice of rhyme was no doubt encouraged by the solo *Charlie* (see next).

Charlie The origins of this are far from straightforward. An isolated claim for it as American services slang appeared in 1946, but no subsequent supporting evidence has been brought forward. It's first recorded in British English in the mid-1950s. One theory of its origin is that it's a cut-down version of **Charlie Hunt**, rhyming slang for *cunt* (presupposing a softening of its meaning, as with *berk*). Charlie Hunt evidently had some currency as an insult-rhyme in the early 20th century, but it seems never to have been as popular as the synonymous **Joe Hunt**. Julian Franklyn in his *Dictionary of Rhyming Slang* (1960) suggests that the reason for this may have been that although the shortened form **Joey** could be freely used in this sense, there was some resistance to calling someone a 'Charlie' since it could also be interpreted as 'ponce' (see *Charlie Ronce* at **SEX**). It's not clear whether the need for such scruples had simply faded out by the middle of the 20th century, or whether *Charlie* 'a fool' is just a jocular use of the male first name, with no rhyming antecedents. But either way, it was in widespread use in British slang in the 1950s and 1960s (which strongly suggests a services origin in the Second World War—it's possible that the 1946 report mistakenly identified it as American rather than British). Commonly preceded by *proper* or *right*:

> The plebeian engineer was a proper Charlie to let himself be roped in for it.
> —*Listener* (1957)

I felt a right Charlie coming through the customs in this lot.
—Alan Simpson & Ray Galton *Four Hancock Scripts* (1961)

Foolishness, Stupidity, and Madness

When it comes to insults, silliness, and madness are simply at opposite ends of the same continuum, not in separate semantic camps, and rhyming slang spans both, with stupidity in the middle:

Silly

Auntie Lily Standardly reduced to **auntie**.

   daffadowndilly or **daffydowndilly** Co-opting the dialectal and colloquial name for the daffodil, and no doubt also feeding off *daffy* 'foolish', a relative of *daft* that was current in English dialect in the late 19th century (and probably well before that), and *dilly* 'foolish', another English dialectal form (perhaps a blend of *daft* and *silly*), subsequently taken up by Australian English.

   Harry and Billy A 1990s rhyme, virtually always heard in the reduced form **harry**.

   Piccadilly After the fashionable thoroughfare in the West End of London (which itself is said to have got its name from the *pickadils* (collars or hem trimmings) sold by a 17th-century tailor called Baker who lived nearby). In speech nearly always reduced to **picca**.

   Uncle Willie A mid-19th-century rhyme which survives to the present day. Perhaps the husband of Auntie Lily.

Barmy

Dad's Army From the name of the popular BBC television sitcom about the Home Guard during the Second World War, first broadcast in 1968.

   lakes of Killarney From the three lakes (the largest of which is Lough Leane) around Killarney in the southwest of Ireland, which have been a noted beauty spot since the mid-18th century. The rhyme is approximate, but as it's almost always reduced to **lakes** it doesn't really matter.

   Salvation Army A late 19th-century rhyme (the name was adopted for the evangelistic Christian movement in 1878).

Potty

mazawattee From the name of a brand of tea popular in Britain in the 19th and early 20th centuries.

Thick

king dick Earlier used as a rhyme for *brick*, so some comparison of mental capacities may be implicit ('as thick as a brick' is a not uncommon simile).

Paddy and Mick Incorporating the stereotype of Irish stupidity.

Paddy Quick An earlier rhyme than **Paddy and Mick**, dating from the mid-19th century, but probably exploiting the same prejudice.

Rick and Dick First recorded in the 1960s.

Batty

Carlo Gatti Current in the first third of the 20th century, when the firm of Carlo Gatti, suppliers of ice to London restaurants, was in business. Almost always shortened to **carlo**.

Bonkers

marbles and conkers After two childhood games traditional in rhymeland. Generally reduced to **marbles**.

Yarra

An Australian slang synonym of *insane*, from the mental hospital at Yarra Bend, Victoria. The rhyme on **cock sparrow**, traditional perky Cockney bird, may be a dig at the Poms. First recorded in the 1960s.

Mad

mum and dad A 20th-century rhyme in use in both Britain and Australia.

Mental

Radio Rental First recorded in the 1970s, and based on the name of a television and video rental firm. Usually shortened to **radio**.

Nonsense

Tripe

cherry ripe From the cherry-seller's traditional street-cry, made famous in Robert Herrick's lyric (1648). Usually shortened to **cherry**.

Twaddle

tosh and waddle A late 19th-century Australian rhyme, in the guise of a deconstructed blend (tosh + *waddle* = *twaddle*). The identity of the first element is problematical. *Tosh* 'nonsense', the obvious candidate, apparently originated as Oxford University slang in the 1890s, which is chronologically tight, and it would be unusual to use a synonym of the rhymed word in a rhyme. There were other slang terms *tosh* around at the end of the 19th century, meaning variously 'a pocket', 'a hat', 'half-a-crown', and 'a penis'.

Baloney

macaroni A largely Australian rhyme, first recorded in 1924. Elsewhere, often interpreted as a rhyme on *pony* (itself a rhyme—see next):

> What is flashed from the projector overhead will be the same old macaroni.
> —Joseph von Sternberg *Fun in a Chinese Laundry* (1965)

Crap

pony and trap Like the word it rhymes, a metaphorical application of the literal sense (see *Defecation* at **IN THE LAV**). Usually shortened to **pony**.

Balls, Bollocks

For **cobblers** and other testicular rhymes used for 'nonsense', see *Testicles* at **THE BODY AND ITS PARTS**.

Sex

Observe human sexual behaviour through the perspective-glass of rhyming slang and what do we see? The romantic fulfilment of love's dream? Not quite. The mature and equal enjoyment of sexual pleasure between man and woman (or other pairings)? You must be joking. In the rhyming slangster's world, sexual intercourse is well represented, but only in the guise of euphemisms concealing (or perhaps really emphasizing) the more graphic end of copulatory vocabulary. Otherwise, the main preoccupations seem to be with erections (some signs of anxiety here, perhaps?) and masturbation. There is a great abundance of rhymes for *prostitute*, and homosexuality is casually sniggered at or coldly scorned.

In other words, this is sex looked at from a male angle—particularly (although perhaps not exclusively) from the angle of a late 19th- or early 20th-century male of conservative outlook, accustomed to sexual superiority, apt to see sex in terms of receiving rather than giving or reciprocating gratification, decidedly 'old man'. But what else was to be expected? Slang is a mirror of its makers, and as the rhyming slang in many other fields demonstrates, women mostly are not part of the game.

Courtship and Romance

But to get the niceties out of the way first—some elements of old-fashioned wooing and winning do find their way into rhyming slang. For instance, the:

Sweetheart

A word that shows its age, and its rhymes have passed into history. Note that both implicitly stand for 'girlfriend', not 'boyfriend':

jam tart A coinage of the mid-19th century that has been the starting point of a chain of lexical developments. In its original meaning it has long since died out, but it seems rapidly to have broadened out its application to 'young woman', and this usage survives in Australian English:

> The Pope's a Jew if that jam tart doesn't root like a rattlesnake.
> —*Private Eye* (1969)

By at least the 1860s *tart* had detached itself from the rhyming pair, still with the original meaning '(female) sweetheart', and by the 1880s it was being used in the derogatory sense, 'promiscuous or immoral woman', familiar today.

merryheart A sentimental coinage with a feeble rhyme; it never had the legs for a long career.

As in straight vocabulary, many rhyming-slang synonyms for *girl*, *boy*, *young woman*, etc. double as 'girlfriend', 'boyfriend'; see **PEOPLE AND THE HUMAN CONDITION**.

Kisses

hit and miss A coinage of the 1960s, apparently based on the tentative efforts of a beginner (although there may also be a memory here of the 'hit' and 'miss' verdicts in the 1960s BBC television programme *Juke Box Jury*). In its shortened form **hit** it turns aggressive, especially when used as a verb.

plates and dishes Only plural, and a rather approximate rhyme.

Tooting Bec For light kisses only: it rhymes with *peck*. Usually abbreviated to **Tooting**. It comes from the name of a locality in southwest London (for its history see **FOOD AND DRINK**, where it also operates as a rhyme).

Cuddling

mix and muddle A cosy domestic image? Or perhaps a need to consult the manual.

Hot Sex

Randy

port and brandy Appropriate enough for the early effects of alcohol, although glossing over the later ones. A 20th-century creation, but the port dates it.

In the same league as *randy* is *hot*, which in rhyming slang becomes:

pass in the pot Thus recorded in print, although *piss* would seem to be more idiomatic and logical. A product of the late 19th century, which could explain any euphemistic tinkering with the vowel.

Seduction

John Bull Used in the expression *go (out) on the John Bull*, that is, *on the pull*, looking for sexual conquests.

Sexual intercourse

Never actually rhymed itself, not surprisingly, but there is no shortage of more or less graphic or euphemistic slang alternatives for rhyming slangers to choose from, most notably *fuck*. The most popular rhyming vehicle is *duck*. This has inspired **Aylesbury duck**, **Donald Duck** (an Australianism of the 1960s, based on the irascible Walt Disney cartoon character; successful enough to be regularly shortened to **Donald**), **flying duck** (after the plaster birds that fly eternally up the walls of British lower-middle-class homes in the post-Second World War era), **roasted duck**, **rubber duck**, and **Russian duck** (first recorded in the 1970s). Of these, Aylesbury duck and flying duck are used metaphorically, standing in for the F-word in *not give a fuck*, and rubber duck usually turns up in expletives, but the rest are used literally.

The most persistent, and productive, of these *duck*-rhymes, though, is **goose and duck**, which originated around the middle of the 19th century, probably in America. It seems likely that it was the starting point of US slang *goose* 'to have sex with', which is first recorded in 1879 and continues in use:

> The old man who owns the place is crippled or something. Kolb gooses his wife once in a while.
> —Richard Jessup *Sailor* (1969)

This in turn may have been the origin of *goose* 'to poke someone between the buttocks', which emerged between the two world wars.

Some other *fuck*-rhymes:

Friar Tuck Dating from the 1940s, and exploiting the sensuality of Robin Hood's tubby monachal companion.

Joe Buck An Australian contribution, first recorded in the 1930s. Not a real person.

push in the truck An inspiration of the haulage industry, apparently from the 1930s. The scenario can be left to the imagination.

trolley and truck A venerable example, dating back to the 1910s and well enough established to be regularly shortened to **trolley**.

Of the various alternatives to *fuck*, the most productive numerically is the comparatively mild *sex* (first recorded in the sense 'sexual intercourse' in 1929):

Oedipus Rex From the title of Sophocles' play, but no doubt inspired chiefly by the link in everyone's mind (thanks to Sigmund Freud) between Oedipus and sex. Dating from the 1970s.

Shell-Mex From the name of the oil company established in the UK in 1920 to market the products of Shell and Mexican Eagle, a British oil company whose Mexican oil fields had been bought by Shell in 1919.

T. Rex From the name of a British rock band of the late 1960s and early 1970s, whose hits included the 1968 album 'My People were Fair and had Sky in their Hair, but now they're Content to Wear Stars on their Brows'. (Their name in turn came from the dinosaur *Tyrannosaurus rex*).

Cunt is vulgarly used as a metonym for 'sexual intercourse', and rhyming slang follows suit: **grumble and grunt** and **Sir Berkeley** (short for Sir Berkeley Hunt) come into this category.

In Australia the preferred colloquialism is *root*, which yields **juicy fruit** and **wellington** (short for **wellington boot**).

Some other assorted rhymes:

bag of coke Based on *poke*, which is first recorded in the sense 'act of sexual intercourse' in 1902.

barney moke Originally a pickpockets' rhyme for *poke* 'pocket', but latterly some use for 'sexual intercourse'.

Joe McBride Rhyming with *ride*, a metaphor for sexual intercourse which dates back to the Middle Ages.

me and you Based on *screw*, which is first recorded in the sexual sense in the 1920s.

Melvyn Bragg A no doubt unwanted compliment to the British novelist and broadcaster Lord Bragg (1939–), based on *shag*.

To copulate

balaclava The rhyme is with *charver*, a slang synonym for *copulate* of late-19th-century vintage which was acquired from Polari, the secret language of travelling actors and showmen.

cattle truck Almost always reduced to **cattle**, and widely used not just literally but in the range of figurative and expletive roles of its model *fuck*: *cattled* has made a modest niche for itself as 'spoilt, ruined, defeated', etc.

rock and roll A coinage of the 1990s, based on the expression *get one's hole* (of a man) 'to have sex' (which itself relies, of course, on long-established slang *hole* 'vagina').

Oral sex

flying sixty-six A curious rhyme with a complex history. The immediate model is *French tricks*, slang of mid-19th-century vintage for 'oral sex' based on the stereotype of the French as addicted to such beastly/naughty practices. But there may well also have been some inspiration from *flying sixty-nine*, denoting mutual oral-genital stimulation (the number in this case suggests in graphic form the position of the couples). And the general pattern of *flying* plus a numeral may owe something to such mid-20th-century US Army slang usages as *flying twenty* and *flying twenty-five* for the first pay instalment given to recruits in training.

plate of ham The rhyme is with slang *gam* 'to fellate'. This in turn is an abbreviation of the synonymous *gamahuche*, prostitutes' slang of the mid 19th century which was acquired from French *gamahucher*:

> Barry tells me that all those Americans have got crabs. G. launched into a great
> account of a queen who got them in the moustache because of a plate of ham.
> —Kenneth Williams *Diaries* **25** August **1968** (1993)

Since the 1950s the abbreviated **plate** has become so familiar, particularly
as a verb, that its rhyming-slang origins have tended to fade into the
background.

slice of ham A variation on plate of ham which has never caught on to
the same extent

Erection

The number of rhymes devoted to the successfully erected penis cannot but
prompt psychological speculations about the fragile confidence of their male
coiners. Only one seems to have been based on *erection* itself: **general
election**, which offers ample scope for puns involving 'standing' for
parliament and 'members' of parliament. By far the most popular rhyme-
base is *horn*, a vulgarism which dates back at least to Shakespeare's time;
and it is probably not a coincidence that the rhyming word chosen is often
morn, suggesting associations with slang *pride of the morning* 'an erection on
waking':

colleen bawn A 19th-century rhyme, but it survives in the eroded form
colly. Those who speak of 'having a colly on' perhaps do not realize that the
original is an Anglicized form of Irish *cailín bán* 'white or fair woman'. It
owes its rhyming-slang status to a character of that name, the heroine of
Julius Benedict's opera *The Lily of Killarney*, which was first produced at
Covent Garden in 1862.

early morn A fairly open reference to the erection that persists from
dreams to waking.

flake of corn An inversion of the name of the popular breakfast cereal (so
we are back with the early morning scenario), and generally abbreviated to
flake ('to have a flake on').

hail, smiling morn A poetic example from the 1970s, perhaps recalling
'Hail, thou ever-blessed morn!' from Edward Caswall's Christmas hymn 'See,
amid the winter's snow' (1858), and possibly even Milton's 'Sure pledge of
day, that crownst the smiling Morn With thy bright Circlet' from *Paradise
Lost* (1667).

Marquis of Lorne Apparently a 1960s semantic adaptation of a rhyme
which had been in use since the 19th century for 'penis'. Marquis of Lorne is
a subsidiary title of the dukes of Argyll (see *A file* at **HOUSEHOLD MATTERS**); its
rhyming status was no doubt promoted by a number of pubs bearing the
same name.

Mountains of Mourne A 20th-century creation, somewhat self-
aggrandizing perhaps, based on the name of the range of craggy hills in
Northern Ireland.

popcorn A popular addition to the vocabulary of erections in the 20th century, and often abbreviated familiarly to **poppy**.

September morn A coinage of the 1970s, apparently based on the name of a painting (1912) by Paul Chabas of a young woman bathing naked. It achieved widespread notoriety when censors tried to ban the exhibition of a reproduction of it in the US.

Sunday morn Hinting at a frequent Sunday morning occupation.

The above do not quite exhaust the possibilities of *erection*:

crouton A 1990s inspiration, rhyming with *root-on*, itself a fairly new creation based on the well-established slang *root* 'erection' and *hard-on* 'erection'.

full-blown Stallone A double rhyme on *bone*, exploiting the name of US film star Sylvester Stallone (1946–), famous for his impersonation of the impeccably macho Rambo. A rhyme of the 1990s.

Yasser A US coinage of the 1990s with fairly complex antecedents. It is short for *Yasser Crack-a-fat*, a punning alteration of the name of the Palestinian leader Yasser Arafat (1929–). To *crack a fat* is a slang expression meaning 'to achieve an erection'.

Semen

On the street, as it were, semen is *spunk*, and that is the word that gets most of the rhyming attention. The earliest rhyme, dating from the late 19th century, is **Maria Monk**, based, appropriately enough, on the name of the anonymous 1836 anti-Catholic pornographic novel *Awful disclosures of Maria Monk, a narrative of her sufferings in the Hotel Dieu nunnery at Montreal*. This was presumably the model on which were based the somewhat later **Victoria Monk** (a variation on the name of the music-hall entertainer Victoria Monks (1884–1927), best known for her rendition of 'Won't you come home, Bill Bailey?'), the considerably later **Thelonius Monk** (from the name of the US jazz pianist (1917–82)), and the anonymous **Harry Monk**. Introducing some welcome variety is the 1990s Scottish rhyme **pineapple chunk**.

As an alternative to *spunk* there is *come*, which has inspired the bizarre **Pedigree Chum** (from the name of a brand of dogfood).

Condom

reggie and ronnie The rhyme is with *johnny*, a British colloquial euphemism for *condom* since the 1960s; the reference is to the Kray brothers (Reggie (1933–2000) and Ronnie (1933–95)), a pair of 1960s London gangland bosses; and the rationale is that the Krays extorted money in exchange for 'protection'.

wise monkey A rhyme based on slang *flunky* 'condom'.

Sexual satisfaction

After all that, a man may be considered to have had his 'oats'—in rhyming slang **John O'Groats**, from the name of the locality popularly (though erroneously) considered to be the most northerly point in mainland Britain.

In Solitary

Masturbation

Masturbation is a major concern of rhyming slangsters, to judge from the number of rhymes it has been accorded. The word itself does not figure; that job goes mainly to the much-easier-to-rhyme *wank*, a slang synonym first recorded at the end of the 19th century.

Of the many options, the most popular is *bank*, which has an inviting array of potential partners. Probably the earliest pairing is **Barclay's Bank**, which dates from the 1930s. It is regularly abbreviated to **Barclay's**:

> Quite the barclays before bed. Masturbatory success is the result of imaginative conceit.
> —Kenneth Williams *Diaries* 12 August 1976 (1993)

> He [Kenneth Williams] relied on 'the Barclays' . . . for gratification.
> —*Independent on Sunday* (1993)

Other financial institutions to be so honoured are **Allied Irish** (an Irish creation of the 1990s), **Yorkshire penny bank**, and the more lowly **piggy bank** (generally shortened to **piggy**). And sharing the rhyme is **Jodrell** (short for *Jodrell Bank*, the name of the site in Cheshire where a pioneering radio telescope was opened in 1957).

But other rhymes have had considerable success too, notably **J. Arthur Rank** and **Sherman tank**. The former (usually shortened to **J. Arthur** or even **Arthur**) commemorates the British film magnate (1888–1972) who founded the Rank Organization; the latter (frequently just **Sherman**) comes from a US tank (named after US General W. T. Sherman (1820–91)) much used during the Second World War:

> You settle down for a discreet Sherman and suddenly it's 'Sands of Iwo Jima'!
> —*Guardian* (1995)

Some further *wank* contenders:

ham shank A suggestive-sounding coinage of the 1990s.

Levy and Frank From the name of an old firm of London pub and restaurant proprietors, Levy and Franks. The shortened form **Levy** is often used as a verb, 'to masturbate'.

shabba A 1990s verbal rhyme based on *Shabba Ranks*, the stage-name of reggae star Rextion Gordon (1965–   ).

taxi rank Another rhyme often used, in full or abbreviated to **taxi**, as a verb.

But *wank* does not have a monopoly on the rhymes. There is competition from that old stand-by *toss* (most familiar in *toss off*), which produces **polish and gloss** (often just **polish**, or, borrowing the particle, **polish off**), conjuring up apposite imagery. And *strop* yields **whip and top** (generally shortened to **whip**); in this context masturbation is **Christmas shopping**. Most bizarrely inventive of all, though, is the 1990s creation **drain Charles Dickens**. The basic rhyme is with *chickens*, but the underlying inspiration is the (extremely numerous) range of off-the-wall expressions meaning 'to masturbate' which flowered in the late 20th century—and specifically *choke the chicken* and *drain the monster*.

Virtually all the rhymes based on *wanker* are exclusively used metaphorically rather than literally, so see *Wanker* at **PEOPLE AND THE HUMAN CONDITION**.

Commercial Sex

Rhymes for men who live on the earnings of prostitutes outnumber those for the prostitutes themselves, so it seems reasonable to suppose that rhyming slang in this area is mainly the invention of insiders, rather than of, say, the punters (for rhymes for *punter* see *A customer* at **MONEY AND COMMERCE**)—although the clientele make free use of the *prostitute*-rhymes.

Prostitute

In the heyday of rhyming slang, in the late 19th and early 20th centuries, *whore* was still a fairly standard term for 'prostitute', so it is not surprising that the majority of rhymes denoting female sex-workers are based on it:

boat and oar First recorded in the 1940s, but condemned by Julian Franklyn in *A Dictionary of Rhyming Slang* (1960) as 'a rather weak rhyme'—presumably because *oar* is identical to the /h/-less pronunciation of *whore*.

bolt the door Usually reduced to **bolt**—bottom-of-the-market hookers were accorded the cruel epithet 'old bolts'.

Doug McClure From the name of the American film and television actor (1935–95), perhaps best known for his appearance in such schlock science fantasies as *The Land that Time Forgot* (1975) and *At the Earth's Core* (1976).

Apparently representing a pronunciation /hʊə/, still current in some varieties of English.

Jane Shore A late-19th-century creation, presumably of some historically minded rhyming slangster who was aware that the original Jane Shore (d. 1527) was the mistress of Edward IV. Standardly shortened to **jane**.

Roger Moore A possibly unwelcome tribute to the suave English actor (1927–), portrayer of the Saint and James Bond.

Rory O'More Much more familiar in domestic contexts as a rhyme for *door* and *floor* (see under Structural Elements at **HOUSEHOLD MATTERS**), but some late 19th-century use for *whore*.

six to four A rhyme from the 1950s, based on the bookies' odds (quite possibly, as Ray Puxley suggests in his *Cockney Rabbit* (1992), the punter's chances of picking up something nasty from the encounter).

sloop of war A superannuated rhyme from the mid-19th century. A later creation in the same vein was **tug of war**.

two by four Another 1950s creation. A *two by four* is (originally in US English) a post or batten measuring two inches by four in cross-section, and the term subsequently came to be applied to anything small or insignificant.

The word *prostitute* itself has not attracted rhyming slangers, the only successful hit being the Australian **mallee root** (a mallee is a type of small eucalyptus tree; *root* is a favourite Australianism for 'to have sex (with)'). There have been some takers for the now past-it *moll*: **kewpie** (short for *kewpie doll*, the name of a small chubby doll with a topknot of hair, registered as a US trademark in 1912) and **paper doll** (coined in the 1960s, and used in the context of amateur as much as professional promiscuity). The unfortunate **Melvyn Bragg** comes in for it again (see under **SEXUAL INTERCOURSE** above), his rhyme on *slag* again not necessarily implying payment. But the most significant contribution has come from *tail*, old-established collective slang for 'women as objects of sexual desire'. Rhymed, it becomes **brass nail**, whose shortened form **brass** (first recorded in 1934) has found a niche for itself well beyond its rhyming-slang origins:

> If Mr. Willis thought she was a brass, he had got another think coming. . . If you looked at those brown eyes you could see she was innocent as a baby.
> —Noel Streatfeild *Aunt Clara* (1952)

> His old woman who was a brass on the game.
> —Frank Norman *Bang to Rights* (1958)

Homosexual prostitutes

burton Short for Burton-on-Trent, which is rhyming slang for *rent*—and *rent* denotes homosexual prostitution. A usage of the 1960s and 70s.

nigh enough The rhyme is with *puff* 'homosexual', which also produced (with no commercial overtones) **nice enough** (see under *Poof* at **HOMOSEXUALITY**).

Prostitution

On the bottle originally connoted specifically homosexual prostitution (*bottle* being short for **bottle and glass**, rhyming slang for *arse*). In US slang it broadened out to apply to any sort of prostitution.

Pimps

In British rhyming-slang circles, *ponce* is evidently the salient term, not *pimp*, because it has the lion's share of the rhymes:

alphonse Apparently an underworld favourite of the 1950s. It has broadened out in meaning to cover anyone who sponges off others.

candle-sconce or **candle and sconce** First recorded in the 1920s, when people can be expected to have been familiar with what a sconce is (it is a sort of candlestick). Often shortened to **candle**, and used, like alphonse, with reference to any sponger.

Charlie Ronce A widely used rhyme since at least the 1930s, and very common too in its curtailed form **Charlie**. Another member of the family in the same line of business is **Joe Ronce**.

Joe Bonce A 1930s coinage, and possibly a variation on the contemporaneous Joe Ronce.

ronson Not exactly rhyming slang, but inspired by it. It is a pun on Charlie Ronce or Joe Ronce, based on the name of the firm that makes cigarette lighters. A usage of the 1950s.

In Australian English, the preferred term is *hoon*. It is first recorded in the late 1930s, but its origins are obscure. It has given Australian rhyming slangsters a field day:

blue moon Dating from the 1970s. A still more romantic-sounding contemporary variant is **silvery moon**

dish ran away with the spoon The longest piece of rhyming slang on record, lifted (perhaps ironically) from the mid–18th-century nursery rhyme 'Hey diddle diddle! The cat and the fiddle. The cow jumped over the moon'. The vintage is 1970s.

egg and spoon The original rhyme seems to have been with *goon* 'fool', but *hoon* soon got in on the act.

silver spoon This one was first applied to *moon*, but there is no keeping *hoon* out. Possibly some subliminal reference to a silver spoon as a symbol of unearned wealth.

terry toon An Australian rhyme from the 1970s, based on *Terrytoons*, the name of a US company that produced animated cartoons, founded by Paul Terry. In production between 1915 and 1968, its best-known character was Mighty Mouse.

Compared with these two, *pimp* gets comparatively short shrift: just the rather contemptuous **fish and shrimp**, and the altogether more interesting

McGimp. This originated in US English in the early 20th century (it is first recorded in 1914). No reference to a particular person is apparently involved, but the *Mc* may have been suggested by the somewhat earlier US underworld slang *mack* 'pimp' (first recorded in 1903, but the related verb *mack* 'to work as a pimp' is known from the 1880s), which itself probably came from French *maquerelle*. It survived well into the second half of the 20th century, often in worn-down forms suggested by spellings such as **M'Gimp** and **magimp**:

> One of the dance-hall bums . . . insisted Louis . . . was . . . a M'Gimp.
> —W. R. Burnett *The Asphalt Jungle* (1949)

Brothel

timothy An Australianism of early 1950s vintage. Its origins are not certain, but rhyming slang seems a plausible conjecture—possibly from **timothy grass** for *arse* or **timothy titmouse** for *house*:

> I'm like the proverbial moll in the timothy. You've talked me into it.
> —D. R. Stuart *Wedgetail View* (1978)

Homosexuality

The rhyming-slang lexicon of homosexuals is not the place to go for political correctness. Latterly some variations on *gay* have begun to appear, but for the most part it is stuck in the world of *poofs* and *queers*. Their sting is partly drawn by the joky disguise of the rhyme, but it cannot altogether conceal the vein of contempt.

Poof

The rhymes suggest variation in the source word between *poof* /pʊf/ and *puff* /pʌf/. *Puff* is first recorded in this sense in the first decade of the 20th century (*poof* goes back to the mid-19th century), and written examples of it persist into at least the 1970s, but it seems likely that the more recent ones conceal a pronunciation /pʊf/. **Nellie Duff, nice enough** and the like confirm (in a Southern English pronunciation) that /pʌf/ was once current, but there probably was not much life left in it by the middle of the 20th century.

horse's hoof Some 20th-century usage, but always second fiddle to **iron hoof**

iron hoof First recorded in the 1930s, but well before the end of the decade the abbreviated form **iron** had established itself, and went on to become a leading London slang term for 'homosexual':

> You gets into bed and goes straight off to kip, never touched me you didn't, you
> great iron.
> —James Curtis *The Gilt Kid* (1936)

> Gorblimey, 'e's an *iron*, did'n yeh know?
> —Eric Partridge *Adventuring among Words* (1961)

Opportunities for double entendres abounded:

> Julius Caesar [Kenneth Williams]: I usually have the blow wave. Hengist Pod
> [Kenneth Connor, in the persona of a barber]: Yes, well, I'm no good at that, sir, but I
> know where I am with the iron.
> —*Carry On, Cleo* (1964)

So divorced from its rhyming-slang roots did iron become, in fact, that it
was adopted as the basis of a new rhyme, **Lenny the Lion**—a comparatively
rare case of a two-layer rhyme (Lenny the Lion was a ventriloquist's dummy
lion popular on British television in the 1950s, and the rhyme is
contemporaneous)

jam duff A duff is a sort of dumpling or suet pudding—but perhaps the
rhymer was thinking mainly of the confection known as a *jam puff*.

Nelly Duff A rhyme best known as the starting point of *not on your Nelly*
'not likely, certainly not' (*duff* rhymes with *puff* = *life*—'not on your life'),
which dates from around 1940, but there seems to have been some currency
for 'homosexual' too. It may lie behind slang *Nelly* 'effeminate man,
homosexual' (He . . . puffed daintily on a long cigarette as he watched the nellies
cruising to the 'tearoom', Kim Platt *The Pushbutton Butterfly* (1970)), although **Nellie
Dean** is another possible source (see QUEEN below), and there are
chronological problems with both.

nice enough Easy to imagine this one camply delivered. The similar **nigh
enough** is applied specifically to homosexual prostitutes (see above).

Poofter

An originally Australian elaboration on *poof* which has evoked the hostile
Australian rhyme **cloven hoofter**.

Queer

Queer as derogatory slang for 'homosexual' dates from the mid 1920s,
providing a useful cut-off date for the rhymes based on it:

Brighton pier Often abbreviated to **Brighton**—not inappropriately, given
the Sussex seaside resort's reputation as a gay capital. First recorded in the
1950s (although the rhyme itself, in *queer*'s earlier sense 'ill', was around in
the 1850s).

chandelier This generally gets compressed to **shandy**.

ginger beer Going back to the 1920s, and very common in its shortened
form **ginger**.

jeer or **jere** Perhaps a memory of old thieves' cant *jere* 'turd', a relic of the 16th century, which itself came from Romany *jeer* 'excrement'.

King Lear Not surprisingly, a favourite of the theatrical profession.

Queen

haricot Short for haricot bean, an Australian creation of the 1960s.

in between Another Australianism, emphasizing the intermediate status of homosexuals.

Nellie Dean Reportedly some use for 'homosexual' (and a possible source for slang *Nelly* 'effeminate man, homosexual'; see *Nelly Duff* under **POOF** above), but mainly this old music-hall favourite stands for 'greens' (see under *Veg* at **FOOD AND DRINK**).

pork and bean Usage is usually plural for this 1960s Australian coinage.

Nancy

song and dance A product of the First World War years, based of course on the abbreviated form *nance*. It fell from favour in the middle years of the 20th century as its model gradually gave way to *queer*.

tickle your fancy Current in the 1940s and 1950s. Ray Puxley in *Cockney Rabbit* (1992) suggests a couplet from the song 'Billy Boy' as a possible source: 'Did Nancy tickle your fancy, Oh my darling Billy boy?'—with 'Nancy' subversively amended to 'a nancy'.

Sod

Tommy Dodd A product of a period (roughly the mid-19th to the mid-20th century) when *sod* (short for *sodomite*) was still in contemptuous use for 'homosexual'. There seems to have been no particular person in mind, and in fact it had been used earlier as a rhyme for *odd* in the game of coin-tossing.

Bent

Duke of Kent A specific application of a general rhyme for *bent*, and not known to have been based on any particular holder of that title.

Stoke-on-Trent First recorded in the 1970s, and reportedly used as a noun, not an adjective (the nominal use of *bent* in this sense dates from the 1950s). From the name of the city in Staffordshire, England.

Homo

Perry Como *Homo* as a contemptuous term for a homosexual came in in the 1920s, and lasted until insulting gays became socially unacceptable in the 1970s. This product of its latter days is based on the name of the catatonically laid-back US crooner (1912–2001). No personal imputation is intended.

Dyke

Raleigh bike From the name of a British make of bicycle. Quite possibly some heavy-handed pun is intended, given the slang use of *bike* for 'promiscuous woman'.

Gay

C&A An early rhyme for *gay*, first recorded in the 1950s, when the usage of *gay* was still largely restricted to the homosexual community. *C&A* is the name of a chain of large middleish-market clothing shops founded in Holland in 1841 by Clemens and August Brenninkmeyer (hence the name). The first British branch was opened in 1922, in Oxford Street, London.

Darling Buds of May From the title of a novel (1958) by H. E. Bates (which itself was based on the line from Shakespeare's Sonnet 18: Rough winds do shake the darling buds of May), but it did not take off as rhyming slang until the novel was turned into a successful British television series in the early 1990s. The shortened **darling buds** makes a suitably camp salutation.

Doris Day From the name of the wholesome US singer and film star (1924–) who became something of a gay icon.

Howard's Way From the name of a British television series of the 1980s, which aimed to be a sort of British answer to *Dallas* and *Dynasty*—middle-class opulent soap (and a tad camp).

Crime and Punishment

Part of the image of rhyming slang is that it inhabits a slightly dodgy area on the borders of legality, the world of Cockney chancers, duckers and divers, and small-time crooks. As such it might be expected to be replete with synonyms for various criminal practices and the machinery of detection and punishment. In truth, rhyming slang is proportionally no richer in this area of vocabulary than any other sort of slang, but it still covers a comprehensive range of human sin and—especially—retribution.

Dishonest, corrupt

Bent

Duke of Kent A widely used rhyme in all senses of the word *bent*, but in this context it generally refers to police officers who have succumbed to the temptations of bribery and corruption.

 Jackie Trent A 1990s rhyme, after the singer and lyricist of popular ballads (1940–).

 See also *Jimmy Young* at **BRIBE**.

Criminals

A crook

babbling brook Some currency in Australian English between the 1920s and the 1960s, but it always played second fiddle to babbling brook 'a cook' (see **FOOD AND DRINK**).

 Joe Hook Not based on a real person, but inspired by slang *hook* for 'a pickpocket or other thief'. Current from the 1930s. An occasional alternative is **Joe Rook** (perhaps with a memory of *rook* 'to defraud').

A villain

Used colloquially for 'a criminal' (as opposed to its long-term standard meaning 'a wicked person') from around 1960, which fits in with the period during which the Conservative politician **Harold Macmillan** (1894–1986) was British prime minister, from 1957 to 1963. The rhyme is purely convenient, and makes no suggestion of wrongdoing beyond what is normally imputed to politicians.

Gang members

Often known with chilling euphemism as 'the boys', which provided the basis for the rhyme **san toys**, current in the 1930s. *San Toy* was originally the name of a brand of small cigar.

A thief

Much the most successful and widely known 'thief' rhyme is **tea leaf**, first recorded in 1903 and still with some life in it at the beginning of the 21st century.

> The badinage . . . was more picturesque . . . 'You dirty old tea-leaf.'
> —Arnold Bennett *Imperial Palace* (1930)

> A tea-leaf wouldn't find the key on your person if he broke in.
> —Douglas Clark *The Gimmel Flask* (1977)

> 'Can't be too careful nowadays, you know. Lots of tea leaves about—know what I mean?' 'Excuse me?' 'Tea leaves—thieves.'
> —*The Limey* (1999)

It was no doubt around in the 19th century, like its first cousin **tea-leafing** 'thieving':

> He could do more than his share at tea-leafing, which denotes the picking up of unconsidered trifles.
> —C. Rook *Hooligan Nights* (1899)

An occasional alternative to tea leaf has been **autumn leaf**.

The main rhyming competitor to *leaf* has been *beef*. It's produced **corned beef** and **leg of beef**, but its most curious offspring is **hot beef**. Since the 18th century *cry beef* and the like had been used to give the alarm ('They whiddle [i.e. utter, divulge] beef and we must brush', they cry *thief* and we must get away. *The Life and Adventures of Bampfylde Moore Carew* (1745)), and *beef* seems to have been generally interpreted as a rhyme on *thief*—though whether that was actually so is a moot point. By the middle of the 19th century it had developed into **hot beef**, used as an equivalent to 'Stop thief!', that overoptimistic injunction to a fleeing criminal:

> It was now that he first experienced 'hot beef'—which is the Jago idiom denoting the plight of one harried by the cry 'Stop thief'.
> —Arthur Morrison *A Child of the Jago* (1896)

> 'Hot beef, hot beef,' cried the schoolboys. 'Catch him . . .'
> —Gwendoline Butler *A Coffin for Pandora* (1973)

To 'give a thief hot beef' was to run after them shouting 'Stop thief!'

The most recent addition to the thieves' kitchen is **Edward Heath** (more usually, and familiarly, **Ted Heath**), perpetuating the criminal associations of Conservative prime ministers (see *Harold Macmillan* at **A VILLAIN**). Sir Edward (1916–) was premier from 1970 to 1974. The rhyme reflects the traditional 'Cockney' pronunciation of /θ/ as /f/.

Celluloid

Harold Lloyd Nothing to do with the cinema, but referring to the abbreviated form *loid*, a slang term for a piece of celluloid or plastic used by housebreakers for illegally opening Yale locks. After Harold Lloyd (1893–1971), star of early silent film comedies. Apparently some use in the abbreviated form **Lloyd**, although that is phonetically indistinguishable from *loid*.

A pickpocket

'Pickpocket' rhymes depend on a range of now largely superannuated *pickpocket* slang synonyms. The earliest may be **cockie's clip**, a late 19th-century Australian rhyme based on *dip* 'a pickpocket' (a *cockie* is a small farmer in Australian English). **Joe Rourke** rhymes with *fork*, which was slang for 'a pickpocket' from the late 17th to the 19th centuries. And in the 20th century, picking pockets was a **bottle of fizz** (i.e. champagne), rhyming with *whizz* 'pickpocketing' (*on the whizz* 'picking pockets' became **on the bottle**).

A fence

eighteen pence A common way of referring to one shilling and sixpence in old money, which suggests a rather meagre return for the burglar selling his booty to the fence.

A child molester

Uncle Lester A 1990s rhyme, even though by then *abuser* had largely replaced *molester* as the politically correct euphemism. The formulation capitalizes on the preponderance of family members as sexual attackers of children.

Crime

To steal

Colloquially, *pinch*, which is the basis of the well-known pre-metric rhyme **half-inch**. First recorded in 1925, it has since spread into British English at large:

> Half-inching is venial, in certain lines of goods.
> —T. E. Lawrence *The Mint* (1950)

> If people are going to go around half-inching planets the situation is pretty serious.
> —*Times* (1972)

Inch, 1990s US campus slang, is probably an independent creation.

In New Zealand in the 1970s, *snitch* 'to steal' was the model, producing the rhyme **half-hitch** (originally the name of a type of knot).

Stolen goods

little red ridings A 1950s and 1960s usage, shortened from a presumed earlier Little Red Riding Hoods, after the extremely honest fairy-tale character whose grannie got eaten by a wolf.

Fraud

hey-diddle-diddle The rhyme is with *fiddle*: an embezzler or fraudulent converter is 'on the hey-diddle-diddle'. The inspiration was no doubt the title of the 18th-century nursery rhyme 'Hey! diddle diddle! The cat and the fiddle' (*diddle-diddle* was originally an imitation of the sound of a violin). But *diddle* itself was already well established in the sense 'to cheat' by the early 19th century and probably played its part too, as it certainly did in the late 19th-century rhyme **Jerry Diddle**.

Nelson Riddle Also rhyming with *fiddle*, and commemorating the doubtless completely upright American composer and musical arranger Nelson Riddle (1921–85).

A fake

cornflake From the term for the breakfast cereal (which itself came on the scene in the first decade of the 20th century).

Sexton Blake Coined at the end of the 19th century from the name of the fictional English detective created by 'Hal Meredith' (pen-name of Harry Blyth) in the magazine *The Halfpenny Marvel* in the 1890s. It came to wider public attention in the latter part of the 20th century thanks to the work of the English copier Tom Keating (1917–84), who used it to characterize the many hundreds of fake Constables, Turners, Renoirs, etc. with which for a time he bamboozled the art world:

> 'You mean those dresses are Sexton Blakes?' 'Are they fakes? Machine finishing, synthetic fabrics . . .'
> —Barry Purchese *Minder* (1983)

A falsified entry, especially in a bookmaker's records, is known as an **oliver** (first recorded in the 1970s). It's short for Oliver Twist (from the name of the Charles Dickens novel (1838)), a rhyme based on *fist* in its metaphorical association with handwriting.

In British underworld slang, items that are fakes are characterized as *snide*, which finds an appropriate rhyme in **Jekyll and Hyde**, from Robert Louis Stevenson's tale of good and evil, *Dr Jekyll and Mr Hide* (1886):

> All these in here are pukka; we'll keep the Jekylls in the safe.
> —*In Deep* BBC1 (2002)

Bribery

In 20th-century British slang a bribe is a *bung*, which inspired the rhyme **Jimmy Young** (often **Jimmy** for short), after the pop ballad singer turned radio disc jockey and chat-show host (1923–) whose Radio 2 *Jimmy Young Programme* became a long-running hit in the latter part of the 20th century.

An Informer

This despised species has a number of uncomplimentary names in the underworld, and naturally enough it's these rather than *informer* that get the rhymes. The most widely used present-day term (so widely known, indeed, that it has passed into the general language) is **grass**. First recorded in 1932, it seems likely that it is itself a product of rhyming slang. It is generally claimed to be an abbreviation of an earlier **grasshopper**. That has a well-documented history as a rhyme for *copper* (see at **A POLICE OFFICER**), but *copper* is semantically unpromising. It could be, though, that the rhyme in this context is based on *shopper* 'someone who shops (i.e. gives information on) criminals to the police'. Since its early days it has blossomed into a verb, and a subsidiary noun *grasser* has been formed from it:

> Tell you the details and then you'll do the gaff on your jack . . . or else turn grass.
> —James Curtis *The Gilt Kid* (1936)

> 'How reliable was the original information?' 'As reliable as any information is from a grasser.'
> —Roderic Jeffries *Traitor's Crime* (1968)

There are other theories that have been put forward to account for *grass*. It has been suggested that it's short for *grass-snake*—*snake*, and more particularly *snake in the grass*, being a familiar metaphor for a treacherous person—and it's been linked with another 'informer'-rhyme, **grass in the park** (based on *nark*), although it seems more likely that that was inspired by **grass** than vice versa. Whatever its origin, *grass* quickly became so firmly established that it in turn was rhymed into slang in the 1950s, with **duck's arse** (not an anatomical term, but the name of a men's hairstyle then in fashion among teddy boys).

The most frequently rhymed word for 'an informer' is *nark*, a piece of slang which goes back to the mid-19th century and was derived from

Romany *nak* 'nose'. Based on it are **carpark** (dating from the 1960s); **grass in the park** (possibly an extension of *grass*—see above); **Hyde Park** (from the name of the royal park on the edge of Mayfair); and **Noah's Ark** (first recorded in 1898 and in wide use in the first half of the 20th century; Julian Franklyn in his *Dictionary of Rhyming Slang* (1960) reports that it was often Spoonerized to *'oah's Nark*, implying 'whore's nark'—a greater insult, but a neutralization of the rhyme).

As an alternative to these there is **Johnnie Walker**, originally applied simply to someone who talks a lot (see *Johnnie Walker* at COMMUNICATION), but subsequently suggesting 'someone who talks to the police'.

Australian English has some choice 'informer'-rhymes: **cabbage-tree hat** (rhyming on *rat*—the literal meaning is 'a hat made from the leaves of the cabbage palm'); **chocolate frog** (rhyming on *dog*); and, most widespread of all, **Moreton Bay fig**. First recorded in 1953, and generally shortened to **Moreton Bay** (Fifty percent of the Drug Squad's arrests are based on information received and woebetide a user, supplier or anyone else who becomes a dog, a gig or, as the police term it, a Moreton Bay. *Bulletin* (Sydney) (1984)), this is based on *fizgig*, or *gig* for short, an Australian slang term for 'an informer' dating back to the late 19th century. The Moreton Bay fig is a type of fig tree that grows at Moreton Bay, at the mouth of the Brisbane River in Queensland.

If a verb rhyme rather than a noun is wanted, there is **lollipop** (sometimes **lolly** for short), based on *shop* 'to inform on someone to the police'.

The Police

In Australian rhyming slang the police are **ducks and geese**, but that is a comparatively rare example in this area of a rhyme based on standard terminology. Most rhymes have other slang as their starting point—in the case of the police, *the filth*, which becomes **Uncle Wilf** (in 'Cockney', *filth* is /fɪlf/), or *the (Old) Bill*, rhymed as **Beecham's Pill**, after the celebrated proprietary tablets introduced by Thomas Beecham in 1850 (generally shortened to *the* **Beechams**), or occasionally as **Jack and Jill**.

A police officer

The most widely used base is *cop*, which has inspired at various times **ginger pop** (generally shortened to **ginger**), **greasy mop** (an Australian rhyme, often just **greasy**), **lollipop** (never in common use), **pork chop** (no doubt a thinly veiled reference to slang *pigs* for 'police'), and **string and top**. Much the most prolific of these *cop* rhymes, though, is the Australian and New Zealand **John Hop**:

A couple of John-Hops arrived to investigate the accident.
—G. Cross *George and the Widda-woman* (1981)

First recorded in 1905, it does not refer to any particular person, and is probably just an arbitrary extension of the earlier slang *John* 'a policeman' (itself short for *johndarm*, from French *gendarme*), to create a rhyme. It soon came to be contracted to **jonnop** (He's not a bad sort for a jonnop. Adelaide Lubbock *Australian Roundabout* (1963)), and the widespread modern Australian use of **John** for 'policeman' ('I'll fetch the johns in the mornin'!' she shrieked. 'Layin' into a white woman!' Patrick White *Riders in the Chariot* (1961)) may be as much an abbreviation of John Hop as a survival of the original usage.

The unshortened *copper* was the basis for **bottle and stopper**, first recorded in US English in 1919 but apparently not used in Britain until the 1950s. Often shortened to **bottle**:

A class neighborhood, the bottles bust you on sight.
—Malcolm Braly *It's Cold Out There* (1966)

It also lies behind **grasshopper**, first recorded in 1893 and in use until the middle of the 20th century:

The criminal classes always speak of policemen as 'grasshoppers'.
—*Daily Chronicle* (1907)

club and stick A 20th-century rhyme based on the mainly US slang *dick* for 'a policeman', and no doubt inspired by the American policeman's nightstick.

hammer and saw An American rhyme of the inter-war period, based on *officer of the law*:

Down there I ran into a whole flock of hammer and saws and had to go overboard in China Basin, swimming up to a pier, being ranked again by a watchman there.
—Dashiel Hammett *The Big Knockover* (1929)

hot scone An Australian rhyme dating from the 1920s, taking *John* 'a policeman' as its basis (see **JOHN HOP** above).

Joe Goss Originally and primarily a rhyme for *boss*, but also used in Australian English for 'a policeman'.

The Flying Squad

Sweeney Todd A widely recognized rhyme, especially in its shortened version **the Sweeney**, thanks mainly, no doubt, to the use of the latter as the title of a popular (and notoriously violent) British televison drama series (1975–8) about the Flying Squad, presented by Thames TV and starring John Thaw as the unruly DI Jack Regan:

Was designed—as they say in The Sweeney—to put the frighteners on Labour knockers.
—*Guardian Weekly* (1977)

Sweeney Todd was the name of a fictitious murderous barber of Fleet Street, London, who slit his customers' throats and made meat pies from their flesh. He first made his appearance in a play by George Dibdin Pitt (1799–1855). The term *flying squad* for a police rapid-reaction force is first recorded in 1927, and it had attracted the rhyme by the mid-1930s.

Scotland Yard

bladder of lard Just as *Scotland Yard* becomes colloquially *the Yard*, so bladder of yard is usually shortened to **the bladder**. Mainly in use between the 1920s and the 1950s, when the headquarters of the Metropolitan Police was situated in a street in Westminster called New Scotland Yard.

To follow a suspect

In the jargon of police and criminals, generally to *tail*, which in rhyming slang becomes **hammer and nail**—or simply **hammer**.

An arrest

Colloquially, a *pull*, which is rhymed as **John Bull**. A 20th-century coinage, based on the name of the archetypal Englishman, which by the 1980s had become shortened to **John**.

On Trial

A judge

Barnaby Rudge An early 20th-century rhyme, from a time when the criminal classes were perhaps more familiar with the works of Dickens than they are now (it's the title of an 1841 Dickens novel set in the period of the Gordon Riots in the 1780s, and its choice may have had something to do with the novel's sub-theme of the evils of capital punishment).
  chocolate fudge Usually shortened to **chocolate**.
  inky smudge A late 19th-century rhyme which survived into the 1930s.
  smear and smudge A 20th-century rhyme.

A magistrate

garden gate First recorded in the 1850s, and it lingered on into the 20th century, but rhymers have found it more fruitful to work with the slang synonym *beak*:
  bubble and squeak After the dish of fried leftover potatoes and greens (which itself came from the sound of the cooking). Generally abbreviated to

bubble (a miscreant appearing in a magistrate's court is 'up before the bubble').

   once a week A 20th-century rhyme, presumably coined by someone who appeared before the magistrate on a regular basis.

Bail

holy nail Dating from the late 19th century, and conjuring up not altogether apposite images of the nails on Christ's cross.

   Royal Mail From the name of the British postal service.

Prison and Punishment

Jail

The great majority of 'prison'-rhymes are based on *jail*: **bucket and pail** (usually shortened to **bucket**—someone who's in prison is 'in the bucket'); **ginger ale** (again, commoner as plain **ginger**); **jug and pail** (there is no connection with slang *jug* 'prison', which predates it by a good hundred years, and was originally short for *Stone Jug*, an 18th- and 19th-century nickname for Newgate Prison); **moan and wail** (an American example from the 1940s, presumably reflecting the inmates' state of mind); **Royal Mail** (more usually meaning 'bail'—see above); and **sorrowful tale** (dating from the mid-19th century, and often applied specifically to three months' imprisonment).

   The commonest alternative is the *nick*, which is the basis of **cow's lick** (from the 1960s; originally a term for a curl of hair which stands up as if it had been licked by a cow); **Moby Dick** (a late 19th-century rhyme, latterly more commonly used for *sick*—see *Moby Dick* at **ILLNESS**); and **shovel and pick** (usually **the shovel**, and perhaps a reference to the tools of hard labour).

   Slang *stir* for 'prison' produced **Joe Gurr**, or just plain **Joe** (first recorded in the 1930s); and the now obsolete *the steel* (from *Bastille*) was the basis of **fillet of veal**, which dates back to the mid-19th century.

Imprisonment

For the inmates, serving your sentence is doing *time*, and that produced a rhyme whose shortened form is now so firmly embedded in British English that its rhyming origins have almost been forgotten. It started off as **bird-lime** (a term for a sort of sticky substance applied to branches to trap birds). That appears to date from the middle of the 19th century, and it was still in use a hundred years later:

> In the past Charley's done his 'birdlime' but he was given time off for good
> behaviour.
> —*Radio Times* (1962)

By at least the 1920s, though, it had been shortened to **bird**, and it's in
that guise that it has become more widely known among readers and
viewers of crime fiction:

> Hell of a long time the next bit of bird was going to be unless he got done for
> suspect.
> —James Curtis *They Drive by Night* (1938)

> Having done his bird, as imprisonment is called in the best circles.
> —*Listener* (1953)

Specific lengths of sentence are denoted by an almost poetic array of
synonyms in prison slang, and some of them are, or may be, of rhyming
origin. **Woodener** 'one month' (in use in the 1940s and 1950s) is short for
wooden spoon, a rhyme based on *moon*, 19th-century prison slang for 'a
one-month sentence' (no doubt also with a nod to the wooden spoon
formerly issued to prisoners). Late 19th-century **carpet** 'three months' is
probably short for the synonymous **carpet-bag**, rhyming with *drag*, prison
slang for 'a three-month sentence' from the late 18th century onwards.
Carpet-bag is not recorded until the 1930s, though, and an alternative
theory put forward for **carpet** is that three months was the time it took to
produce a carpet in the prison workshop. See also *sorrowful tale* at JAIL.

A prison officer

The polite and standard term is *warder*, which got its rhyme in the early
20th century from **Harry Lauder** (1870–1950), the Scottish music-hall
entertainer. To most inmates, though, their guardians are the *screws*, which
has been abundantly rhymed: as **flue** (an unusually brief single-syllable
rhyme from the 1940s and 1950s); **four by two** (a New Zealand rhyme, more
familiarly applied in Britain to a Jew—see *four by two* at JEW); **kangaroo** (in
use since the 1920s and not exclusively Australian, although the shortened
form **kanga**—first recorded in 1953—is); and **little boy blue** (from the
nursery rhyme of that title, and presumably also with an eye to the colour of
a prison officer's uniform).

The senior warder—that much loved figure—is the *chief*, rhymed as
corned beef (an ironic choice, as it also stands for 'thief'—see *corned beef* at A
THIEF) and various other combinations with *beef*, including **bully beef** (long
obsolete), **plate of beef**, and (much the commonest) **ham and beef**:

> There's the ham-and-beef and tickety-boo making rounds.
> —J. Phelan *Murder by Numbers* (1941)

The prison governor is termed affectionately the *guv*, which in rhyming
slang of the 1940s and 1950s became **light of love**.

A cell

flowery dell A rhyme which has reached a wider audience through television prison sitcoms and dramas, thereby ensuring its long-term survival. It dates back at least to the 1920s, and even then, those in the know were shortening it to **flowery**:

> I talked to him of his 'flowery'.
> —E. Jervis *Twentyfive Years in Six Prisons* (1925)

> Found aht on the Moor, . . . that if you have a new play to read weekends in the flowery . . . you can kid yourself you're having a Saturday night aht.
> —T. Clayton *Men in Prison* (1970)

The choice of such a fragrant rhyme may well be simply ironic, but there could also be a connection with 19th-century intinerant traders' slang *flowery dell* for 'a room in an inn'.

The electric chair

I don't care Recorded as a rhyme for *chair* by David Maurer in his 1944 article 'Australian Rhyming Argot in the American Underworld', and conjecturally originally a whistling-in-the-dark reference to the electric chair.

Parole

jam roll A rhyme dating from the 1970s. A prisoner awaiting release on parole is 'up for his jam roll'.

On the run

hot cross bun The usual rules of abbreviation apply: anyone who has escaped from prison (or indeed from marital bliss) is said to be 'on the **hot cross**'.

Weapons

Rhyming slang's relevance to weaponry is largely in the context of criminal violence rather than the battlefield, so it's convenient to group rhymes for weapons together here:

Firearms

fire alarms Mainly an army usage, referring to rifles.

A gun

hot cross bun A cosy domestic name for something that can blow your head off.

A pistol

lady from Bristol Possibly originating in Australia, but the reason behind the strange metaphor is not known.

A shooter

Phil the Fluter Commemorating the hero of the Irish ballad 'Phil the Fluter's Ball'. The slang use of *shooter* for 'a gun' dates from the middle of the 19th century.

A rod

Tommy Dodd US slang *rod* for 'a gun' dates from around the turn of the 20th century. The rhyme (for the origins of which see *Sod* at SEX) is first recorded in the 1920s.

A blade

In this context, a knife or razor for inflicting damage on human soft tissue:

   first aid A blackly humorous reference to the measures called for after the blade's use.

   shovel and spade Usually reduced to **shovel**, and suggesting gruesome images of 'digging' into the skin.

A razor

For rhymes on *razor* as applied to an offensive weapon, see *A razor* at HOUSEHOLD MATTERS.

A sword

my gawd A 19th-century rhyme, which the 20th century didn't have much call for.

Animals

When it comes to the rest of animate creation, rhyming slangsters' horizons are not extensive. Their invention tends to stretch no further than creatures that impinge directly on their own lives: which for the most part means, frankly, ones you can bet on, ones you can eat, and ones that come into intimate and irritating contact with you—plus, in Australia, ones that bite you. The ubiquitous cat rates only two rhymes, but dogs are much more richly endowed—thanks largely to a single breed, the greyhound. And in the rhymers' world, the animals that loom by far the largest are fleas and lice, followed closely by bedbugs.

Vermin

Inhabitants of the crumbling inner-city housing where rhyming slang thrived and grew in the London of the 19th and early 20th centuries shared their homes, their beds, their clothes, and often their bodies with a host of unwelcome but hard-to-evict visitors—insects and rodents that made their lives a misery. Add to this the experience of the verminous trenches of the First World War, and it is little wonder that these irritants provoked a significant verbal reaction:

Fleas

Almost as if they have been granted a grudging kinship, fleas are commonly rhymed with human names. An obvious but alarming choice is *Lee*—alarming because most of the rhymes turn out to be the same as ones for *tea*. Into this category come **Jenny Lee**, **Nancy Lee**, and even dear old **Rosie Lee**. What keeps the association from becoming too intimate is that the *flea*-rhymes are generally pluralized—always so in the case of another member of the *Lee* family, **Willy Lees** (an Australian contribution, dating from the 1920s). Going beyond this cosy family circle we find the long-obsolete 19th-century **Phil McBee** and the Australian **Jack Rees**.

Of the other alternatives, **you and me** goes back to the 19th century, and did not survive long into the 20th; the almost equally venerable and disused **Bonny Dundee** is reported as being a speciality of the theatrical profession; **stand at ease** (an inappropriate injunction to someone who has just been bitten) betrays its First World War military antecedents; and the curious

Australian **two UEs** possibly owes its origins to Australian slang *hughie* 'act of vomiting'.

Lice

Lice is a rather posh name for those unpleasant little parasites that cling to human beings and suck their blood. Most rhyming slangers know them more colloquially as *crabs*, often referring specifically to the crab-louse, which specializes in infesting the pubic hair. Since the mid-20th century **taxicabs** has been a popular rhyme (**taxis** for short), replacing the earlier **hansom cabs**. In the 1930s **Beattie and Babs** was all the rage, taking rather unfair advantage of the names of a pair of music-hall entertainers of that time. **Dribs and drabs** has widespread appeal, in Australia as well as Britain, as does **Sandy McNab** (shades of being 'nabbed' by the louse).

For *lice* itself, the choice is between the 19th-century **boys on ice** and the Australian **white mice**. (Literal lice usually work in gangs, so a reference to a singular *louse* can generally be counted on as metaphorical; this is borne out by the usage of the rhyme **cat and mouse**, for 'despicable person'.)

Bedbugs

Steam tug did the job (often in the devolved form **steamer**) in the 19th and early 20th centuries, after which the decline of the bedbug lessened the need for it, and it took up other rhyming duties elsewhere (see under FOOL). The alternative **tom tug** has a similar profile. The comfortably domestic-sounding **hearthrug** is a 20th-century contribution.

Rat

bowler hat Used for the rodent, but also applied metaphorically to a treacherous person (which is the only application for **cocked hat**, and for the Australian **tit-for-tat**, denoting particularly a trade-union scab).

Mouse

Maxwell House A comparatively recent rhyme based on the name of a brand of instant coffee (rather than on that of the headquarters of the fraudulent tycoon Robert Maxwell (1923–91)).

On the Track

Horse

Sauce is the key word when it comes to rhyming *horse*, and the favourite flavour of all is **tomato sauce**. First recorded in 1905, it remains popular in Britain, Australia, and New Zealand:

> 'Nice weak tomato sauce ta be puttin' money on,' said the Wrecker
> —J. Alard *He Who Shoots Last* (1968)

In practice the rhyme seems most often to be applied (as in the above quote) to nags that trail in after the rest have gone home—a target shared by the synonymous **apple sauce** and **bottle of sauce**.

Equally slow is the **plate-rack**, a 19th-century rhyme based on the fairly derogatory *hack*. The image of the slats of the plate-rack brings the poor gaunt-ribbed creature vividly to life.

The true Cockney rhyme, though, is **Charing Cross**. Dating back to the mid-19th century, when for Londoners *cross* was still decidedly /krɔːs/, it survived well into the 20th century, often in the abbreviated form **Charing**. Here we are not so much at the racetrack as with Londoners' working horses—draymen's draught horses, cabbies' hard-worked hacks, and so on. The name comes from an area to the east of Trafalgar Square, so called from the Eleanor Cross erected there at the end of the 13th century.

Dog

Although most *dog*-rhymes can have a general application, the great majority of their time is spent at the greyhound track; and a good few of them convert into synonyms for this most popular of working men's diversions—*the dogs*.

The commonest and, to modern eyes, the greatest curiosity is **cherry hog**—but that is just what 19th-century Londoners used to call cherry stones. A night out at **the cherries** is spent at the dog track.

Log, though, is the most widely rhymed word—again, not promising much in the way of speed. **Christmas log** is a popular choice, alternating with **Yuletide log**, both recalling the traditional lump of wood burnt at Christmas time and also the log-shaped cake based on it. Australian variations on the theme are **chock and log** and (ominously suggesting the unlikelihood of a burst in the finishing straight) **hollow log**.

London fog sometimes stands in for cherry hog (recalling a major feature of the London climate in the 19th century and the first two-thirds of the 20th), as does **golliwog**, regardless of political correctness (the dog-races are *the golliwogs*, or *the gollies*).

Trouble in Australia

Nature tends to be more proactive in Australia than in London—or at least the things that bite you are larger and potentially more fatal. Hence Aussie rhymers' preoccupation with sharks and snakes:

Shark

Joan of Arc Current in the 1940s and 1950s. From the name of the French national heroine (1412–31) who was burnt at the stake by the English for being a witch and heretic.

Joe Marks Current in the 1930s and 1940s, for the plural *sharks*. No particular Joe Marks—perhaps he was a distant relative of **Joe Blake** 'snake'.

Marcus Clarke From the name of the Australian writer (1846–81) best known for his novel set in early Australian penal settlements, *For the Term of his Natural Life* (1874).

Noah's Ark First recorded in 1945, and by far the most widely used *shark*-rhyme:

> 'Poor blighter, what about the "Noah's Arks"?' voices exclaimed.
> —*Dit* (Melbourne) (1945)

> The sun-bronzed ones refused to dunk their pinkies in the surf while the Noah's Ark was also in it
> —John Hepworth *His Book* (1978)

Commonly curtailed to **Noah's** (usually in the plural form *Noahs*):

> A lotta them beaches in Oz are full of Noahs.
> —Barry Humphries *Bazza comes into his Own* (1979)

> 'I'll tell you what's worse than the Noahs', said Edgar. 'What about those bloody dragon-flies?'
> —*Bulletin* (Sydney) (1982)

Snake

Snakes all belong to the *Blake* family. Minor members are **George Blake** (from the Englishman (1922–94) who spied for the Soviet Union) and **Sexton Blake** (much better known for rhyming with *fake*—see CRIME AND PUNISHMENT), but the head of the family is undoubtedly **Joe Blake**. First recorded in the first decade of the 20th century, it is merely a made-up name for the convenience of the rhyme, not based on any actual person:

> I understand the common Joe Blake to which we refer as a grass snake isn't a snake at all—it's a worm!
> —*North Australian Monthly* (1963)

> We've camped . . . with the Joe Blakes, the goannas, the flies, and 4000 skinny jumbucks.
> —*Sunday Mail Magazine* (Brisbane) (1970)

> I'd never heard of anyone actually being bitten by a 'joe blake' in the hills.
> —P. Barton *Bastards I have Known* (1981)

The plural form often enters into the metaphorical scenario of 'seeing snakes', denoting the effects of excessive alcohol consumption (see under *Delirium tremens* at **ALCOHOL AND OTHER DRUGS**):

> I saw a lot of *Joe Blakes*, but I don't know if they were dinkum or just the after effects of the grog.
> —J. Meredith *Learn to talk Old Jack Lang* (1905)

Assorted Other Mammals, Birds, and Insects

Beetles

pins and needles A distinctly approximate-looking rhyme, although it has been claimed it represents a genuine pronunciation /'biːdlz/.

Cat

ball of fat A vivid evocation of the overfed domestic moggie ensconced by the hearth.

brown hat First recorded in the late 19th century, but it does not seem to have survived long into the 20th.

Donkey

Jerusalem artichoke The rhyme is with *moke*, from the mid-19th century a widely used colloquialism for 'donkey', not least among the East End costermongers who used donkeys to pull their carts. **Jerusalem** was a common abbreviation (possibly encouraged by an association with Christ riding through Jersualem on a donkey). (A slang term for a mule is *Jerusalem cuckoo*, from its raucous bray.)

Fly

meat pie Conjuring up uncomfortable images of fly-blown window displays in grocers' shops. Also used in the plural to denote trouser flies (see **CLOTHING**).

Nellie Bligh A multi-purpose rhyme which among its other applications has *meat pie* (see *Pie* at **FOOD AND DRINK**).

Leeches

cries and screeches An Australian rhyme, evoking the reaction when a leech attaches itself to you.

Pig

Lord Wigg An uncomplimentary reference to the British Labour politician George (later Lord) Wigg (1900–83), whose role as inquisitor-in-chief to prime minister Harold Wilson brought him fairly general unpopularity.

Sparrow

bow and arrow A solitary rhyme for the quintessential Cockney bird, first recorded in the late 19th century.

Spider

sit beside her A convenient ready-made rhyme from the nursery rhyme 'Little Miss Muffet': 'Down came a spider and sat down beside her'. Inspiration is claimed, too, from old-fashioned outdoor lavatories, which occupants generally had to share with a few spiders.

Squirrel

nice one, Cyril From a catchphrase popular in Britain in the 1970s. It originated as a line in a television advertisement for 'Wonderloaf', and was subsequently taken up by football fans as a chant aimed at the Tottenham Hotspur player Cyril Knowles.

For rhymes for animals used as food, see FOOD AND DRINK.

Food and Drink

Anyone searching for linguistic confirmation of the stereotypical diet of the London working classes in the 19th and 20th centuries need look no further than their rhyming slang. This is a world where tea reigns unchallenged (sixteen rhymes, as against just two for coffee); where bread and butter is a major subsistence item, supplemented by a bit of cheese if you are lucky (butter and cheese significantly outnumber other foodstuffs in the rhymes contrived for them); where meat in all its forms (**stop thief, billy button, hop it and scram, Bernhard Langers,** and so on) yields no ground to fruit and veg; where pies and stews, fish and chips and winkles are the comfortably familiar staples, and there is not a quiche in sight (although curry has been allowed to join the pantheon).

Food

Food itself can be **in the mood** or **in the nude** (the latter apparently a facetious alteration of the former), or **don't be rude**. As often as not, though, a slang alternative to *food* is the basis of the rhyme. Probably the most ancient of these is *peck*, originally 16th-century thieves' cant and used until the early 20th century as an equivalent of *grub* (it probably came from the idea of 'pecking' up food, as a peckish person would like to do): the rhyming slang version was **Tooting Bec**, or just **Tooting** for short, from the name of the northerly part of Tooting, in the south London borough of Wandsworth (*Bec* is a relic of a time, in the early Middle Ages, when the area was held by the Benedictine Abbey of Saint Mary of Bec in Normandy). Then there was *scran*, a word of uncertain ancestry used from the early 19th to the mid-20th century for a snack, and especially a workman's portable lunch: in rhyme it became **Tommy O'Rann** (possibly an allusion to the Irishness of many navvies and other labourers), or sometimes alternatively **Johnny Rann**. Rather more recent is *nosh*, which does not seem to have made its way into English from Yiddish until the 1950s, and then soon progressed to the rhyme **mouthwash**.

To *eat* is **tidy and neat**, but this rhyming-slang format is unwieldy for verbs, and it usually becomes just **tidy**—or even (with its rhyming origins presumably forgotten) **tidy up** (as in 'You can't go out till you've tidied up your dinner'). But perhaps you are on a **Brixton riot**—a 'diet'.

For eaters-out, the rhyme between *waiter* and *potato* has proved hard to resist (it depends of course on *potato* being /pəˈteɪtə/, not /pəˈteɪtəʊ/). Probably the oldest variation on the theme is **hot potato**, which dates back to the late 19th century. It was joined in the 20th century by **cold potato**, and some authorities claim a distinction between hot potato for a speedy and efficient waiter and cold potato for a lugubrious and dilatory one—but there is no evidence for it, and it sounds too good to be true. Other 20th-century variants are **roast potato** (often compressed to **roastie**) and **baked potato**.

The *cook*'s rhyme, though, is firmly established, at any rate in Australian and New Zealand English: he is a **babbling brook**. And it generally is a 'he', too, for the term is mainly applied to someone catering for a party of sheep-shearers or stockmen, or to an army cook:

> Local good cooks asked for the recipe, but minds boggled at the quantities the army's babbling-brook recited for their benefit
> —*Sunday Mail* (Brisbane) (1981)

Commonly shortened to **babbler** (first recorded in 1904, which predates the earliest record of **babbling brook** by nine years):

> We worked it out that the old babbler made 112,000 rock cakes during those four months
> —*Weekly News* (Auckland) (1963)

and still further to **bab** (first recorded in 1936):

> The bab's present rate for cooking for more than seven is £14 4*s*. 11*d*., *plus* keep and overtime for Sundays and holidays
> —*Bulletin* (Sydney) (1959)

There is even a verb formed from it: *babble* 'to cook':

> I've bin babblin' for fifty-four years. Cookin' all sorts o' scran—yairs, from wombats to steers
> —*Bulletin* (Sydney) (1938)

Meat

The rhyming slang of meat is not exactly a cornucopia, but as befits the argot of a decidedly non-vegetarian culture, each main variety is represented. And as a cover term for *meat* itself there is **hands and feet**—a metaphor which does not bear too close contemplation, especially in its frequent abbreviated form **hands**.

At the behest of modern tastes, selective breeding seems to be on course to eliminate most fat from meat, but in the 19th and early 20th centuries *fat* was king, and who else should be its rhyming partner but **Jack Sprat**—as in the nursery rhyme:

> Jack Sprat could eat no fat, His wife could eat no lean.

Beef

itchy teeth A rhyme depending on the 'Cockney' pronunciation /tiːf/.

stop thief Dating from the mid-19th century, and reputedly applied only to a stolen joint, not to a legitimately acquired piece of beef (Stop Thief, meat stolen. 'I have got this piece of stop thief.' I stole this piece of raw meat. Th[ieves]. 'Ducange Anglicus' *The Vulgar Tongue* (1857))—though this may well be a post-hoc rationalization. *Stop thief* is the traditional (since the early 18th century) cry of someone calling on anyone in the vicinity to stop a runaway thief, and with neat circularity **hot beef** has been used as rhyming slang for *it* (see *hot beef* at CRIME AND PUNISHMENT).

Steak

ben flake Recorded in the 1850s in both Britain and the US, but it does not seem to have survived beyond the early years of the 20th century.

Joe Blake Probably the most widespread and long-lasting of the *steak*-rhymes. There was no particular Joe Blake; he is just a convenient rhyme.

quiver and shake A 20th-century Australianism, possibly provoked by eating some steak that was past its sell-by date.

Veronica Lake Commemorating the Hollywood film star (1919–73) famous in the 1940s especially for her peek-a-boo hairstyle.

Steak and kidney

Kate and Sidney An early rhyme (first known in print from 1914, and the earliest record of *steak and kidney* itself is only from the 1860s, when Mrs Beeton gave a recipe for the pudding), and one whose quirky humour seems to have kept it in fashion ever since:

> Beefsteak pudding? Phew! A pity Johnny's not here, Ma! Remember how he used to go for your Kate and Sidney?
> —Marguerite Steen (1949)

Not just rhyming slang, but also a partial spoonerism, transposing the *s* and the *k* of *steak and kidney*. Mainly applied to the pudding, it seems, but also available for the pie.

Dripping

Very non-PC in the 21st century, crammed as they are not only with the worst possible sort of fat but also quite conceivably with BSE, in the 19th and early 20th centuries the congealed meltings of a roast joint (in theory any meat, in practice usually beef) were regularly and enthusiastically devoured, typically spread on bread or toast. Gallows humour seized on a rhyme with **Doctor Crippen**, from the murderer (Dr Hawley Harvey

Crippen, 1862–1910) who became a national celebrity in the 1900s for killing his wife, fleeing justice with his young lover dressed as a boy, and being captured with the aid of the new-fangled wireless.

Mutton

Billy Button Dating from the mid-19th century, but it gradually faded from use as mutton disappeared from the British diet (or was dressed up verbally as *lamb*). *Billy Button* was the traditional generic name of an itinerant tailor.

Lamb

Uncle Sam No particular connection with the personification of the United States (who goes back to the early 19th century), merely a convenient rhyme.

Pork

Duchess of York Apparently a quite recent rhyme, and therefore presumably inspired by the Duchess of York (1959–) who was the wife of Prince Andrew. No derogatory association with the stereotypical fatness of pork is surely intended.

knife and fork A longer established rhyme, and suitably gastronomic in its allusion.

Mickey Rourke An unsolicited linguistic memorial to the Hollywood actor (1955–).

Pig's trotters

Gillie Potters From the name of the English comedian Gillie Potter (1887–1975), and declining in currency as his memory has waned. The rhyme has also been applied facetiously to the human feet.

Ham

hop it and scram *Scram* in the sense 'to go away quickly' is not recorded in British English before the 1930s, providing a useful *terminus a quo*. Usually reduced to **hop it**.

Seringapatam From the name of the capital of the former princely state of Mysore in southwestern India, which became familiarized to English-speakers when the city was beseiged and captured by the British in 1799. Decidedly a 19th-century rhyme, and latterly apparently used only in partnership with **plasterer's trowel** (see CHICKEN).

trolley and tram Commemorating two modes of urban public transport in Britain in the early and middle years of the 20th century. First the tram and then the trolley bus were supplanted by the motor bus.

Sausages

Sausage is not easy to rhyme, and anyway rhyming-slang cultures often seem to have alternative terms—Cockneys' *bags of mystery*, for instance, and Australians' *snags*. But *banger* (first recorded in 1919) is at first sight far more enticing to the rhymster. The only rhyme to have gained even some small currency, though, seems to have been **Berhard Langer**, after the German Ryder Cup golfer (1957–). **Coat-hanger** has apparently been used in the same sense, but its main rhyming partner is *banger* 'old car'. Then there is the *saveloy*, that spicy sausage much beloved of Londoners in the 19th and 20th centuries: it became **girl and boy** as early as the 1850s, and later **Myrna Loy**, after the Hollywood actress (1905–93).

Chicken

In the heyday of rhyming slang, chicken was not so habitually on people's tables as it became in the post-Second World War years of factory farming. Rhymers have had one stab at it, though, producing, with a fine disregard for accuracy, **Charlie Dicken**, from the name of England's most celebrated novelist, Charles Dickens (1812–70). From the days (i.e. up to the early 20th century) when chicken for the table was still commonly referred to as *fowl* comes **plasterer's trowel**, which apparently was used only in partnership with Seringapatam to denote 'chicken and ham' (see HAM).

Turkey

bubbly jock An antiquated 19th-century rhyme based on *turkey cock*, and no doubt inspired by the bird's noisy gobbling. *Bubbly Jocks* was used as a rather unfriendly nickname of the Royal Scots Greys, a British army regiment.

Pinky and Perky From the name of a pair of puppet pigs who became popular on television in Britain in the late 1950s and early 1960s, particularly for their electronically manipulated high-pitched singing. Usually shortened to **Pinky**.

Stew

A basic culinary concept—unspecified meat cooked at a slow boil in a pan, usually with a few vegetables—but apparently not lexicalized as a 'stew' until the late 18th century. It soon got the rhyming treatment with the curious **bonnets so blue**, which is first recorded in the 1850s but had probably died out by the end of the century; it was often used specifically for Irish stew, which is a shade deviant geographically, since in the past the literal 'blue bonnet' was particularly associated with Scotland. Somewhat later came **Battle of Waterloo**, often **Waterloo** for short (unusually for rhyming slang losing the first element rather than the last). The metaphorical sense of *stew*, 'state of anxiety', is of almost equal antiquity with the literal one, and it has been claimed that it has its own rhyme in *how d'ye do*. This is chronologically plausible, as *how d'ye do* is first recorded in the 1830s, but the semantics do not really quite fit: a *how d'ye do* is more of a generally embarrassing or confused state of affairs than a personal state of anxiety. Also contentious is the status of **boys in blue**: some claim it has been used for a literal stew, others that it can only be a metaphorical one.

And finally, the inevitable accompaniment to meat:

Gravy

Evidently a forces' favourite, or at least there was no shortage of it in service canteens: **army and navy** dates from the First World War period, the less common **Royal Navy** from somewhat later.

Fish

Not surprisingly, when it comes to fish, the habitat of rhyming slang is the chip shop and the whelk stall: this is the world of cod and winkles, not sea bass and palourdes. The rhymes for *fish* in general set the tone: from the early 20th century you could have **Andy McNish** (if there was an original Andy, his identity has been lost); and somewhat later there was **Lilian Gish** (from the name of the long-lived Hollywood actress (1896–1993)). Australia contributes **dirty dish**.

Cod

The main fishy partner for chips, but not the most fragrant of tributes to the British film actor **Richard Todd** (1919–), doyen of stiff-upper-lip roles in war movies.

Eel

Quintessential Cockney fare in jellied form (see *Mother Kelly* at FRUIT), so it finds an appropriate rhyme in **Tommy Steele** (1936–), the London-born entertainer who in the late 1950s was the first home-grown British rock-'n'-roll star.

Haddock

Another chip shop favourite, with a pair of fairly relevant rhymes: **Bessie Braddock**, from the post-Second World War Labour member of parliament for Liverpool Exchange (1899–1970) whose girth suggested not infrequent visits to the chippie; and **Fanny Cradock**, from the presenter of television cookery programmes (1909–94; née Primrose-Pechey) famous for her intimidating manner and green-dyed mashed potato.

Kipper

It would have taken particular strong-mindedness to resist the rhyme with **Jack the Ripper**, especially since the splitting open of the herring is a gruesome echo of the Whitechapel murderer's way with his victims in 1888. An infrequent American alternative is **New York nipper**.

Mussel

As good an excuse as any for rhymsters to contemplate **Jane Russell**, from the Hollywood film star (1921–) famous for her bust.

Prawn

Prawns did not really become a front-line foodstuff until the 1950s, with the advent of the prawn cocktail (until then, the ordinary man in the street would be far more likely to encounter shrimps), so their rhyme is appropriate to the moment: **Frankie Vaughan**, from the British song-and-dance man (1928–99) with the roguish grin, who first came to fame in that decade.

Shrimp

Shrimps with bread and butter would have made a good Londoner's tea in the days of **Colonel Blimp**, originally a cartoon character invented in the 1930s by David Low and later adopted as the generic name of a pompous reactionary or bigot.

Winkle

Winkles, and the whole etiquette of pin-extraction, are very much part of Cockney culture (there is even a song about them, full of lightly veiled innuendo: 'I can't get my winkle out, isn't it a sin; the more I try to get it out, the further it goes in'). In rhyming slang they become **grannie's wrinkles**, popularly **grannies**.

Soup

bowl the hoop An ancient reminder of Victorian soup-kitchens for the poor, from the days when bowling an iron hoop along the road was a favourite childhood game.

  loop the loop An Australian rhyme. The expression *loop the loop* dates from the early years of the 20th century; it was originally applied to a sort of fairground switchback ride, and later came to be used for an aerobatics manoeuvre.

From the Dairy

Rhyming slang laughs at cholesterol. Products of the dairy are copiously and enthusiastically synonymized. It may be true that most *butter*-rhymes refer tacitly to bread and butter, but butter is butter, and there are no fewer than fourteen of them (and only one, note, for *margarine*). *Cheese* weighs in with an impressive seven. We are reminded that in the 19th and early 20th centuries, cheese and butter, along with bread, were major staple foods of working people.

Butter

Bread goes with *butter* as surely as butter goes with bread—indeed the combination, with its institutionalized meaning 'bread spread with butter', goes back at least to the early 17th century. It is not too surprising, therefore, that although the majority of *butter*-rhymes probably started out referring simply to butter, they generally ended up meaning 'bread and butter' (despite a lack of any supporting rhyme in the first element).

One little nexus of rhymes revolves around *gutter* (reflecting the incompetent ventriloquist's pronunciation of the word). There is the Australian **kerb and gutter**, but most of them suggest a curious scenario involving possibly drunken abjection: **lay me in the gutter**, **roll me in the gutter**, and **slip in the gutter**. All three go back to the early 20th century, and the second was in common enough use to acquire the shortened form **roll me**.

Another group exploits rhyming vocalizations: **cough and splutter**, **lisp and stutter**, **mutter and stutter**, **stammer and stutter**, **mumble and mutter** (**mumble** for short). The commonest of these, dating from the early 20th century, was probably **stammer and stutter**:

> How would the QM go if he was faced with an order like this . . . a couple of pounds of stammer and stutter with a bottle of dead horse.
> —*Puckapunyal: Official Journal of the 17th Australian Infantry Brigade* (1940)

Then there are the names, mostly fictitious as far as is known: **Dan Tucker**, dating back to the mid-19th century, and his American cousin (and equally dodgy rhyme) **Danny Rucker**; **Gordon Hutter**, New Zealand rhyming slang and the one real person in this select club—Gordon Hutter was a racing and wrestling commentator in the 1930s and 1940s; and **Johnnie Nutter**, also from the 19th century.

That leaves **pull down the shutter**, a late 19th-century rhyme, and the bizarre and obsolete **potash and perlmutter**, based on the name of a play by the US dramatist Montague Glass which was first performed in London in 1914.

Margarine

little and large Rhyming slangers eat butter, not any sort of namby-pamby substitute, so *margarine* manages only a single rhyme. It is 20th-century, but it is not clear if any reference was intended, originally or subsequently, to the English comedy double act made up of Sid Little and Eddie Large who were popular in the 1980s.

Cheese

Annie Louise An Australian contribution, from the 20th century.

balmy breeze Usually cut to **balmy**. A variation on the theme is **evening breeze**, which apparently existed also in the elaborated form **sweet evening breeze**.

bended knees Probably dating from the late 19th century, and generally shortened to **bended**. Apparently in common use among tramps, and one theory has it that it refers to the difficulty of obtaining cheese.

cough and sneeze From the late 19th century. Reputedly mainly a retailer's rather than a customer's term, and hopefully not reflecting what went on over the cheese counter.

flying trapeze Also late 19th-century, and presumably inspired by the 1868 song by George Leybourne, immensely popular at the time, whose first two lines run: He'd fly through the air with the greatest of ease, A daring young man on the flying trapeze.

John Cleese From the gangling English comedy actor and writer (1939–) who came to fame in the *Monty Python* television series. Not an inappropriate rhyme for the man who created Basil Fawlty, the hotelier from hell who regularly terrorized the dining room.

stand at ease Apparently a coinage from the trenches of the First World War.

Eggs

arm and leg Never any extensive currency, and probably finally driven out by the expression *an arm and a leg*, meaning 'an extortionate price', with which it clashes metrically.

borrow and beg A late 19th-century rhyme which was reportedly revived during the Second World War, when scarcity meant that eggs could only be had by borrowing or begging.

Scotch peg Mainly and originally (from the late 19th century) 'leg', but apparently some use for 'egg' in the 20th century. A variation on the *peg* theme is **tent peg**.

Milk

Milk does not offer many rhymes, so *silk* is exploited for all it is worth. The earliest example, from the 19th century, is **yellow silk**, a hyperbolic epithet perhaps at odds with some of the watered-down, adulterated milk sold at that period. By the 20th century, when **satin and silk** appeared, it may have deserved the name more. **Soft as silk** is an Australian contribution.

A late 19th-century alternative to these was **Charlie Dilke**, after the British Liberal politician Sir Charles Dilke (1843–1911), whose career was prematurely terminated in 1885 by his involvement in a divorce case.

The only name the 20th century had to offer was **Acker Bilk**, commemorating a jazz clarinettist (1929–) who enjoyed some popular success in Britain in the 1960s.

Veg

The greengrocer's stall scarcely produces a cornucopia of rhyming slang—a reflection of the comparatively low regard in which vegetables were held in Britain in the recent past—but at least veg does better than fruit. Nothing fancy, mind. None of the supermarkets' new queer gear, and little that would find its way into a salad. We stick with tried and trusted staples: cabbages, carrots, greens—and, of course, the potato.

Potatoes

The actual word *potato* has been sparingly rhymed. By far the older of the two efforts is **navigator**, which dates back at least to the 1850s. In the 19th century, street sellers used to cry out 'Navigator scot!' (= potatoes hot) to advertise their baked potatoes. The navigator the rhymer had in mind was presumably not a nautical one, but one of the labourers (*navvies* for short) who built the canals and railways of Victorian Britain. Large numbers of them were Irish, and the connection with the potato, thought of as the stereotypical Irish vegetable, is no doubt not fortuitous.

A more recent alternative is **Spanish waiter**, a living tribute to the loyalty of the British to their favourite vegetable even when on holiday in Spain. Both this and navigator depend on the 'Cockney' pronunciation of *potato* as /pə'teɪtə/.

Somewhat easier to rhyme, and more comfortably familiar, is *spud*, a word for 'potato' which dates back to the middle of the 19th century. Spuds can be **rosebuds** (rather OTT, and often shortened to **roses**, which is no less flowery; it dates from the late 19th century, and was apparently popular in the British Army during the First World War); or **Captain Bloods** (an Australian contribution: the obvious derivation is from Captain Peter Blood, the fictional pirate created in 1922 by Rafael Sabatini and played on screen in 1935 by Errol Flynn, but given the Australian connection, a more likely source may be the gory nickname 'Captain Blood' bestowed on the 20th-century Australian Rules footballer Jack Dyer); or **steele rudds** (also Australian, from *Steele Rudd*, the pen-name of Australian writer Arthur Hoey Davis (1868–1935), whose 'Dad and Dave' characters (see *Shave* at HOUSEHOLD MATTERS) have passed into Australian folklore); or **Roy Hudds** (from the name of the London comedian Roy Hudd (1936–), not averse to the occasional rhyme himself).

Chips

jockey's whips A reapplication of a rhyme originally used for *kip* (see *Sleep* at HOUSEHOLD MATTERS). Usually abbreviated to **jockeys**.

   lucky dips Definitely the rhyme of choice for the 21st century. Possibly from an underlying scenario of dipping into an improvised 'bag' of newsprint (or, in these cleaned-up, hygenic times, a real paper bag) and pulling out one's takeaway chips.

   nigger's lips A shock-tactic rhyme apparently current in the 1970s and 1980s, but its chances of long-term survival were never high.

Crisps

Crisps were around at the end of the 19th century, but the actual word *crisp* is not recorded until the 1920s, providing a *terminus a quo* for the rhyme **will o' the wisps**. In everyday use this is generally curtailed to **willers**.

Greens

Greens are perhaps the quintessential rhyming slanger's vegetable; one of the components of the traditional meat and two veg is certain to be something covered by the term—Brussel tops, spring greens, or most likely cabbage. Their unloved status (especially among children, who stereotypically need to be thumbscrewed into eating them) is best reflected in the rhyme **has beens**, which apparently started life as prison slang. Alternatives are **God save the Queens** and **Nellie Deans**—the latter presumably inspired by the heroine of Harry Armstrong's popular song of the early 20th century favoured by the sentimentally drunk: There's an old mill by the stream, Nellie Dean, Where we used to sit and dream, Nellie Dean.

Cabbage

Cabbage itself, on the other hand, rates only one rhyme, the purely fictitious **Joe Savage**—perhaps reflecting a shortage of suitable rhyming partners. It dates back to the mid–19th century, and is long since obsolete.

Brussels sprouts

cockles and mussels The rhyme, of course, is with the standard colloquial shortening *Brussels*, not with the full form.

Carrots

The partner for boiled beef in traditional English cuisine gets the rhyme **polly parrots**.

Onions

corns and bunions Dating from the late 19th century, and forming a reciprocal pair with **Spanish onion**, rhyming slang for 'bunion'. Reportedly applied not just to literal onions, but also to metaphorical ones—hence 'to know your corns and bunions'.

Peas

you and mes Peas do not figure highly enough in the Cockney scheme of things to merit a rhyme; this is an Australianism.

Beans

kings and queens In practice this always refers to baked beans. In rhyming slang, beans on toast becomes **kings on holy ghost**.

Spinach

Woolwich and Greenwich From two localities in southeast London, both parts of the London borough of Greenwich. Primarily a greengrocers' term, it dates from the late 19th century. The alternative formulation **Charlton and Greenwich** picks up on another area of southeast London.

Fruit

Fruit gets even shorter shrift from rhyming slangsters than vegetables. Perhaps it is for wimps. Even those two stalwarts of the genre, apples and pears (as in 'stairs'), get only two rhymes between them. All the stranger that something as apparently exotic as the pomegranate should get the nod.

Apple

Whitechapel From the area of east London probably most famous, or notorious, for being the scene of the Jack the Ripper murders in 1888. A more apposite connection, though, may be with Spitalfields fruit and vegetable market, just to the north of Whitechapel Road, which remained in business until 1991.

Pear

teddy bear The teddy bear did not come into existence until 1906 (its name inspired by US President Theodore ('Teddy') Roosevelt, an enthusiastic bear-hunter), fixing the rhyme firmly in the 20th century.

Banana

Gertie Gitana A now forgotten tribute to an early 20th-century music-hall singer (1888–1957). According to Julian Franklyn, *Dictionary of Rhyming Slang* (1960), 'Have a banana', the refrain of the popular music-hall song *Let's all go down the Strand*, was often replaced by audiences with 'Gertie Gitana' in the first two or three decades of the century.

Rajputana An ephemeral mid-20th-century example from the London Docks, after a P&O cargo vessel of the time. The rhyme was purely fortuitous—the ship did not carry bananas.

Pomegranate

Tommy Rabbit A decidedly approximate rhyme from the late 19th century. At that time, pomegranates were far from uncommon, but as they became more exotic fruit, their rhyme vanished from memory.

Prune

Rangoon Given its reputation as a laxative, the prune could scarcely have hoped to escape the rhyming slang treatment. It has been speculated that the choice of Rangoon (former name of Yangon), capital of Myanmar (formerly Burma), may reflect the stomach upsets that afflict visitors to that part of the world.

Sultana

salty banana A surreal Australianism (Australia is a major producer of sultanas). The gastronomically inappropriate *salty* is a variation on the first syllable of *sultana*.

Nuts

fat guts Presumably a reference to the effect of a surfeit of nuts on the eater.

And, because it is generally fruit-flavoured, a place may be found here for:

Jelly

Mother Kelly Inspired by the owner of the doorstep in the popular sentimental song 'On Mother Kelly's Doorstep' (1925), by George A. Stevens. Actually, not just fruit jelly, but also the medium of that favourite rhyming slangster's delicacy, jellied eels.

In the Bakery

Baker

long acre First recorded in the mid-19th century, and no longer much used. Long Acre is a street in central London, near Covent Garden; it has no particular connection with baking.

Flour

half an hour An Australianism, first recorded in the 1940s.

Bread

lump of lead Not a tribute to the baker's art. In British rhyming slang, lump of lead means 'head' (see THE BODY AND ITS PARTS); this usage is Australian.

 needle and thread First recorded in 1859, and continuing in use well into the 20th century. Reportedly often used in its abbreviated form **needle** in combination with **stammer** (short for stammer and stutter 'butter'). A contemporary variation **skein of thread** stood for 'loaf of bread'.

 strike me dead Dating from the late 19th century, and often shortened to **strike me**.

 Uncle Fred Reportedly used mainly to children. An Australian relative is **Uncle Ned**.

And to spread on your bread and butter (see FROM THE DAIRY):

Jam

The longest established rhymes are **Amsterdam** (from the Dutch city; usually shortened to **amster**, but with no suggestion of eating rodents) and **gor-damn** (*gor* from the euphemistic alteration of *god*). Twentieth-century alternatives include **baby's pram**, **bus and tram**, and the Australian **Tom and Sam**.

Crust (of bread)

you must An encouragement to children to eat their crusts, which they are traditionally reluctant to do.

Toast

fig and post A British Army coinage of the Second World War period and perhaps partially a spooneristic inversion of **pig and roast**.

   holy ghost Current since the 1940s, and the best survivor of the three rhymes:

> Waiters began screaming, 'Holy Ghost for Two', 'Holy Ghost for Four' . . . My simple task was to provide toast demanded from the bedrooms, where the famous occupants were hungry after the delights of the night and screamed for attention. As I lit my oven, using my new dexterity to extract hundreds of slices of Holy Ghost and thrust them at the shrieking line of waiters, my lie-abed mornings in Arundel Terrace seemed irrecoverable.
> —John Osborne, *A Better Class of Person* (1981)

   pig and roast A British Army coinage of the Second World War period, said to be an ironic comparison of the fare available to officers and to other ranks.

Roll

Nat King Cole Celebrating the velvet-voiced US singer and pianist (1919–65).

Pie

In practice, these rhymes generally refer specifically to a meat pie— particularly the Australian ones, where the meat pie is a heritage item. Into the latter category come **dog's eye** (first recorded in the 1960s, and perhaps recalling Australian slang *tinned dog* 'tinned meat'), **Nazi spy** (not surprisingly a Second World War coinage, and suggesting a grisly fate for any spy caught in Australia), and **Nellie Bligh** (after the 'other woman' in the sentimental ballad *Frankie and Johnnie*), often **Nellie** for short:

> *Nellie at Expo 67.* An Australian meat pie is to be sent to Expo '67
> —*Kings Cross Whisper* (Sydney) (1967)

   British offerings include **smack in the eye** (also recorded in America), the distinctly unappetizing **scabby eye**, and (presumably a result of the smack in the eye) **black eye**—all again mainly referring to meat pies.

Crust (of a pie)

Australians even have a rhyme for pie-crusts, and not one that makes them sound very appetizing: **dirt, grime, and dust**.

Pasty

cheap and nasty A 20th-century Australianism, reflecting widely held opinion on the contents of (shop-bought) pasties. To British eyes, the rhyme seems to point towards a pronunciation /ˈpɑːsti/, but in Australian English *nasty* is quite likely to be /ˈnasti/, so things are not so straightforward as they seem.

Cake

give and take From the mid-19th century, and no longer in use by the end of the 20th.

Joe Blake Possibly from the late 19th century, but never in very widespread use.

put and take The rhyme comes from a sort of gambling game played with a six-sided top, which was introduced in the early 1920s.

Sexton Blake Commemorating the fictional English detective created by 'Hal Meredith' (pen-name of Harry Blyth) in the magazine *The Halfpenny Marvel* in the 1890s. In quite common use in the early 20th century, but it gradually lost out to its alternative rhyming application, *fake* (see *A fake* at CRIME AND PUNISHMENT).

Swan Lake From the Tchaikovsky ballet (1876), probably the best known of all 19th-century romantic ballets. Often shortened to **swan**.

Condiments and Spices

Sauce

But in the world of rhyming slang, unlikely to be béchamel or ravigote: these are rhymes that accompany tomato sauce and HP. British English opts for **rocking horse**, which denotes not only literal sauce but also its metaphorical offshoot, 'cheek, effrontery'. Australian English has **dead horse**, applied specifically to 'tomato sauce'; the expression was presumably appropriated, with no particular relevance, from the idiom *work (off) a dead horse* 'to work for wages which all go in paying off old debts':

> How would the QM go if he was faced with an order like this . . . a couple of pounds of stammer and stutter with a bottle of dead horse.
> —*Puckapunyal: Official Journal of the 17th Australian Infantry Brigade* (1940)

> Remember that fabulous 1960s Railway Refreshment Room cuisine (poi, peas, and dead 'orse).
> —J. Borthwick *Off the Rails* (1996)

Pickle(s)

The singular version gets **slap and tickle**, a colloquial euphemism for amorous boisterousness which dates from the 1920s. For the plural there is **Harvey Nichols**, from the name of the Knightsbridge clothing store (latterly with an up-market food department).

Salt

The most orthographically orthodox rhyme is **squad halt**, of obviously military origin. It dates from the 19th century, but First World War square-bashing gave it its biggest boost. Australian English since the 1970s has had **Harold Holt** (matching the pronunciation /sɒlt/), from the Australian prime minister (1908–67) who drowned in a swimming accident.

Betraying an /l/-less pronunciation of *salt* are **Earls Court** (from the area of southwest London heavily populated in the 1960s and 1970s by more or less permanent Australian immigrants) and **Hampton Court** (from the royal palace on the Thames near Kingston; commonly shortened to **Hampton**).

Pepper

High stepper dates back at least to the First World War period; it appropriates a 19th-century expression for an elegant or fashionable person. The less appetizing alternative is **dirty leper**, often shortened to **dirt** (perhaps suggested by the appearance of ground black pepper).

Cloves

A spice which survived in English cuisine (e.g. in apple pies) when many others fell by the wayside in the plain-Jane early 20th century. The rhyme **kitchen stoves**, though, is Australian.

A rather wider range of spices than rhyming slang offers is needed for:

Curry

River Murray The Australian contribution, taking the name of Australia's principal river, which forms the Victoria-New South Wales boundary.

Ruby Murray From the name of the popular Irish singer (1935–96) of the late 1950s and early 1960s, whose hits included 'Let Me Go, Lover' and 'Happy Days and Lonely Nights'. The take-away curry craze did not really begin in Britain before the 1970s, but the memory was still green enough to make **Ruby** an obvious choice.

Balti

Basil Fawlty A cruel choice of rhyme for what is typically a restaurant dish, commemorating the hotelier from hell, anti-hero of John Cleese's BBC television sitcom *Fawlty Towers* (1975–9).

And with the curry:

Rice

Both the contributions are products of the 'Indian takeaway' era, and exploit the worst stereotypes of the restaurants' menus and kitchens with black humour: **rats and mice**, whose abbreviated version **rats** allows the witty customer to order, e.g., 'prawn biryani and rats'; and **three blind mice** (from the nursery rhyme), an equally alarming item on the menu.

Beverages (non-alcoholic)

Water

A single theme with variations for this soberest of potations: the common denominator is the rhyme on *daughter*, but it has a wide array of combinations. Perhaps the most widely used is **fisherman's daughter**, which dates from the late 19th century; frequently shortened to **fisherman's**, which might accompany a request for a scotch. Alternatives are **darling daughter** and the less complimentary **dirty daughter**; **miller's daughter** (also late 19th-century); **mother and daughter** (earlier still, and probably obsolete by the end of the 19th century); **ratcatcher's daughter**; and **squatter's daughter** (an Australian version).

Tea

If there were any doubt that tea is rhyming slangers' favourite drink, just look at the number of rhymes: no fewer than sixteen, in contrast to two for *coffee* and just one for *cocoa*.

By far the best known is **Rosie Lee** (or **Rosy Lee**), which has transcended the parochial boundaries of rhyming slang and entered the general language. First recorded in the 1920s, it probably originated in the British Army during the First World War; it has remained current ever since:

> We were having a cup of rosy lee.
> —Alfred Draper *Swansong for a Rare Bird* (1970)

It is equally, if not more familiar in its shortened form **Rosie/Rosy**:

> This is the best cup of rosy I get all day, Janey.
> —Allan Prior *Z Cars Again* (1964)

It is tempting to link it with *Gypsy Rose Lee*, the stage-name of the American stripper Rose Louise Hovick, but as she was not born until 1914 she can scarcely have been its source. It may, however, lie behind the Australian **gypsy lee**, first recorded in the 1930s.

The name *Lee* is the most popular of all rhymes for 'tea'. Other combinations in which it appears include **Betty Lee** (recorded in US English in the 1940s), **Dicky Lee** (an Australian version), **Jenny Lee** (a 19th-century formation, well predating the British Labour politician Jennie Lee (1904–88) but possibly reinforced by her name), **Jimmy Lee** (another Australianism), and **Nancy Lee** (last heard of in the 1930s). Also into this category comes **peter and lee**, recorded in the 1990s for a 'cup of tea'; it is based on *Peters and Lee*, the stage name of the 1970s British singing duo Lennie Peters (1939–92) and Dianne Lee (1950–) (but it should be used with caution, as it also does rhyming duty for 'pee' (see *Urination* at **IN THE LAV**)).

Many of these names can appear with the alternative spelling *Lea*, which is the only possibility when it comes to **River Lea**, a 19th-century rhyme based on the name of the river that flows down through Essex into the Thames at Canning Town.

Other *tea*-rhymes:

bug and flea Usually used in the plural for 'cups of tea', but not very appetizing.

George Bohee Current in the first half of the 20th century, and based on the name of a well-known banjo player (probably reinforced by *bohea* (pronounced /bəʊˈhiː/), the term for a type of black tea from China).

Jack Shea The pronunciation is /ʃeɪ/, which at first sight seems an implausible rhyme, but this is a 19th-century Irish creation, so *tea* is /teɪ/. In Australian English the term came to be applied (latterly often in the form *jackshay*) to a tin vessel used for brewing tea and incorporating a smaller vessel for drinking.

Mother Machree An Australian contribution, based on the title of a sentimental 19th-century ballad by Rida Johnson Young.

sailors on the sea Recorded in north London in the late 1950s, and familiar enough then to be shortened to **sailors**, but it is not clear if it was ever widely current elsewhere.

split pea Dating from the mid-19th century, but apparently not surviving into the 20th.

sweet pea A 19th-century rhyme which was also applied to *whisky* (see under **ALCOHOL AND OTHER DRUGS**), so it needed to be used with care.

you and me Probably the most widely used rhyme after **Rosie Lee**. It goes back to the 19th century.

One more 'tea'-rhyme, based on the colloquial synonym *char*: **there you are**.

Coffee

There are not many rhymes for *coffee*—in fact, *toffee* is just about it. Rhyming slangers have therefore had to make do with **Everton toffee** (first recorded in 1857; **Everton** for short) or the rather rarer **sticky toffee**. The epithet 'Everton' comes from a suburb of Liverpool where the toffee was first made, in the mid-18th century; its choice for the rhyme may have been reinforced by the fact that the toffee is made with cream or a substitute (as cream is added to coffee).

Cocoa

orinoko A rhyme with an odd history. Ostensibly it is a version of *Orinoco*, the name of a river in South America. Doubt has been cast, though, on the likelihood of such a choice for Cockney rhyming slang, and it may be that in reality it is a garbled variant of *Oroonoko*, the title of a play by Aphra Behn (1668). Adaptations of this continued to appear on stage in succeeding centuries, and in the late 17th and early 18th centuries *oronoko*, or *orinoko*, was used as (?rhyming) slang for 'tobacco' (see TOBACCO). In the 19th century *orinoko* turns up as a rhyme for 'poker' (see HOUSEHOLD MATTERS), which may provide a link with the 'cocoa'-rhyme.

Coke

holy smoke Not a very appropriate-sounding rhyme, but it makes sense when you know that it was originally applied to the sort of coke burnt as a fuel. *Coke* for *Coca-Cola* came into use as early as the first decade of the 20th century. (See also *Rum* at **ALCOHOL AND OTHER DRUGS**.)

See also *Milk* at **FROM THE DAIRY**.

Mealtimes

The main meal (literally) for rhyming slangers is *dinner*. The term denotes the chief meal of the day, regardless of timing—which in practice is likely to be the middle of the day. Hence the preponderance of rhymes for:

Dinner

The main rhyme-theme is the surname *Skinner*. Variations on it, none of them apparently linked to an actual person, include **Charley Skinner** (from the mid-19th century, and long since obsolete), **Jimmy** (or **Jim**) **Skinner** (British, but also recorded in US English), **Joe Skinner**, **John Skinner**, and **Ned Skinner** (first recorded in the mid-19th century). In the same family is **Lilley and Skinner**, from the name of the British firm of shoe manufacturers and retailers founded in 1835.

A more sombre note is struck by a pair of 19th-century rhymes: **glorious sinner** and **saint and sinner**. Both have the whiff of Victorian religious tracts.

A worldly alternative is offered by the Australian **Derby winner**.

Lunch

Judy and Punch A rather strained effort, which is usually shortened to **Judy**.

    kidney punch Commonly just **kidney**, which is altogether more appetizing—you could pop into a pub for 'a bit of kidney', which might well be a pie and a pint.

Supper

Tommy Tupper Probably an alteration (to fit the rhyme better) of an earlier (19th-century) **Tommy Tucker**, which in turn was presumably based on the nursery-rhyme character: 'Little Tommy Tucker sang for his supper'.

Venues

Café

Colonel Gaddafi From the name of the revolutionary socialist leader of Libya (1942–), a widely known figure in the West as a result of his demonization by Western governments.

And finally, after all this plenty:

Starving

A choice between **Lee Marvin** (from the US film actor (1924–87)) and **Hank Marvin** (from the British guitarist (1941–), long-time stalwart of Cliff Richard's backing group The Shadows.

Alcohol and other Drugs

The profile of the rhyming slangster's good night out reveals itself in the following pages: a copious variety of synonyms for a wide range of alcoholic drinks, and a lot of ways of saying 'drunk'. But examine the rhymes a little more closely and the pattern becomes more precise: this is a world where beer rules, and cigarettes and whisky, and perhaps even more emphatically gin. Not much attention to wine is paid here, and although one or two later 20th-century favourites put in a token appearance (lager, for instance, and Bacardi), this collection was essentially put together in the days when the gin-shop and the British working man's pub served a severely limited repertoire of booze. The plentiful consumption of cigarettes is faithfully reflected in the number of rhymes they attract, and even snuff is well represented. The second half of the 20th century played catch-up in terms of other recreational drugs, but they still have a lot of leeway to make up.

Alcohol

Even rhyming slangers' ingenuity baulks at *alcohol* (possibly something could have been done with *doll*, or perhaps even more appropriately *loll*), so *booze* it is:

mud and ooze A discouraging Australianism of the 20th century.

pick and choose Generally shortened to **pick**—someone who is *on the pick* is in the process of getting drunk. The implied fastidiousness becomes progressively less appropriate.

River Ouse There are three rivers in England called *Ouse*, and it is not clear which one was intended here (although given the frequent spelling *Ooze*, probably no one cares much):

> The place still bulging with smoke and river ooze.
> —Robin Cook *The Crust on its Uppers* (1962)

It is unusual in that both its elements can be used independently: *on the river* and *on the ouse* both mean 'on a drinking spree'.

win or lose Ray Puxley in *Cockney Rabbit* (1992) quotes a racegoer's rhyme: 'Win or lose we have our booze/But when we win we drink gin'.

Drink
....

Drink is one of those innocent-looking words that depend for their impact upon their context—and as far as rhyming slang is concerned, the context is almost always 'prospective intoxication'.

bit of blink A late-19th-century invention which seems to have died out by the time of the First World War.

cuff link A 20th-century Australian creation.

Engelbert Humperdink A rhyme of the 1960s, when the English pop singer Engelbert Humperdink (1936–) first came to fame. His real name is Gerry Dorsey—his more florid stage-name (usually shortened by rhyming slangsters to **Engelbert**) was borrowed from the 19th-century German composer of the opera *Hansel and Gretel*.

kitchen sink Also Australian—in British rhyming slang it means 'stink'.

pen and ink Yet another Australianism—a pattern may be beginning to emerge. Apparently coined in the 1960s, and also used in New Zealand (We wander over to the bar for a pen and ink. *N.Z. Truth* (Wellington) (1963)). Again it utilizes what in Britain is a rhyme for *stink*.

tiddlywink The historical strands of this word and its shortened form **tiddly** are confusingly intermeshed, and it is not at all clear how it started out. It is first recorded in the 1840s as a term for a small unlicensed pub or beer-shop, and we do not hear of it in the sense 'drink' until the 1880s:

> 'Now, Jack, I'm goin' to get a tiddley wink of pig's ear . . . '. A tiddley wink of pig's ear! . . . What does it mean? Simply this. . .a workman . . . goes to get a drink of beer.
> —D. W. Barrett *Life & Work among the Navvies* (1880)

However, Hotten records the abbreviation, in the form *titley*, in his *Dictionary of Modern Slang* (1859), meaning 'drink', so we can safely assume tiddlywink was around then too. It seems to have largely faded out by the 20th century, but the short version went from strength to strength:

> It took two 'ot tiddleys to warm 'er.
> —*Punch* (1895)

> It wasn't oysters that she really wanted, but . . . tiddly.
> —E. V. Lucas *Down the Sky* (1930)

It is said to apply mainly to spirits rather than beer (a claim repeated by Julian Franklyn in his *Dictionary of Rhyming Slang* (1960)), but to the extent that this is true it is probably a late development, influenced by *tiddly* 'tiny' (which is first recorded in 1868); as can be seen from the 1880 quote above, its original users were quite happy for it to refer to beer.

Tiddly is first recorded as an adjective, meaning (euphemistically) 'drunk', in 1905, so it is perfectly plausible that it may have been spun off the noun tiddly. As for the game known as 'tiddlywinks', this seems to have inherited the name (originally trademarked as *Tiddledy-Winks*) in the 1880s from a sort of game played with dominoes. *Tiddlywink* in this sense is first recorded in 1857, but its connection with the rhyming slang remains obscure.

tumble down the sink An early 19th-century creation whose graphic implications of after-effects perhaps helped it to survive well into the 20th century. It is rather unwieldy for everyday use, though, and it was commonly shortened to **tumbledown** (first recorded in the specific sense 'grog' (watered-down rum), but by the late 19th century applied broadly to any type of alcoholic drink), or even just **tumble**. Tumble can also be used as a verb, 'to have a drink'.

Then there are the colloquial synonyms for *drink*, which can get in on the rhyming slang act. *Lush*, meaning 'strong drink', dates from the late 18th century. It yields **comb and brush**, perhaps hinting at what the drinker may later be in need of. It has also been used as a verb, meaning 'to treat someone to a drink', and it later followed the semantic development of *lush* itself into 'drunkard' (see below under INTOXICATION). *Soak* for a 'drink' or 'drinking bout' is late 17th- to mid-19th-century slang, and it got **suit and cloak** as its rhyme. **Arthur Scargill** immortalizes the British mining trade-union leader (1938–) as a rhyme for *gargle*. Then there is **Jonathan Ross**, a late 20th-century term for a 'drink', and especially 'beer', which celebrates the British television personality of that name: its origins are unclear, but one theory makes it rhyme with *toss* (as in—it is most charitably explained—'*toss* back a drink'); another links it with the suggestion of gayness in Ross's flamboyant style and dress sense, although the rhyme in that case would not be directly with *Ross* but between *queer* and *beer*.

Places to Drink

Bar

jack tar A 20th-century creation, and latterly familiar mainly in its shortened form **jack**. A *jack tar* was originally a sailor (from the tar with which 18th-century sailors waterproofed their trousers), and sailors are not exactly unknown in bars.

near and far Applied to a bar-room in a pub, and in use roughly between the late 19th century and the 1920s. One conjecture links it with the tantalizing inaccessibility of the bar when the room is crowded. When you finally get there you can order some **far and near** (see under BEER).

there you are A 19th-century coinage, but rather ousted in the 20th by the highly contrasted application to *tea* (see under *Tea* at FOOD AND DRINK).

Tommy Farr In memory of the Welsh-born British heavyweight boxing champion of that name (1914–86).

A slang synonym for *bar* in the pre-Second World War period was *ramp*, and this got the rhyming treatment with **postage stamp**—possibly inspired partly by the humorous 19th-century use of *postage stamp* to denote any pub or hotel named the 'Queen's Head' (from the head of Queen Victoria on postage stamps).

A bar *stool* is likely to become an **April fool**.

Pub

nuclear sub A late 20th-century alternative to the all-pervasive rub-a-dub (see next):

> He then orders an aristotle of the most ping-pong tiddly in the nuclear sub.
> —*Lock, Stock, and Two Smoking Barrels* (1998)

rub-a-dub First recorded in this (presumably original) form in the 1920s, but some of its many embellishments and alterations locate its beginnings in the 1890s at the latest. Since then it has established itself in both British and particularly Australian rhyming slang, in a wide array of variants, as *the* word for *pub*. *Rub-a-dub* was originally (from the late 18th century) an onomatopoeic representation of the sound of a drum-roll, but it may be that the immediate inspiration for the rhyme was the opening line of the nursery rhyme 'Rub-a-dub-dub, three men in a tub' (although the rhyme variant **rub-a-dub-dub** is not recorded before the 1940s):

> I gazed upon the motley crowd Within this 'rub-a-dub'.
> —'Mixer' *Transport Workers' Song Book* [a New Zealand source] (*c*1926)

> He could fathom why rub-a-dub meant a pub.
> —Henry Slesar *Bridge of Lions* (1963)

> Let's grab some Kate and Sydney and a pint of apple fritter at the rub-a-dub-dub.
> —*National Times* (Australia) (1971)

In Britain, the favourite tactic of shortening rhyming slang produces **rubber**. Australian English, on the other hand, has opted for variants on the theme, notably **rubbity-dub** or **rubbedy-dub** and various abbreviations and permutations—**rubbity**, **rubbedy**, **rubberdy**, **rubberty**, **rubby-dub**, **rubby**, **rubbie**:

> And I will lay an oil-rag to a pound of 'Darling Pea' He gallops straightaway towards a 'rubbie' for a 'spree'.
> —*Worker* (Sydney) (1897)

> His home is 'the rubby dub', his occupation 'the joint'.
> —*Bulletin* (Sydney) (1898)

> Others swamp their earnings at the wayside rubby, and then have themselves to blame that they are every year humping bluey.
> —E. S. Sorenson *Life in the Australian Backblocks* (1911)

> Overheard in a Melbourne rupperty.
> —*Action Front: Journal, 2/2 Field Regiment* (1944)

> 'What is a rubbity?' Joe said scornfully, 'Rubbity-dub.'
> —Nino Culotta *They're a Weird Mob* (1957)

> How about a gargle? Down to the rubberdy, come on.
> —D'Arcy Niland *Call me when the Cross turns over* (1957)

> 'Ow about we ducks into the rubbitty-dub for a quick 'un?
> —Blue Garland *The Pitt Street Prospector* (1969)

> I met another of the Fennels down at the rubbidy.
> —Kenneth Giles *Murder Pluperfect (1970)*

> There's the story of the barman in the rubbedy.
> —*Australian Post* (1971)

> 'Been down to the rubbity lately?' 'No, I haven't hit the hops for a couple of weeks.'
> —Alexander Buzo *Rooted* (1973)

> They are hopeful the prince (if not the princess) will grace them with a royal
> presence around the bar of one of the local 'rubbidies' over Easter.
> —*Daily Telegraph* (**Sydney**) (1983)

More colloquially, a pub is a *boozer* (a late 19th-century coinage), and this is
rhymed as **battlecruiser** (first heard in the 1940s, but enduring to the end of
the 20th century: He's gone down the battlecruiser to watch the end of a football game.
Lock, Stock, and Two Smoking Barrels (1998)), or occasionally as **cabin cruiser**
(conjuring associations with floating gin palaces).

Beer and Cider

As the stereotypical tipple of the rhyming classes, beer not surprisingly,
once all its various types and brands are taken into account, easily
outnumbers all other alcoholic drinks for rhymes:

Beer

Britney Spears After the female US teen pop star Britney Spears (1982–)
who achieved fame at the turn of the 21st century. The form of the name
invites the rhyme with *beers*, and this is carried through into the abbreviated
version **Britneys**:

> After a couple of Britneys (beers) a Jay Kay (takeaway) might be SClub7 (heaven).
> —*The Sun* (2001)

Charlie Freer A late 19th-century rhyme which faded out in the early 20th.
Christmas cheer Generally abbreviated to **Christmas**.
Crimea A 19th-century rhyme used mainly in the British Army, and
surviving only as long as there were those with memories of the Crimean
War (1854–56) to appreciate it.
far and near A popular rhyme from the 19th century, although never
quite challenging the supremacy of **pig's ear**. Note the rhyme of the
inverted near and far with *bar* (see under PLACES TO DRINK).

fusilier A 19th-century British Army rhyme, obsolete well before the First World War.

Germaine Greer An Australian coinage of 1980s vintage, dedicated (presumably without permission) to the Australian feminist writer of that name (1939–).

never fear A mid-19th-century creation that had largely died out by the 20th. Possibly inspired by the idea of Dutch courage.

oh, my dear A long-defunct 19th-century rhyme, but in its heyday any London barmaid would have recognized an order for a 'pint of oh'.

pig's ear Dating from the late 19th century, but with a great deal more stamina than other contemporary *beer*-rhymes:

> But the most of the fiver would go in the old pig's ear.
> —James Curtis *The Gilt Kid* (1936)

> In the pub you can ask for a pint of *pig's ear* (beer).
> —Peter Wright *The Language of British Industry* (1974)

Routinely shortened to **pigs**. As far as the written record shows, the other slang uses of *pig's ear* (to mean 'mess, chaos, balls-up', and in the contemptuous exclamation *in a pig's ear*) are both later than this rhyme.

red steer A US rhyme from the 1940s.

Ale

Daily Mail From the name of the British daily newspaper, and rhyming with *ale* in its role as a generic substitute for *beer*. Often shortened to **daily**.

ship in full sail First recorded in the 1850s, and generally taken to stand for a 'pint of ale'. The abbreviation **ship** continued to be recognized as a 'pint of beer' well into the 20th century.

Brown ale

up and down The rhyme, of course, is with *brown* (it is also used for *brown* in more general contexts, but beer is the main referent).

Light ale

Ale is taken as read—all the rhymes are based on *light*:

Chalky White Generally a **chalky** for short. From the standard nickname for anyone surnamed 'White'.

day and night A late 19th-century creation which continued fitfully in currency in the 20th.

silent night Presumably inspired by the Christmas carol of that name.

stage fright A theatrical rhyme—reputedly from a scenario of beer as a pre-performance nerve-settler, but that is probably a post-hoc rationalization.

Mild

Marty Wilde From the stage-name of the British rock-'n'-roll star Marty Wilde (1939– ; real name Reginald Smith) of the 1950s and 1960s (when people still drank 'mild').

Bitter

apple fritter An old-established rhyme with some 20th-century use.

Gary Glitter From the stage-name of the flamboyant British pop singer and convicted paedophile Paul Gadd (1940–). Standardly shortened to **Gary**. A 1980s application of the rhyme, later superseded by a less complimentary one (see *The anus* under THE BODY AND ITS PARTS).

giggle and titter Presumably alluding to the effects of too much of the original—no less appropriately in the abbreviated form **giggle**. A variation on the same theme is **laugh and titter**.

Tex Ritter From the name of a star of early US westerns (1905–74). When it was still familiar, a pint of bitter would be the result of an order for a 'pint of **Tex**'.

Stout

in and out A 20th-century rhyme, often denoting specifically a 'bottle of stout'.

salmon and trout One of a wide range of applications for this fishy rhyme, but probably the best established.

See also GUINNESS below.

Lager

Forsyte Saga A 1970s rhyme, inspired not by the original John Galsworthy novel sequence (1906–30) centred on an upper-middle-class English family of the time, but by the popular BBC television version.

Porter

An old term, denoting a type of heavy dark brown beer, and the rhymes for it are correspondingly well past their prime:

hod of mortar From the 19th century; usually interpreted as a 'pot of porter'.

Liffey water Again, 19th century. The River Liffey flows through Dublin; on its bank is the Guinness brewery.

Burton

lace curtain A genteel rhyme for a term derived from *Burton-on-Trent*, the name of the Staffordshire town that is a centre of the brewing industry. It is (or was) usually applied specifically to a type of strong dark ale, or to the products of Messrs. Bass & Co.

Shandy

Amos and Andy A lo-alcohol use for a rhyme more usually applied to *brandy* (see under **SPIRITS**)—Amos and Andy lite.

Andy Pandy From the name of the puppet familiar to millions of British baby-boomers from its appearances on BBC's *Watch with Mother* (1953–7). A suitably innocent-sounding rhyme for a not very intoxicating drink.

Beano and Dandy From the name of two children's comics popular in Britain in the second half of the 20th century. Again, the rhyme emphasizes that this is not a drink for grown men.

Mahatma Gandhi Another appropriation of a rhyme apparently originally applied to *brandy* (see under **SPIRITS**)—in this case quite an appropriate one, since Gandhi was a teetotaller.

napper tandy A 20th-century Australian coinage, in honour of the Irish revolutionary hero James Napper Tandy (1740–1803), whose fame is perpetuated in the ballad 'The Wearing of the Green'.

The brand-names of some beers have become so well known that they verge on the generic. When that happens they can easily attract the attention of rhyming slangsters. In Britain in the second half of the 19th century the name of the brewers *Bass* & Co. of Burton-on-Trent, with their universally recognized red-triangle logo, became almost synonymous with *beer*—you simply asked for 'a bottle of Bass' (The first signs of returning vitality given by the Prince was to ask feebly for a bottle of 'Bass'. *Daily Chronicle* (1909)). The rhymers were not slow in responding: from the late 19th century to the 1930s an order for **beggar boy's ass** (or **beggar boy's** for short) would have produced the required result in a London pub (note that this is ostensibly *ass* 'donkey', to rhyme with *Bass* /bas/, but a rhyme with *ass*/*arse* 'buttocks' would not have been out of the question in 19th-century London). Another popular beer in the London area was made by the brewers Ben Truman, and the familiar abbreviation *Ben* produced a couple of much-used rhymes: **jenny wren** and (anticipating the morning after) **never again**. The wonder-working beer *Double Diamond* gets a look in with **Simple Simon**, a rhyme borrowed from the more valuable single variety (see *A diamond* at **CLOTHING**). Still near the top of the beer league is *Guinness*, whose rhyme **photo finish** (often shortened to **photo**) suggests a slight slurring of speech. And the latest contender, the lager *Stella* (*Artois*), has pulled in a number of candidates, including **Nelson Mandela** (from the name of the South African statesman (1918–)), **Uri Geller** (from the name of the spoon-bending Israeli illusionist (1946–)), and **David Mellor** (from the name of the British Conservative politician (1949–) who enjoyed a certain notoriety for various sexual exploits in the 1990s).

The quantity in which beer is served can also engender rhymes. 'A *pint*' in the right context is instantly recognized as 'a pint of beer', and mid-19th-century rhyming slang turned it into **top joint** (to 21st-century eyes this might seem to suggest a 'Cockney' pronunciation /pɔɪnt/ rhyming with *joint* /dʒɔɪnt/, but in fact it probably reflects the old pronunciation /dʒʌɪnt/ for *joint*, which still lingered on in popular London dialect of the 19th century). **Pimple and wart** for *quart* had some currency from the late 19th century to the mid-20th, when it was still common to buy beer in quarts (two pints) at a pub (the rhyme also applies, somewhat confusingly, to *port*—see at WINE below). And in Australia, **lily of lagoona** denotes beer as well as the type of tall glass, known as a *schooner*, in which it is served (from the popular 1912 song 'Lily of Laguna'). Aussies of greater capacity may well prefer an **Auntie Meg** (rhyming with *keg*).

Cider

runner and rider From the vocabulary of horse-racing—a horse that is entered in a race, and its rider.

Spirits

Gin

From the beginning of the 18th century until it started to move up-market in the 20th, gin was a major route to intoxication for the poor ('Drunk for a penny, dead drunk for tuppence' was its motto). It is no surprise, therefore, that there is a richer legacy of rhymes in this area than for any other sort of spirits:

Brian O'Linn or **Brian O'Lynn** A mid-19th-century coinage based on a hypothetical Irishman. It was widely used in the second half of the century, commonly in the abbreviated form **Brian** (or even **Bri**: customers in the gin-shop would order a 'quartern o' Bri'—a quarter pint of gin). Early in the 20th century association with a popular song of the time, 'Father O'Flynn', seems to have produced the hybrid rhyme **Brian O'Flynn**, and there is even evidence of Father O'Flynn itself being used for *gin*.

bung it in Popular between the two world wars, often in the curtailed form **bung it**. For those who like more gin than tonic.

Father O'Flynn See under BRIAN O'LINN.

Gunga Din An Australian rhyme, invoking the eponymous hero of Rudyard Kipling's poem 'Gunga Din' (1892) (for the details, see under *Chin* at THE BODY AND ITS PARTS, for which Gunga Din is more familiar as a rhyme in Britain).

Huckleberry Finn Another Australian literary rhyme, this time based on the name of the young boy who is the central charcter of Mark Twain's novel *The Adventures of Huckleberry Finn* (1884).

Lincoln's Inn From the name of one of London's Inns of Court. Popular in the late 19th century, but it faded out in the early 20th, and had disappeared before Lincoln's Inn Fields became a notorious resort of winos.

needle and pin Probably the best-established of all *gin*-rhymes. It is not recorded before 1937, but it survived to the end of the 20th century:

> You owe him some needle and pin–gin.
> —James Leasor *A Host of Extras* (1973)

Commonly shortened to **needle**.

Nell Gwyn A worthy memorial for Charles II's mistress (1650–87), one-time orange-seller and actress.

nose and chin A late 19th-century rhyme, not widely used.

paraffin An unappetizing 20th-century rhyme favoured in South Africa.

Ralph Lynn Based on the name of the British actor (1882–1964), and current mainly during the period of his popularity, the 1920s to the 1940s, when he starred in many of the Ben Travers farces.

thick and thin Recorded in US English in the 1920s.

Vera Lynn From the name of the British singer (1917–) famous for her morale-raising performances for the troops during the Second World War. Perhaps the most widely used *gin*-rhyme in the latter part of the 20th century. Commonly shortened to **Vera**.

And to go with it:

Tonic

Philharmonic What better orchestral accompaniment could Vera Lynn have?

> So it's a Vera and Philharmonic for the lady, and an orange juice for you.
> —Leon Griffith *Minder* (1979)

Brandy

Amos and Andy Current in the 1940s and 1950s, and based on a US radio and television comedy show popular at that time which featured two negro characters called 'Amos and Andy', played by the white actors Freeman Gosden and Charles Correll.

Charley Randy A 19th-century rhyme (from a time when cheap brandy was a common working-man's drink), which had virtually died out by 1900.

fine and dandy A 19th-century rhyme with some residual use in the 20th. That *fine* is a French term for 'brandy' is probably coincidental.

Jack Dandy or **Jack-a-Dandy** More mid–19th-century rhymes which failed to see it through to the 20th. *Jack-a-Dandy* also means 'will-o'-the-wisp, marsh gas', and Julian Franklyn in his *Dictionary of Rhyming Slang* puts forward a somewhat far-fetched theory linking the blue flames of burning brandy and burning marsh gas.

Mahatma Gandhi From the name of the Indian nationalist leader and independence campaigner Mohandas K. Gandhi (1869–1948), called *Mahatma* 'Great Soul'. Never a very popular rhyme since, as Ray Puxley points out in his *Cockney Rabbit* (1992), *Mahatma* is outside the usual patterns of Cockney phonology, and nor is it particularly appropriate, Gandhi having been a teetotaller. Also applied to *shandy* (see under **BEER AND CIDER** above).

sugar candy Current from the mid-19th century until roughly the 1920s.

Rum

dad and mum A homely Australian rhyme, also applied specifically to the mixed drink made with the cordial Bonox and rum.

finger and thumb A very widespread rhyme during the second half of the 19th century and into the early years of the 20th, although after that it went into a decline. Generally shortened to **finger** (a quarter pint of rum was 'a quartern o' finger').

kingdom come A rhyme with some currency in the 20th century.

thimble and thumb A less often encountered variant of finger and thumb. Usually in the abbreviated form **thimble**.

tom thumb After the diminutive fairy-tale hero, and generally reduced still further to **tom**. It often refers specifically to a 'tot' (small measure) of rum.

As white rum became fashionable in the latter part of the 20th century, the brand name *Bacardi* (star of a billion Bacardi and Cokes) garnered a couple of rhymes: **kiss me, Hardy** (from the alleged last words of Horatio Nelson, but suggestive enough for a young modern audience) and **Laurel and Hardy** (from the early-20th-century film comedy duo of Stan Laurel (1890–1965) and Oliver Hardy (1892–1957); generally shortened to **Laurel**, so a Bacardi and Coke becomes a *Laurel and Holy* (see holy smoke under *Coke* at **FOOD AND DRINK**)—coincidentally reminiscent of the pub name 'Holly and Laurel').

Whisky

With a limited set of possibilities to choose from and an eye to appropriateness, it is little wonder that rhyming slangers have seldom bothered to look beyond *frisky* when dealing with *whisky*. The combinations include **bright and frisky** (possibly favoured as a conscious replacement for gay and frisky; the shortened form is metamorphosed orthographically into the place-name **Brighton**), **Charley Frisky** (a personification popular in the 19th century), **gay and frisky** (first recorded in the 1920s, but increasingly impractical as the main meaning of *gay* has shifted), **I'm so frisky** (somewhat bizarre, but common enough to be frequently used in the shortened version **I'm so**), and **young and frisky** (an Australian variant).

As an alternative there is the rather desperate **sweet pea**, but it is preferable to cut straight to *Scotch*, which has two or three rhymes to choose from: **gold watch** (quite widely used from the 19th century onwards (Stick a gold watch in there for me Mags, eh? Get one yourself Russell Lewis *Without Motive* (2000)); probably directly inspired by Waterbury watch), **pimple and blotch** (generally shortened to **pimple**), and **Waterbury watch** (from the brand of watch made in Waterbury, Connecticut, USA; popular in the late 19th century and up to the Second World War).

Soda

Both brandy and whisky may be preferred with a splash of soda water. The superannuated high-society rhyme **fashoda** was inspired by the so-called 'Fashoda Incident' of 1898, a confrontation between British and French forces at Fashoda in Egyptian Sudan over the countries' rival claims in the area. It goes specifically with *brandy*: wags in gentlemen's clubs of the time would facetiously order a 'brandy and fashoda'. For 'whisky and soda' the particular rhyme is, or was, **Major Loder**, a tribute to a certain Major Eustace Loder, who owned the amazingly successful late 19th-century racehorse Pretty Polly. For an independent rhyme we have to go to **Quasimodo** (from the name of the hunchback bell-ringer in Victor Hugo's *Notre-Dame de Paris* (1831)), often curtailed to simply **Quasi**; or to **Voda**, an abbreviation of *Vodaphone*, the name of a British mobile-phone service.

Short

The use of *short* for a glass of (usually undiluted) spirits dates from the early 19th century. In rhyming slang it becomes **magistrate's court**—perhaps a tribute to the source of the licence for the place where you are drinking the shorts, but more likely foreshadowing where you may end up tomorrow morning.

Ice

If you require rhyming ice in your spirits you have a choice between **sugar and spice** and **Vincent Price** (from the name of the chilling star (1911–93) of Hollywood horror movies; usually just **Vincent**).

Wine

Wine does not loom large in rhyming slang's alcoholic universe, so to mitigate its insignificance this section also covers sherry and port.

Table wine

Until virtually the last quarter of the 20th century wine simply did not impinge on the British rhyming classes sufficiently for them to take notice of it. Of the rhymes that have been coined for *wine*, nearly half originated in Australia, where wine production is a major industry. And of the two rhymes for *claret*, one is exclusively and the other almost exclusively applied to its slang sense 'blood' (see at THE BODY AND ITS PARTS).

Calvin Klein A rhyme from the 1990s, when wine had become fashionable and could be paired with the US fashion designer Calvin Klein (1942–).

honky tonk An Australian rhyme based on *plonk* (see next) and applied specifically to inferior wine. A *honky tonk* was originally a cheap seedy bar.

plinkety plonk A fanciful rhyme spun from French *vin blanc* 'white wine' by Australian troops serving in France during the First World War:

> Nosey and Nobby shared a bottle of plinketty plonk, as *vin blanc* was called.
> —Henry Williamson *Patriot's Progress* (1930)

It formed the basis of the now widely used colloquial *plonk* for 'cheap wine' (first recorded in 1933).

rise and shine Presumably from the armed forces' vernacular early-morning injunction to get out of bed and about your duties, first recorded during the First World War period. Not very appropriate for someone who has been on the wine the night before.

River Tyne Not offering a complimentary comparison with the contents of the bottle—this is strictly reserved for the *vin de table* end of the market.

Sherry

derry-down-derry Reportedly mainly theatrical slang—a more suitable habitat for this 16th-century poetic refrain than the barracks or the market-place. Often shortened to **DDD** or **three Ds**.

Londonderry Recorded in the middle of the 19th century, but little evidence since then. From the name of the city in Northern Ireland (*Derry* to Republicans).

Woolwich ferry Inspired by the ferry which plies the River Thames between Woolwich on the south bank and London City Airport on the north.

Port

didn't ought Mimicking the feigned reluctance of ladies offered a glass of port (and lemon—the scene is inner-city pub, not aristocratic dining table). First recorded in the late 19th century, and still around in the 1940s.

long and short Possibly a reference to port drunk neat ('short') or mixed with lemonade ('long').

pimple and wart An alternative application for what was originally a rhyme for *quart* (see under BEER AND CIDER).

Containers

See under *Bottle*, *Glass*, and *Pot* at HOUSEHOLD MATTERS.

Intoxication

You may begin just by satisfying a modest **there first** 'thirst' (common in the army in the First World War, and evoking the rush to the bar), or more recently a **Geoff Hurst** (from the name of the West Ham footballer (1941–) and 1966 World Cup Final hat-trick scorer), but you could end up:

Drunk

elephant's trunk A venerable rhyme, first recorded in 1859, but one which soldiered on successfully through the 20th century to the present day:

> He came home and he found the artful dodger elephant trunk in the bread and butter (He found the lodger drunk in the gutter).
> —*Evening Standard* (1931)

Its popularity has probably been aided by a subliminal suggestion of the pink elephants that manifest themselves in drunken reverie. Commonly abbreviated to **elephants**:

> *Elephant's trunk*: drunk. The phrase became incomprehensible by the dropping of the rhyming. 'Oh he's elephants' (i.e., intoxicated) will, in time to come, exercise many an etymologist.
> —J. R. Ware *Passing English of the Victorian Era* (1909)

An occasional variant on the theme is **jumbo's trunk**.

Molly the Monk An Australian usage of the 1960s and 1970s, usually shortened to **Molly**.

> Ophelia was more than a little bit Molly the Monk after Parkinson had been loosening her up a bit with three bottles of Quelltaler hock.
> —*Kings Cross Whisper* (Sydney) (1973)

out the monk A New Zealand expression of uncertain origin, first recorded in the 1940s. It is applied to unconsciousness or sleep, but usually when these are the result of drunkenness, so it seems a reasonable supposition that it started out as a rhyme for *drunk*.

salt junk A 19th-century rhyme which barely survived into the 20th, although its abbreviation **salted** was more robust. The term was originally a contemptuous reference to the salt beef served to sailors on board ship, which no doubt gave them a great thirst. . .

Various synonyms for *drunk* have been rhymed, notably *full*, which in 1960s Australian English inspired **John Bull** (from the name of the English nation personified); *barmy*, rhymed as **Salvation Army**; and the euphemistic *merry*, which got its rhyme **Tom and Jerry** not from the cat and mouse featuring in the Warner Bros. animated cartoons of that name, but from a pair of fictional early 19th-century rakes, created by the author Pierce Egan (1772–1849), who became bywords for drunkenness. But easily the most prolific of all is:

Pissed

A usage which emerged in the 1920s, providing a useful cut-off date for all the rhymes based on it:

Adrian Quist Probably the leading Australian 'drunk'-rhyme, although it is not recorded before 1978. From the name of the Australian tennis player (1913–91), who with John Bromwich won the Wimbledon men's doubles title in 1950:

> I'm on the turps again—got Adrian Quist somethin' terrible the other night.
> —*Australian* (1978)

> They didn't look particularly decorous . . . collapsed, Adrian Quist, as the racing men say, under the hedge.
> —*Sydney Morning Herald* (1982)

booed and hissed First recorded in the 1980s.

Brahms and Liszt An arbitrary use of the names of two notable and reasonably sober European composers, Johannes Brahms (1833–97) and Franz Liszt (1811–86). Current since the 1930s and retaining its popularity during the rest of the 20th century, particularly in its abbreviated form **Brahms**:

> 'It's six o'clock. The air is clear. No carbon monoxide.' 'Are you Brahms?'
> —Leon Griffith *Minder* (1979)

> Do you remember the first time you got . . . a bit Brahms? . . . My five cousins took me out round the pubs and I got ill on Pernod and blackcurrant.
> —*P.S.* (1989)

fog and mist A neat encapsulation of alcoholic stupor. Claimed as the origin of *foggy* 'intoxicated', but as that is first recorded in 1823 and the rhyme cannot be pre-20th-century, the etymology will not wash. It is probably just a straightforward metaphorical extension of *foggy* 'obscured by fog'.

hand and fist A 20th-century coinage, always used in full.

hit and missed First recorded in the 1960s, and, like hand and fist, never abbreviated.

Mozart and Liszt A variant on **Brahms and Liszt**, substituting the composer Wolfgang Amadeus Mozart (1756–91) (for the authentic 'Cockney' touch, say /ˈməʊzɑːt/, not /ˈməʊtzɑːt/). First recorded in 1961, and popular in Australia as well as England:

> Everybody thought I was *Mozart and Liszt*, falling flat on my *Khyber Pass* like that.
> —Ronnie Barker *Fletcher's Book of Rhyming Slang* (1979)

Schindler's List From the name of the popular 1993 film adapted from Thomas Keneally's *Schindler's Ark* (1982), about a German businessman's efforts to save his Jewish employees from the Nazis. Largely a middle-class rather than a working man's rhyme. Usually shortened to **Schindler's**.

Scotch mist Probably based on the original literal *Scotch mist* 'fine light drizzle', as the later sarcastic use for 'something insubstantial or imagined' is not recorded before the 1940s.

Drunkard

Not itself rhymed, but there is no shortage of synonyms to fill the role:

comb and brush Rhyming with *lush*. That originally meant 'alcohol', and so did **comb and brush** (see under **ALCOHOL**), but when it moved on semantically, the rhyme went with it.

Georgie Best From the name of the Irish footballer (1946–) as notorious for his drinking exploits as he was famous for his mercurial soccer skills. The actual rhyme is with *pest*, but the subtext is always 'drunken pest'.

Kennedy rot A 20th-century Australian rhyme with *sot*.

Drinking session

Leo Sayer A 1990s coinage based on the name of the pop singer (1948–). It rhymes with *all-dayer*.

See also *on the river* and *on the ouse* under **RIVER OUSE** above.

Delirium tremens

Colloquially 'the *shakes*', which is what forms the basis of the rhymes:

currant cakes It is not clear whether this precedes or was derived from the rather more broadly applied **currant-cakey** 'shaky', which dates from around 1900.

ducks and drakes An Australian coinage of the 1960s.

Joe Blakes Reported in Australian and New Zealand English since the late 19th century in the general sense 'shakes', but the specific application to alcoholic delirium is not recorded until the 1940s, when a rhyming connection begins to be made with *snakes*—the sort you see when in the grip of the D.T.s (**Joe Blake** has been an Australian rhyme for a literal *snake* since around 1900—see under *Snake* at **ANIMALS**):

> You feel nothin' when you're on a bender. . . You get the Joe Blakes bad after a few
> weeks.
> —Alan Marshall *These are my People* (1944)

> As Phil arrived, a shooter sufferng from a bad attack of the morning after 'Joe
> Blakes' was trying to take aim.
> —W. G. Howcroft *This Side Rabbit Proof Fence* (1971)

To be *out the joe* is to have passed out drunk.

rattlesnakes Often shortened to **rattles**, which goes well with the much longer-established slang *rattled* 'drunk'.

And when it comes to deciding whose turn it is to get the drinks in:

Shout

Wally Grout An Australian rhyme, commemorating Wally Grout (1927–68), who kept wicket for Australia between 1958 and 1965 (and in that capacity was always 'shouting' for lbw and catches).

Tobacco

Coming on stream when snuff was still widely used, rhyming slang was in full swing to record the high-watermark of 20th-century cigarette consumption, from the First World War period onwards.

Tobacco

All the rhymes depend, of course, on the 'Cockney' pronunciation /tə'bakə/:

hi jimmy knacker From the name of a children's street game of some antiquity, similar to leapfrog.

nosey my knacker This bizarre rhyme is first recorded by Henry Mayhew in his *London Labour and the London Poor* (1851) ('Ducange Anglicus' in *The Vulgar Tongue* (1857) and John Hotten in his *Dictionary of Modern Slang* (1859) both give the slightly different form **noser my knacker**). Julian Franklyn in his *Dictionary of Rhyming Slang* (1960) offers the unsubstantiated and not altogether convincing theory that it comes from a ribald riposte to people complaining of tobacco smoke—*knacker* being a slang term for 'testicle', it could be interpreted as an invitation to 'smell my balls' (as an alternative to the objectionable fug). Often used in the truncated form **nose-my**.

Tom Thacker Current in the late 19th century. There is no record of a real Tom Thacker on whom it might have been based.

Amongst British prisoners, tobacco is *snout* (a term of uncertain origin, but said to be from the prisoners' subterfuge of rubbing their nose ('snout') to conceal forbidden smoking; first recorded in 1885)—hence:

salmon and trout A rhyme apparently virtually as old as *snout* itself. It enjoyed a revival in popularity in 1990s London youth slang in the shortened form **salmon**, meaning 'cigarette'.

Cigarettes

Cigarette is not a word that figures largely in rhyming slangsters' vocabulary—all those syllables—and it is not surprising that only one rhyme for it has ever caught on: **forgive and forget** (an Australian creation of the 20th century). In the popular dialect of London, a cigarette is almost always a *fag* (in use since the 1880s, and originally usually implying a cheap and nasty cigarette), and that is what has attracted the rhymes over the years:

cough and drag Self-evidently an appropriate reference to the practice of smoking and its effects, and although the actual rhyme is with *fag*, in use it often implies 'an act of smoking a cigarette, a smoke'. A variant on the theme is puff and drag, and see also spit and drag.

do-me-dags A late-19th-century rhyme (for the plural *fags*, of course) based on the name of a children's game. A *dag* was a feat which you challenged others to emulate, and the game 'do my dags' was very similar to 'follow my leader'.

Harry Wragg From the name of a highly successful English jockey (1902–85) whose racing career was at its peak in the 1930s.

oily rag A well-established rhyme, usually truncated to **oily**. The oily rag is a traditional piece of basic equipment for workers who deal with machinery, or with metal that needs polishing, and a cigarette in their hands may come to resemble it.

old nag Used in the trenches in the First World War, but it does not seem to have survived much beyond the 1920s.

puff and drag See at cough and drag above.

spit and drag Originally apparently Royal Navy slang for a 'surreptitious smoke', but later applied to cigarettes. Jonathan Green in his *Cassell Dictionary of Slang* (1998) suggests that it may refer to 'the result of a badly rolled cigarette, from which one spits out the odd strand of tobacco, while dragging . . . down the smoke'. This would not necessarily mean that a rhyme was not also involved, although the alternative version *spit and draw* clearly does not rely on a rhyme.

winkle bag A 1970s coinage, featuring a mollusc dear to Londoners. Often shortened to **winkle**.

An alternative colloquialism is the abbreviation *cig*, first recorded in the 1880s, which is rhymed as **Irish jig** (much better known as a stand-in for *wig*). And two particularly high-selling British brands of the early and middle years of the 20th century received rhymes too:

do me good Rhyming with *Wood*, short for *Woodbine*, a type of fairly cheap cigarette made by W. D. & H. O. Wills. It first appeared in the 1880s, but its popularity was sealed during the First World War, when servicemen in their thousands became addicted to it. The rhyme was probably not ironic: at that time cigarettes were thought (or claimed) to promote good health.

Harry Tates Rhyming with *Weights*, a brand produced by Players. Harry Tate was the stage-name of the popular English music-hall comedian R. M. Hutchison (1872–1940).

Cigarette-end

Victor Trumper An Australian rhyme, based on *dumper*, a colloquialism for 'cigarette-end'. From the name of the brilliant Australian batsman (1877–1915) who flourished briefly at the beginning of the 20th century.

Cigarette paper

Vera Lynn A late 20th-century creation, rhyming on *skin*, a slang term used since the 1960s for cigarette papers for rolling one's own—particularly marijuana cigarettes. A new application for a rhyme most famously applied to *gin* (see at SPIRITS above). Usually shortened to **Vera**:

> Despite a cheeky reference to 'Vera's' . . . , the Shaman disingenuously insisted that the song wasn't about drugs at all. What else could they say?
> —Simon Reynolds *Energy Flash* (1998)

Cigars

Bucks hussar A late 19th-century rhyme, implying 'dashingness'. It did not survive long into the 20th century.

la-di-da or **la-di-dah** First recorded in 1977, and based on the expression implying affectedness or snobbishness (perhaps viewed as appropriate to the upper-crust connotations of the cigar).

> Nerves take over, so a puff or two on a Lusitania cigar. Being too poor to bet or have women, . . . a la-di-dah is my one luxury.
> —John McCririck *Sunday Times Magazine* (1996)

The abbreviated version is generally rendered as **lardy**:

> Middle-aged geezer, . . . big lardy and a carnation.
> —Barry Purchese *Minder* (1983)

Spanish guitar A rhyme common to Britain and the US, with possibly a reference to the Spanishness of Havana. Often shortened to **Spanish**.

Pipe

cherry ripe First recorded in 1859, and continuing in use well into the 20th century. From the cherry-seller's traditional street-cry, made famous in

Robert Herrick's lyric (1648), and no doubt partly suggested by the commonplace cherrywood pipes of the 19th century.

   raw and ripe Recorded in US English in the 1940s.

   Tom Tripe or **Tommy Tripe** A name invented for the sake of the rhyme, which is first recorded in 1859.

   yard of tripe Another mid-19th-century rhyme, first reported by Henry Mayhew in his *London Labour and the London Poor* (1851). The reference is presumably to the stomach tissue of cattle, though hopefully without any notion of putting it in one's pipe and smoking it.

Snuff

blind man's buff First reported in the 1960s, when the days of large-scale snuff-taking were long past.

   hang bluff Recorded in 1857, but long since obsolete.

   Harry Bluff Another mid-19th-century rhyme, but one which survived into the 20th century.

   Lal Brough or **Lally Brough** A rhyme in use in the late 19th and early 20th centuries, when *Lal* or *Lally* was a fairly common pet form of the name *Alice* in Britain. In addition *Lally* had some currency as a generic colloquial term for an old woman, and it may be that the rhyme carries some implication of snuff as an old woman's vice. Conceivably it was even that rare thing, a mainly women's rhyme: Julian Franklyn in his *Dictionary of Rhyming Slang* (1960) reports that **lally** was the inmates' word for 'snuff' in Holloway Prison, London, in the early part of the 20th century.

A light

fly my kite A mid-19th-century rhyme, apparently obsolete by the 20th.

   widow's mite A coinage of the late 19th century which survived into the 20th, often in the shortened form **widow's**.

Smoke

Joe Roke A US rhyme, recorded in 1928 but referring back to the 1890s—but without any evidence as to whether it relates to tobacco smoke, or an act of smoking, or just to smoke in general. An alternative form **Joe Hoke** is reported from the late 1970s.

   laugh and joke A late 19th-century rhyme which lasted at least into the 1950s—and this one definitely denoted 'a smoke'.

Other Recreational Drugs

Drug-taking is not entirely new, but on the whole in the past it has not been a hobby among those who have the rhyming-slang habit—hence the relative sparsity of rhymes in this section. In the great majority of cases the rhymes are based, not surprisingly, on the drugs' various street-names, not on their strict pharmaceutical appellation:

Amphetamines

The rhyme is on their colloquial name *speed*, and two pillars of the entertainment industry are conveniently at hand:

Lou Reed From the name of the US rock star (1942–), still pulling them in in the 1990s.

olly A repeat engagement for Oliver Reed, previously starring as 'weed' (see at CANNABIS below). A 1980s usage.

Cannabis

janet Used in the 1980s as a term for a quarter ounce of cannabis. It is short for *Janet Street-Porter* (*porter*—*quarter*), the name of a British journalist and television personality (1944–).

Jack Flash An Australian coinage of the late 1960s, rhyming with *hash*, short for *hashish*. Possibly inspired by the hero of the Rolling Stones' song 'Jumping Jack Flash' (1968).

Johnny Cash Another Australian contribution, also rhyming with *hash*. Based on the name of the US country singer (1932–).

olly A pet form of *Oliver*, the reference being to *Oliver Reed*, which rhymes with *weed*, slang for 'cannabis'. A 1960s coinage, reflecting on the personal habits of the roistering English actor of that name (1938–99). Later also applied to amphetamines (see above).

Cocaine

Billy Hoke A creation of the 1980s, rhyming with *coke*.

Boutros Boutros-Ghali From the name of the Egyptian statesman (1922–) who was Secretary General of the United Nations in the early 1990s. Based on the slang term *charlie* 'cocaine'.

oats and barley A 1990s rhyme, based on the slang term *charlie* 'cocaine'. The shortened form (which is almost always used, in preference to the full one) rather unusually dispenses with the first element rather than the last: **barley**. Perhaps there was some perceived risk of confusion with *oats* 'sexual gratification'.

Gianluca Vialli From the name of the Italian footballer (1966–) who became well known in Britain after being appointed player-manager of Chelsea in 1998. The rhyme is based on slang *charlie* for 'cocaine':

> Conrad's a cokehead... He give me uppers and cash for some Gianluca...
> Gianluca Vialli—Charlie.
> —*The Bill* (2001)

Crack

applejack A 1980s appropriation of a US term originally denoting 'apple brandy'.

hubba, I'm back A US coinage of the early 1980s. *Hubba* (usually in the double form *hubba, hubba*) is an exclamation of excitement and approval, widely used in US slang since the early 1940s; in combination with *I'm back*, it makes an ironic counterpoint to the suburban cliché 'Honey, I'm home!' *Hubba* can also be used on its own to denote crack cocaine—presumably as a shortening of the rhyme, although that is not altogether clear:

> Jennifer . . . is smoking hubbas, or rocks of crack.
> —*Newsweek* (1988)

Dope

A general term for (illegal) drugs, but also applied specifically to cannabis, heroin, etc., and the rhymes seem to share the vagueness:

bar of soap A 1970s coinage, conjuring up perhaps incongruous images of clean living.

Bob Hope Based on the stage-name of the wisecracking British-born US comedian (1903–) (see under *Soap* at HOUSEHOLD MATTERS), and often applied specifically to cannabis. It is first recorded in the 1960s, and Tony Thorne, in his *Dictionary of Contemporary Slang* (1997), sees in it 'an example of rhyming slang used, and probably coined, by young middle-class soft-drug users in imitation of traditional working-class cockney rhyming slang':

> Then one day someone passed me a bit of Bob Hope. I packed up the drink
> instantly and I haven't been violent once.
> —*Guardian* (1993)

Heroin

hammer and tack An Australian and New Zealand usage of the 1980s, rhyming with *smack*, a slang term for *heroin* since the 1940s.

Salisbury Crag A 1980s coinage based on *scag*, a slang term for *heroin* since the 1960s:

> 'Salisbury Crag' has become rhyming slang in the city. It means skag, heroin.
> —Ian Rankin *Dead Souls* (1999)

Uncle Mac Once again rhyming with *smack*. A 1970s coinage, incongruously and sinisterly commandeering the familiar name of the BBC children's radio presenter from the 1930s to the 1960s (real name Derek McCulloch).

PCP

An abbreviation (actually of *phenylcyclohexylpiperidine*) which denotes the drug phencyclidine, a hallucinogen (known colloquially as 'angel dust'):

busy bee A coinage of the psychedelic 1970s.

Psilocybin

A hallucinogen obtained from a type of mushroom:

simple simon A 1960s rhyme, albeit a rather feeble one: possibly it was suggested by the earlier drug-users' non-rhyming slang *simple simon* 'non-addict'. The ultimate source is, of course, the nursery-rhyme character who met the pieman.

A fix

Jimmy Hix Underworld slang in the 1940s and 1950s, denoting an injection of narcotics.

Tom Mix From the 1960s, and applied to an injection of heroin. Commemorates the US star of silent cowboy films (1880–1940).

Pills

Of the range of rhymes for *pill*, two in particular are often used with the connotation 'tablet of an illicit drug': see jack and jills and Jimmy Hills under Medical treatment at ILLNESS.

A Bad Reaction to Drugs

A bummer

A slang term for a bad trip which dates from the mid 1960s:

John Selwyn A shortening of John Selwyn Gummer, a doubtfully welcome tribute to the former British Conservative politician and minister (1939–).

Household Matters

Rhyming slang is essentially a public rather than a domestic vocabulary, used more in the streets than round the hearth, so the minutiae of household equipment, fixtures, and furnishings do not figure largely in it. But for most of the items you would have found around a working-class or lower-middle-class home in the 19th and early 20th centuries at least one rhyme was coined—and they include, of course, that most archetypal of rhyming slang equivalents, **apples and pairs**.

The Englishman's Castle

House

Mouse is the key word when it comes to rhyming *house*—and not surprisingly, since, certainly in the 19th century, few houses would have been without their share of rodent occupants. Probably the oldest and most widely used is **cat and mouse**; first recorded in the mid-19th century, it provides an appropriate vignette of traditional domestic pest control. In **rat and mouse**, of almost equal antiquity, the unwelcome residents are left to their own devices. US English has its own variation in **trap and mouse**. **Mickey Mouse** (from the universally recognizable Walt Disney cartoon character who first appeared in 1928) apparently enjoyed some early usage in the specialized theatrical senses of *house*, such as '(size of) audience', but mainly it refers to the residence. Australian English opts for his girlfriend **Minnie Mouse**, first recorded in the 1940s.

A step down takes us to **flea and louse**, a mid-19th-century creation which at best connotes a verminous establishment, and is often frankly a brothel.

Home

A pair of rhymes based on *Rome* goes back to the mid-19th century, and has long since retired from active use: **pope of Rome** (an expression that was itself virtually an archaism by the 1800s; often shortened to **pope**) and the curious **top of Rome**. The 20th century added **gates of Rome**, which has survived better.

To keep the place spick and span and avoid any suspicion of being **hundred to thirty** or **two thirty** (*dirty*) you may need to employ a:

Cleaner

semolina The humble charwoman is represented by another unglamorous component of the domestic scene, villain of countless torturous milk puddings in the 19th and 20th centuries.

From the beginning of the 20th century she (or he) will have had the help of a:

Vacuum cleaner

Vancouver From the name of the major city of British Columbia, Canada. The basis of the rhyme is, of course, *Hoover*, which was registered as a trademark in 1927 and subsequently became a generic term for a vacuum cleaner.

But before the arrival of that mod con, there was nothing for it but the:

Brush

19th- and early 20th-century rhymes have a pleasingly Arcadian quality: **song of the thrush** seems to have had a fairly general application, whereas **blackbird and thrush** was usually restricted specifically to a shoe-brush (for applying blacking to boots, naturally), and was even used as a verb in that sense. Fast-forwarding to the end of the 20th century, football replaces ornithology, with **Ian Rush**, from the name of the Liverpool and Wales striker (1961–)—but only for paint brushes.

Broom

bride and groom A rhyme shared with *room* (see STRUCTURAL ELEMENTS), and equally obsolescent.

If washing clothes is part of the brief, then (in the days before tumble-dryers) recourse will have been had to the:

Clothes line

grape vine Julian Franklyn in his *Dictionary of Rhyming Slang* (1960) casts doubt on the authenticity of this item, but other authorities report it as a general rhyme for *line*, though with particular application to clothes lines, and as often used in the shortened form **grape**.

Structural Elements

Room

birch broom An ancient rhyme, first recorded in the 1850s and long defunct. A birch broom, when such things existed, was a besom made of birch twigs.

bride and groom Also 19th-century, but it survived rather longer. Some metaphorical use (as in 'Give me a bit more bride and groom') as well as literal.

shovel and broom Recorded from the 1920s onwards, and in use in America and Australia as well as Britain. Sometimes curtailed to **shovel**.

Floor

Jane Shore Some 19th-century use, but much better known as a rhyme for *whore* (see under *Commercial Sex* at **SEX**).

Mrs Moore From the name of the character immortalized in the Harry Castling and James Walsh song 'Don't have any more, Mrs Moore' (1926)—a plea for reproductive restraint. Often abbreviated to **the Mrs**.

Rory O'More Mainly used for *door*, but originally (in the mid-19th century) it meant 'floor', and in the 20th century it retained some residual use in that sense—mainly metaphorical, in the phrase *on the Rory* 'poor, broke'.

Ceiling

funny feeling A 20th-century replacement of the earlier **fellow feeling**, which seems to have gone out of use by the end of the 19th century.

Door

Strong contention from **George Bernard Shaw**, from the name of the bearded Irish playwright (1856–1950)—generally shortened to **George Bernard** ('Shut the George Bernard, will you?'). But the clear winner is **Rory O'More** (or **Rory O'Moore**). It was originally used for *floor*, but by the end of the 19th century it was being applied to *door*, and eventually it transcended ordinary rhyming-slang usage and became part of the general language. It comes from the name of a legendary Irish rebel, Rory O'More, the eponymous hero of a popular ballad (1826) and novel (1837) by the Irish writer Samuel Lover (1797–1868). Not uncommonly shortened to **Rory**:

> Some lousy berk must have been snooping around the place and found that rory open.
> —James Curtis *The Gilt Kid* (1936)

Key

Jennie Lee In modern usage probably the commonest application of the rhyme that has also been used for *flea* and *tea*. As with the others, any association with the Labour politician (1904–88) of that name is probably a post-hoc reinforcement. Often shortened to **Jennie**.

knobbly knee Reflecting a notable comic icon of 20th-century British working-class culture, the knobbly-knees contest. At holiday camps throughout the 1940s and 1950s, men would counterpoint the female beauty competition with an ugliness contest of their own.

Doormat

tomcat Potentially applicable to any mat, but in practice a tomcat is what you wipe your feet on as you come indoors. First recorded in 1960.

Handle

Harry Randall Apparently used for handles in general, not just door handles. It came into use in the early 20th century, but was soon ousted by the other application of the name, to *candle*. Harry Randall (1860–1932) was an English music-hall comedian popular in the first decades of the 20th century.

Bell

Little Nell After the character of that name (in full Little Nell Trent) in Charles Dickens's *Old Curiosity Shop* (1841). A child beset with Job-like misfortunes, she dies before the end of the book in a scene that has become a byword for pathos. Her name (with its appropriate echoes of *knell*) can in theory be applied to any bell, but it is usually a doorbell.

Window

Not surprisingly, rhymes for *window* reflect the London pronunciation /'wɪndə/, not Standard English /'wɪndəʊ/.

burnt cinder A pre-First World War rhyme which does not seem to have survived the hostilities.

Jenny Linder A curious and rather strained effort, dating from the middle of the 19th century and apparently not surviving long beyond then. It is presumably an adaptation of the name of the Swedish soprano Jenny Lind (1820–87), known as 'the Swedish nightingale', who was very popular around that time.

Polly Flinder A sentimental rhyme popular with soldiers during the First World War period, but apparently not surviving long beyond then. It is based on the character in the nursery rhyme: 'Little Polly Flinders sat among the cinders.'

Tommy Trinder A late 20th-century rhyme featuring the Cockney stand-up comedian (1909–89) whose catch-phrase was 'You lucky people!'

Curtain

Richard Burton From the name of the celebrated (or notorious) Welsh actor (1925–84), and therefore naturally used for theatre curtains, but you can also 'close the Richard Burtons' in the comfort of your own home.

Stairs

apples and pears Arguably the archetypal piece of Cockney rhyming slang, and the one which people who know no other can always quote. It is first recorded in the 1850s, in the form **apple and pears**, but by the 20th century the plural *apples* had become established:

> 'Dirty Ecnop [ponce]! I soon shoved him down the Apples-and-pears.' 'I haven't understood a word of that last sentence,' said Michael. 'Don't you know back-slang and rhyming slang? Oh, it's grand!'
> —Compton Mackenzie *Sinister Street* (1914)

> I 'as my ocean wave an' when I've got my mince-pie properly open I goes down the apples and pears.
> —*John o' London's Weekly* (1934)

Often shortened to just **apples**:

> One of the removal men asked him if a sofa was to go "up the apples".
> —J. G. Bennett *Witness* (1962)

A reported American variant is **peaches and pears**.

Fred Astaires A coinage of the 1940s, from the US dancer and film star Fred Astaire (1899–1987). The image is of a man debonairly dressed in top hat, white tie, and tails dancing elegantly down a sweeping candle-lit stairway, but it has been speculated that the rhyme inspired the later slang *dance* 'to steal from upper-storey rooms'.

stocks and shares A 20th-century rhyme that holds its own, while never challenging the supremacy of apples and pears.

troubles and cares Also 20th-century, and no more successful than stocks and shares.

And to gain access to the property in the first place:

Gate

rickety kate An Australian rhyme, exploiting an adjective that usually goes with *gate* itself.

In the Kitchen

The standard range of traditional pots and pans and cutlery generally have at least one rhyme allotted to them (plus the occasional new arrival, such as the fridge), but the kitchen also generally contains two important items of furniture that can be found in several other rooms in the house:

Table

Betty Grable A creation of the mid-20th century, when the popularity of the US film star and the Second World War forces' pin-up of that name (1916–73) was at its height. Her most bankable feature was her legs (she had them insured for £250,000), so the rhyme is more wittily appropriate than most.

Cain and Abel A rhyme of much longer standing (it is first recorded in 1859), and a long-term survivor. From the two brothers in the Old Testament (Genesis 4), the former of whom killed the latter.

Chair

Fred Astaire An Australian coinage of the 1940s, based on the name of the US dancer and film star (1899–1987). A somewhat sedentary application, less appropriate-seeming than the rhyme with *stairs* (see above).

here and there Not recorded before the 1940s, but quite firmly established in the second half of the 20th century.

I'll be there 20th-century, and reportedly mainly underworld use. It bears a passing resemblance to **I don't care**, used for the electric chair (see CRIME AND PUNISHMENT).

Lionel Blair A rhyme from the 1970s based on the name of the British dancer and all-round entertainer (1931–) probably better known for his link with *flares* (see CLOTHING).

lion's lair A well-established 20th-century rhyme, possibly based on the idea of the chair belonging to the paterfamilias, who must not be disturbed when taking his nap and whose chair you would be unwise to sit in uninvited.

Owen Nares Only for the plural *chairs*, obviously, and based on the name of a British actor (*c*.1888–1943) popular in the early cinema.

Trafalgar Square Apparently a comparatively recent coinage, but a suitably 'London' referent. Generally truncated to **Trafalgar**.

vanity fair Reportedly dating from the 19th century, in which case the model is likely to have been either John Bunyan's original conception of the sinful city, in *Pilgrim's Progress* (1678), or William Thackeray's novel of that name (1848), rather than the fashion magazine (first published in 1914).

Stool

April fool In practice generally applied to the sort of stools you find next to bars, rather than any of the more domesticated varieties.

The kitchen is the natural habitat of cooking utensils, and the everyday crockery and glassware will be kept and used there too:

Plate

Harry Tate An obsolete item, based on the name of a now largely forgotten English music-hall comedian (1872–1940). Even when the memory was still fresh, the rhyme was more familiar in the sense 'state (of nerves)' (see *state* at **BEHAVIOUR, ATTITUDES, AND EMOTIONS**).

one and eight A pre-decimalization coinage, from the days when every British English-speaker knew that 'one and eight' was one shilling and eightpence.

pearly gate Quite a glittering concept, and generally applied to the plates in the best (if not only) dinner service.

Dish

Lilian Gish From the name of the long-lived Hollywood actress (1893–1993), who started in the silent cinema and was still making films in her nineties—and a more dignified use of it than the alternative rhyme *fish* (see **FOOD AND DRINK**).

Cup

dog and pup Generally abbreviated to **dog**—the context usually precludes any confusion with dog = 'phone' (see **COMMUNICATION**).

down and up The Australian version, although the resemblance to *down under* is purely fortuitous.

Saucer

Geoffrey Chaucer Celebrating the first great English poet (*c*.1343–1400), author of the *Canterbury Tales*. A tribute to erudite rhyming slangsters' familiarity with Middle English verse (and it's not as if it were a common pub name).

Mug

barge and tug Favoured by Thames watermen and dock workers. Usually shortened to **barge**.

Bottle

Aristotle From the name of the Greek philosopher (384–322BC):

He then orders an aristotle of the most ping-pong tiddly in the nuclear sub.
—*Lock, Stock, and Two Smoking Barrels* (1998)

The rhyme goes back to the 19th century, and in early use was apparently often shortened to **Arry**—from a no doubt facetious Cockneyfication of the name to '*Arry Stottle*. A later and more long-lasting abbreviation is **arris**, which, partly from the use of **bottle and glass** as rhyming slang for *arse* (see THE BODY AND ITS PARTS) and partly from its own resemblance to *arse*, has come to be used as euphemistic slang for 'buttocks'.

charming mottle A curious Australianism extant from the late 19th century to the early 20th.

Gerry Cottle Based on the name of the 20th-century English circus impresario, and generally shortened to **Gerry**.

Glass

comical farce First recorded in the late 19th century, and on its way out by the time of the First World War.

Hackney Marsh A slightly approximate rhyme, suggesting that the rhymester has perhaps already downed the contents of the glass. A late-19th-century coinage, based on the name of the large area of flat meadowland (long since drained of its water) that lies to the east of Hackney, East London, and in the 21st century is the haunt of weekend footballers. It gradually lost out to the use of its plural form for 'spectacles'.

Khyber Pass Much better known in modern English as a rhyme for *arse* (see at THE BODY AND ITS PARTS), but in the late 19th century it denoted a glass.

Lancashire lass A late 19th-century rhyme, possibly of Northern English origin or inspiration (/glas/ rather than /glɑːs/).

pig's arse A 20th-century Australian contribution.

snake in the grass Perhaps a reference to the treacherous nature of the liquid in the glass. Apparently a secondary use of a rhyme already applied to '(looking) glass' (see below).

weekend pass A 20th-century creation, and no doubt of military origin, weekend passes being something with which servicemen are obsessed.

working class Used for the receptacle, but much commoner in the plural, applied to spectacles (see at THE SENSES).

Pot

red hot An Australian rhyme with specific application to a ten-ounce beer glass—known as a 'pot'.

Sir Walter Scott A resounding rhyme for a humble utensil, appropriating the name of the prolific Scottish novelist (1771–1832). But in fact this is seldom the cooking pot, of 'pots and pans' fame; it is, or was, more likely to be a pot of beer, in the days when people spoke of such things.

Pan

Isle of Man Very often specifically a frying pan—think 'tent pegs sizzling in the Isle of Man'.

Kettle

Hansel and Gretel From the two child-heroes of the Grimms' fairy tale, who incinerated the wicked witch in her oven. The **Hansel** (for short) remains on top of the stove, ready for endless relays of Rosie Lee.

Knife

Knives are multi-role implements, and have many purposes less innocent than peeling fruit. Many of the rhymes had their beginning with *knife* the offensive weapon, military or criminal, and only later moved into the kitchen. **Drum and fife** is a case in point. Its elements proclaim its military band origins (a fife being a small flute that accompanies the drum), but it became firmly domesticated in the course of the 20th century. The usual curtailment operated, producing **drum and**. This came to be reinterpreted as the name **Drummond**, which entered into a long-term partnership with *roce*, the eroded form of roast pork 'fork' (see below)—hence the Cockney's *drummond and roce* 'knife and fork', which, as Julian Franklyn comments in his *Dictionary of Rhyming Slang* (1961), sounds very like an old-established firm of cutlers.

A nexus of *knife*-rhymes is built around *wife* (the compliment is returned with carving knife for *wife*—see RELATIVES AND FRIENDS). Perhaps the leading example was **man and wife**, which seems to have originated in the army in the First World War and then became civilianized to denote mainly a pen-knife. **Charming wife** and **darling wife** were also military creations, but largely stayed that way—the underlying scenario was that you introduced, say, a German sentry to your 'charming wife'. Finally **husband and wife**, first recorded in the 1940s, and generally shortened to **husband**.

Rhymes based on *blade* (e.g. shovel and spade) decidedly belong on the street, not in the kitchen (see *A blade* at CRIME AND PUNISHMENT).

Fork

Duke of York An old rhyme, possibly as early as the 18th century, which has long since abandoned its literal meaning in favour of the metaphorical application of *forks* to 'hands' (see dukes at THE BODY AND ITS PARTS, and see also Joe Rourke at CRIME AND PUNISHMENT).

roast pork Dating probably from the 1920s or 1930s, and appropriate to the carving fork it often denotes. Generally abbreviated to **roast**, whose pronunciation /rəʊs/ has been represented as *roce* in *drummond and roce* 'knife and fork' (see above).

Spoon

blue moon A late 19th-century creation, so inspired by the general notion of the rarely seen blue moon, rather than the popular Rodgers and Hart ballad of that name (1934). It had faded away by the middle of the 20th century.

 high noon Introduced in the 1950s, thanks to the success of the 1952 film *High Noon*, starring Gary Cooper and Grace Kelly.

 Lorna Doone Commemorating the eponymous heroine of the 1869 novel by R. D. Blackmore.

 man on the moon A coinage of the 1960s, inspired by manned space flight rather than the legendary lunar inhabitant (for which see *A loon* at **PEOPLE AND THE HUMAN CONDITION**).

Fridge

London Bridge The word *fridge* did not begin to appear until the late 1920s, providing a cast-iron *terminus a quo* for the rhyme.

Freezer

Freezer in the domestic sense is more recent still (although the word has been used in industrial contexts since the 19th century), but has managed to accumulate two rhymes:

 Julius Caesar From the name of the Roman soldier and statesman (100–44BC).

 Mona Lisa From the English name (in Italian literally 'Lady Lisa') of the most famous picture in the world, painted by Leonardo da Vinci 1503–6.

In the drawers of the kitchen cabinet you can probably find:

Glue

Marylou Apparently a 20th-century coinage, from the female forename.

and:

String

highland fling An Australian application for an item which in British rhyming slang is a verb, denoting 'to sing' (see *To sing* at **AT LEISURE**).

The kitchen may well also be the location of the electricity or gas:

Meter

little peter The inventors of the rhyme probably had in mind criminals' slang *peter* 'safe', a meter holding your grudgingly slotted coins as securely as any strongbox.

In the Bathroom

Bath

hat and scarf Reflecting the pronunciation /bɑːf/ favoured by all true—and would-be—'Cockneys'. And the idea of the behatted and bescarfed bather would no doubt tickle their funny bone too.

For Australians who prefer the term *tub*, there's the rhyme **bib and bub**—commonly used in *have a bib and bub* 'to take a bath'.

Basin

Charley Mason Dating from the late 19th century, but latterly used not so much literally as metaphorically in the sense 'basinful'—that is, 'more than enough'. A slightly more recent alternative is **Jimmy Mason**. Neither represents a real person.

Tap

tree and sap An Australian example from the 20th century.

Plug

little brown jug The expression *brown jug*, connoting a Toby jug or similar ale receptacle, had been around since at least the late 18th century, but this particular formulation was inspired by the song 'Little Brown Jug' (1869), by Joseph E. Winner ('Little brown jug, how I love thee . . .'), which was popularized in Britain in 1939 by Glenn Miller and his orchestra. The original application was probably to the bath plug, but it also came to be used for electric plugs (and, by metaphorical extension, for tampons).

Soap

Hope is the leitmotiv when it comes to rhyming *soap* (perhaps with small boys in mind). Many of the formulations involve a proper name. US prison slang, for example, has **Jimmy Hope**, first recorded in 1912. Australian English favours **Joe Hope**. But the most familiar and most widely used in Britain is **Bob Hope**, from the stage-name (real name Leslie Townes Hope; born (in South London) in 1903) of the US stage and film comic noted for his sharp-edged wise-cracking style. Continuing the optimistic theme are **band of hope** (from *Band of Hope*, the name given in Britain from the late 1840s to associations of young people who had signed the pledge to abstain from alcohol; contracted in Australian English to **bander**); **Cape of Good Hope** (popular in nautical circles); and **land of hope** (presumably from the first words of 'Land of Hope and Glory' (1902), the semi-official English national anthem, verses by A. C. Benson set to music by Elgar).

As an alternative to all this hope, there is, or was, **Charlie Pope**, favoured among soldiers in the First World War trenches.

Carbolic

frisk and frolic An ironically cheerful late 19th-century rhyme for this unloved soap with the penetrating disinfectant smell; now obsolete.

Towel

The name *Powell* lends itself readily to the rhyme, and several notable Powells have been selected (but only if they pronounce themselves /ˈpaʊəl/, of course; /ˈpəʊəlz/, such as Anthony, need not apply). Probably the most widely used late 20th-century example is **Enoch Powell**, from the name of the British politician (1912–98) whose controversial views on race relations found favour in certain quarters of Cockney rhyming-slang territory; popular enough to be regularly shortened to **Enoch**. Also in the frame are the imaginary **Bob Powell** (an Australian creation), **Sandy Powell** (commemorating the red-haired English music-hall and radio comedian Albert ('Sandy') Powell (1900–82)), and **William Powell** (from the name of the US actor (1892–1984) best remembered for his starring role in the *Thin Man* movies in the 1930s and 1940s). A late 19th-century alternative, now obsolete, is **mortar and trowel**.

Drain

Spanish Main From the name once given to the northern coastline of South America, and subsequently to the seas adjacent to this. Possibly suggested by the expression 'main drain', although much contemporary usage seems to be metaphorical, and in the abbreviated form **Spanish**—as in 'The country's going down the Spanish'.

Toilette

Lest it should be thought that all rhyming slangsters are **wattles** (a curtailed version of the mid-20th-century Australian rhyme **wattle and daub**, based on Australian slang *warb* 'a dirty unkempt person'), their inventions abound in terms relating to cleanliness and personal grooming:

A wash

Bob Squash An oldish rhyme applied not just to an instance of washing oneself but also to a public washroom, especially one in a public lavatory.

Usually shortened to **bob**: to *work the bob* was to steal from the pockets of jackets hung up by people having a wash. Also used as a verb, mainly in First World War military slang.

lemon squash An Australian rhyme.

A shower

bag of flour First recorded in the 1970s.

Eiffel Tower A British and Australian rhyme, after the unmistakable Parisian landmark.

Eisenhower From the name of Dwight D. Eisenhower (1890–1969), American Second World War general and later 34th president of the USA (1953–61).

happy hour An Australian rhyme dating from the 1950s. The original *happy hour*, a US naval slang term for 'a period of entertainment and refreshment on board ship', goes back to the First World War period.

Tyrone Power A further Australianism (Australian rhymers seem better acquainted with showers than British ones), based on the name of the Hollywood actor Tyrone Power (1914–58).

Shave

Chas and Dave A noun usage, from the stage name of a Cockney singing duo popular in the 1980s. A rhyming slangsters' in joke: both of the singers are bearded.

dad and dave An Australian verb, commemorating a 1930s radio serial *Dad and Dave*, set in an Australian rural community, which made such a mark on Australian cultural life that its title became a metaphor for an unsophisticated country hick. The two characters were originally created at the end of the 19th century by the Australian writer Steele Rudd (pen-name of Arthur Hoey Davis (1868–1935)) as humorous but aspirational small farmers, but later treatments made them laughing-stocks.

dig in the grave A noun usage which apparently originated in Australia at the beginning of the 20th century, but soon spread to Britain. Its abbreviation **dig** (as in 'to have a dig') was in common use in the middle years of the century. The corresponding verb usage is **dig a grave**.

misbehave An Australian rhyme—not, as might have been expected, for the verb, but for the noun.

ocean wave A noun usage current mainly in the 1920s and 1930s:

> I 'as my ocean wave an' when I've got my mince-pie properly open I goes down the apples and pears.
> —*John o' London's Weekly* (1934)

A razor

Dawn Fraser A 1960s Australian rhyme, honouring the triple Olympic swimming gold-medallist and Australian heroine Dawn Fraser (1937–).

house of fraser Some domestic usage, but the reference is more often to cut-throat razors as used by criminal gangs—and in that context, generally shortened to **howser**. The original inspiration was the British retail chain House of Fraser, onetime owners of Harrods.

Ted Frazer A 1960s rhyme, always applied to the cut-throat type of razor (and not always as used in the bathroom). The identity of Ted Frazer, if he existed, is not known.

A comb

garden gnome First recorded in the 1980s.

ideal home A rhyme dating from the 1950s, and presumably inspired by the Ideal Home Exhibition, an annual British domestic consumer-goods and interior-design show first held in 1908.

Millennium Dome Inspired by the giant domed tent erected in Greenwich, southeast London, to celebrate the new millennium, but no more likely than that reviled structure to survive for the next thousand years. A whiff of punning links the idea of a comb sarcastically with that of a bald 'dome'.

Not much use if you have the misfortune to be:

Bald

Both rhymes suggest a pronunciation /bɔːd/, reflecting a tendency for 'Cockney' *l*s to become *w*s:

Cyril Lord Commemorating the British carpet magnate Cyril Lord (1911–84), a well-known name in the 1950s and 1960s. No doubt the subtle pun (*rug* is slang for 'wig') was intentional.

oh my God Perhaps a reaction to seeing an old friend who's just lost his hair. *God* is /gɔːd/, of course.

In that case, you might try:

A wig

Irish jig First recorded in 1979, and generally reduced to **Irish**:

> I'll take this Irish into custody. You got a plastic bag or something?
> —Leon Griffith *Minder* (1979)

syrup of figs From the powerful fig-based laxative. First recorded in 1981, and not well adapted for the singular form *wig*, but it's almost always abbreviated to **syrup** anyway:

> Any leading neurologist prepared to discuss whether Slappy's memory may have
> been damaged when the subway train doors clamped shut on his syrup should call
> at once.
> —*Guardian* (2000)

> I was totally hoodwinked by *Have I Got News for You*'s fake Elton John (London
> taxi driver Ray, complete with one of Reg's old Versace suits and a cheap syrup
> bought from a market).
> —*Observer* (2001)

Alternatively, you could comb what remaining strands of hair you have
over into:

A flap

wind trap A heartfelt rhyme, reflecting how easily these careful
arrangements are upset by a cruel gust.

And if you prefer to entrust your hair and beard into the hands of another,
there's the:

Barber

Rhymers' imaginations haven't spread beyond *harbour* for this one: the
British have **Dover harbour**, while the Australians have opted for—you've
guessed it—**Sydney harbour**. Less obvious is the Australian **coffs harbour**,
from *Coff's Harbour*, the name of a town and port on the north coast of New
South Wales.

And so to Bed

Bed

roses red A largely Australian alternative to Uncle Ned, presumably inspired
by the traditional verse beginning 'Roses are red, violets are blue . . .'

  Uncle Ned One of the best-established pieces of rhyming slang. First
recorded in 1925, it has achieved familiarity even among non-habitual
rhyme-users:

> Get out of that Uncle Ned, slide into your threads, and come down the nick with us.
> —John Gardner *The Corner Men* (1974)

Often shortened to **uncle**:

> 'You did right, shoving him back in his uncle.' . . . Uncle. Uncle Ned, Cockney
> rhyming slang for bed.
> —Jack Scott *Uprush of Mayhem* (1982)

Or, if you are so inclined, you can rhyme on *sack*, slang for *bed*:

Roberta Flack An Australian coinage of the 1970s, based on the name of the pop songstress (1937–). It tends to follow the idiomatic patterns of *sack* itself: so you can *hit the Roberta*—i.e. 'go to bed'.

Pillow

The key rhyme-word for *pillow* is *willow*—not the most comfortable of concepts. The leading exemplar is **weeping willow**, first recorded in 1880 and surviving well into the 20th century:

> Time young Holly was in bed. . . . Hannah wants your head on your weeping willow, pillow to you.
> —Noel Streatfeild *Curtain Up* (1944)

Variations on the theme are **tit willow**, also from the late 19th century, and the slightly more recent **pussy willow**.

Alternative formulations are **Max Miller**, from the name of the celebrated English stand-up comedian (1894–1963) who might well have pronounced *pillow* /ˈpɪlə/, and **rolling billow**, another 19th-century example.

Mirror

snake in the grass The rhyme goes not, of course, with the non-U *mirror*, but with the now distinctly dated *(looking) glass*. It is first recorded in the 1850s, and faded out with its model. Amateur psychologists may speculate on the motivation: treacherous mirror undermines its owner's delusory self-image, etc. See also *Glass* at **IN THE KITCHEN**.

And before the days of gas and electricity, you would probably have lit your way to bed with a:

Candle

Harry Randall An early 20th-century example, superseding the previous application of the rhyme to *handle* (which see at **STRUCTURAL ELEMENTS** for an account of its origin). Earlier, and now equally obsolete, was **Jack Randall** (or **Jack Randle**), from the name of a noted 19th-century bare-knuckle fighter. Both seem to have enjoyed a surge in popularity during the First World War period, when candles provided much of the illumination in the trenches of the Western Front.

Sleep

If you're **cream-crackered** 'knackered' (I didn't see anybody else walk at all, which is staggering, you're absolutely cream-crackered by then. *Harrow: the School on the Hill* ITV (2001)) or, if you're Australian, **kerried** (short for **Kerry Packered**, from the Australian media magnate Kerry Packer (1937–)), you just want to get to bed for a good sleep. For rhymers, the options are **Little Bo Peep** (or just **Bo Peep**, after the eponymous heroine of the nursery rhyme who mislaid her sheep) and, if you're Australian, **rolling deep**. If, on the other hand, you just want a quick *kip*, there's **feather and flip** (generally reduced to **feather**; 'getting some feather' has appropriate connotations of down-filled pillows); **halfpenny dip** (usually just **halfpenny**, pronounced /ˈheɪpni/); and **jockey's whip** (a rhyme current in the mid-20th century, and often simplified to **jockey's**).

Snore

For the noun there's **lion's roar**, all too obviously apposite, and if you want to express it as a verb, you can use **rain and pour** (the second element is optional: a complaint might well be directed against someone's **raining**).

Heating

A fire

Three strong *fire*-rhyme themes emerge, all of them based on names. In the days when *Maria* was pronounced /məˈrʌɪə/, rather than continentalized to /məˈriːə/, it offered a small range of promising combinations for rhyming slangsters: **Anna Maria**, **Aunt Maria** (both 19th-century rhymes), **ave maria** (from the title of the salutation to the Virgin Mary, which was pronounced /eɪvi məˈrʌɪə/ in English before the restored Latin /aːveɪ məˈriːə/ came into use), plus **black maria** (from the term for a van for carrying prisoners, applied though not to a domestic fire but to one requiring the attention of the fire brigade).

In Australia, the fireplace welcomes the Maguire family: **Andy Maguire**, **Barney Maguire**, and **Molly Maguire**. Their Irish compatriot **Mick O'Dwyer** has filled the same role in Britain.

Many Old Testament male names end in /-ʌɪə/, and two selected for rhyming duty are **Jeremiah** (from the name of the prophet of doom; first recorded in the 1930s, and generally abbreviated to **jerry**) and **Obadiah** (from another Hebrew prophet who has his own Book of the Bible).

Outside the 'names' circle is **I desire**, a rhyme first recorded in 1859 but long since defunct.

Stove

Lane Cove An Australian rhyme, inspired by a harbourside suburb of that name in Sydney.

purple and mauve An alternative Australian formulation, further attesting to the importance of the stove in Australian domestic life.

The fire or the stove may well burn:

Coal

merry old soul From the traditional characterization of Old King Cole. Often shortened to **merry** (a request to 'put another lump of merry on the jerry' can be interpreted by reference to Jeremiah—see above).

or:

Coke

holy smoke The original (and rather more apposite) application of a rhyme which was later transferred to the drink *Coke* (see **FOOD AND DRINK**).

which in due course will produce:

Cinders

Polly Flinders Apparently a new use for a rhyme originally applied in the singular to *window* (see **STRUCTURAL ELEMENTS**).

which you can stir around with your:

Poker

jolly joker A 20th-century coinage, probably with the playing card in mind (though there is no suggestion that the rhyme has ever been applied to 'poker' the game).

   orinoko A 19th-century rhyme, no doubt pronounced /ˌɒrɪˈnəʊkə/. For the curious history of the word and its pairings, see **COCOA** at **FOOD AND DRINK**.

Matches

Most of the rhymes for *matches* exploit, not surprisingly, the appositeness of its connection with *scratches*—scraping the match-head across an abbrasive surface. Hence: **bites and scratches**, **cuts and scratches** (a 19th-century rhyme), **jack scratches** (an Australian contribution), and, in the singular, **itch and scratch** and **press and scratch** (another 19th-century rhyme, and perhaps the most appropriate of them all).

   The only alternative to these is **Colney Hatch**, from the name of a large mental hospital built near Barnet, North London, in 1851. Usually shortened to **colney**.

In the Garden

In the 19th century, London's rhyming classes largely lived in tenements, without the luxury of individual gardens (which is why the rhymes for *grass* listed below referred more to public parks than to private lawns). But the idea of a plot of land is close to the heart of the English, and in the 20th century your average rhyming slangster will have had his bit of garden, where he could cultivate his **uncles and aunts** (*plants*) and think up new rhymes. Those for *garden* itself are all showing their age: **beg your pardon** dates from the late 19th century; **Dolly Varden** is of similar antiquity, and comes from the name of a character in Charles Dickens's *Barnaby Rudge* (1841); and **one and elevenpence three farthing** is a decidedly pre-decimal amount of money, but the rhyme of *farthing* /ˈfaːðən/ with *garden* takes it back even further in time.

Grass

Ernie Marsh A somewhat inexact rhyme from the earliest years of the 20th century. Julian Franklyn in his *Dictionary of Rhyming Slang* (1960) speculates that the unidentified Ernie Marsh may have been a sleeper-out in London parks.

 old iron and brass Adapted from the cry of the rag-and-bone man, collecting unwanted metal. Usually shortened to **old iron**.

A fence

eighteen pence An Australian rhyme of the 1950s, applied to a garden fence. Based on a common formulation for the pre-decimal sum of one shilling and sixpence.

Flowers

Rhyming slang being pre-eminently a street trader's language, it's not surprising that the majority of *flower*-rhymes were coined and used by flower vendors and flower-market workers, rather than by gardeners. **Early hours** is a heartfelt testimony to the pre-dawn rising necessary in the florist's trade, and **happy hours** and **leisure hours** probably just reflect the general feel-good factor of flowers rather than the therapeutic effect of gardening. Also commonly heard in old Covent Garden market was **yours and ours**, as was **April showers** (no doubt inspired by the old proverb 'April showers bring forth May flowers'), although it subsequently escaped into more general usage. Australian rhymers have opted for **Cobar showers**, first recorded in 1959 (Cobar is a copper-mining town in New South Wales).

A poppy

Xerox copy A poppy, but not a live one. The rhyme applies to Remembrance Day poppies, and was coined in Australia in the 1950s (no doubt in allusion to the fact that all such poppies look alike).

In the Toolshed

Tools

April fools Originally, in the 19th century, underworld slang, referring to housebreakers' tools, but by the early 20th century it had become a general term.

crown jewels Mainly in literal use, although it is also a common non-rhyming metaphor for the male genitalia, which of course includes a *tool*.

A hammer

stutter and stammer Usually reduced to **stutter**.

windjammer An Australian contribution, based on the name of a type of sailing vessel.

A nail

monkey's tail Used (usually in the plural) in the carpentry trade.

A saw

bear's paw A general rhyme, not confined to any particular trade.

Denis Law Based on the name of the popular Manchester United and Scotland striker Denis Law (1940–). His sharpness in scoring may well have prompted the rhyme.

mother-in-law A carpenter's term, no doubt with a memory of the mother-in-law figure's reputation as a battle-axe.

A spanner

Elsie Tanner From the name of a character in the never-ending British television soap opera *Coronation Street*. Played by Pat Phoenix, she was the Street's 'tart'.

A drill

Benny Hill Commemorating the English film and television comedian Benny Hill (1924–92).

A file

Duke of Argyll It is not clear which holder of that title was intended, but perhaps the likeliest candidate is the second duke (1678–1748), who was a distinguished general in Marlborough's army during the War of the Spanish Succession. Or maybe it was just a pub name. Long since disused.

Plymouth Argyll From the name of the English Nationwide League football club based in Plymouth, Devon. It was founded in 1886 as Argyle Football Club, and there are various theories as to the origin of its name: the Argyll and Sutherland Highlanders are said to have been stationed in the city at that time, and their footballing skills admired by the locals; then there was the coincidence of the club's first committee meeting being held in Argyle Terrace; probably these both contributed to the name, as did the contemporary fashion for all things Scottish (Argyll, or Argyle, being a former Scottish county), prompted by Queen Victoria's attachment to Scotland.

A shovel

Lord Lovell A navvies' rhyme of the mid-19th century. First recorded in 1857.

A bucket

dip and chuck it An Australian rhyme, evocative of some of the physical activities with which buckets are involved.

Mrs Duckett A usage of the building trade, and also found among fishmongers.

nantucket Recorded in the building industry in the 1970s. Based on the name of Nantucket island, in Massachusetts, USA.

A trowel

Baden-Powell Based on the name of Sir Robert Baden-Powell (1857–1941), founder of the Boy Scout movement, who first came to fame in Britain for his conduct of the defence of Mafeking in 1900. The rhyme depends on the demotic /ˈpaʊəl/ rather than the more refined /ˈpəʊəl/.

bark and growl Recorded in the mid-19th century as a bricklayers' rhyme, particularly among those working on the tunnels and bridges of the new railway system.

Enoch Powell A minor application (mainly among bricklayers) for a rhyme more usually used for *towel* (see *Towel* at **IN THE BATHROOM**). Generally shortened to **Enoch**.

Sandy Powell Likewise, more usually a *towel*-rhyme (see *Towel* at **IN THE BATHROOM**).

A pickaxe

mad mick A well-established Australian rhyme on *pick*, first recorded in 1919. Probably tapping into the stereotype of Irish road-menders:

> I swung a mad-mick there for eighteen months during the depression.
> —T. A. G. Hungerford *Riverslake* (1953)

I won't buy drinks f'r any bloody ganger, just f'r a chance to swing a mad mick.
—F. Huelin *Keep Moving* (1973)

A ladder

Blackadder From the successful BBC television comedy series (1983–9),
starring Rowan Atkinson as various historical incarnations of the
eponymous hero Blackadder.

leaky bladder A condition unsuited to the ascent of high ladders.

Accommodation

It may be that you need to take in:

A lodger

artful dodger First recorded in 1859, so it is chronologically possible that it
could have been inspired by the Artful Dodger, the juvenile pickpocket who
befriends Oliver in Dickens's *Oliver Twist* (1838). But there may well also be a
reference to lodgers' legendary propensity for scooting off without paying
the rent.

jolly roger Presumably from the pirates' skull-and-crossbones flag (the
name is first recorded in the 1780s), although here the subtext could be
another old-time stereotype, randy 'Roger the Lodger'.

who you hope will not get behind with the:

Rent

Burton on Trent A late 19th-century coinage, after the town in Staffordshire
noted as a brewing centre. Ray Puxley in *Cockney Rabbit* (1992) suggests there
may be a link with the liquid which the rent money often got spent on.

Duke of Kent A 20th-century example, and never quite as common as
Burton on Trent.

Lodgings

All these rhymes died out as the practice of temporary living in rented
accommodation gradually became much rarer in the second half of the 20th
century. A further measure of their antiquity is that those for 'lodgings' are
based on the now seldom encountered *digs* and its obsolete source, *diggings*
(which was perhaps derived from the idea of 'entrenching' oneself in a
place).

Charlie Wiggins A 19th-century coinage, used mainly in the theatrical
profession—actors in rep being constantly on the move from one lodging to

another. There appears to have been no particular Charlie Wiggins who inspired it.

Ronnie Biggs A much more recent creation, commemorating the Great Train Robber (1929–) who decamped to Brazil, finally returning to resume his British jail sentence in 2001.

Clothing

The rhyming slang of clothes spans over a century and a half, from the era of bustles and spats (**Johnny Russells** and **Wanstead flats**) to the age of jeans and trainers (**baked beans** and **Claire Rayners**). But in the main it is the earlier period that has left more of a mark: the world of rhyming slang is one where hat-wearing is the norm, where boots are as common as shoes, where braces (**airs and graces**), waistcoats (**Charlie Prescots**), and detachable collars (**Oxford scholars**) are components of everyman's uniform, and where everywoman still wears bloomers (**wicked rumours**), drawers (**Diana Dors**), and stays (**Bryant and Mays**).

Women's garments and accessories are in fact decidedly under-represented in rhyming slang. Unisex items and clothing that can be specifically identified as mainly male more often than not have a generous range of synonyms (eight rhymes for *socks*, for instance, and ten for *coat*), but when it comes to female clothes, *dress* rates a meagre two (plus one for *frock*), as does *bra*. This tends to reinforce the impression of the coinage and use of rhyming slang as being predominantly a male preserve, a product of male cameraderie and self-dramatization. If women were true devotees of rhyming slang, there would surely be at least one rhyme for *handbag*.

Rhyming slang prefers to deal in particularities rather than generalities, so there is only one widely used rhyme for *clothes*: **these and those**. It naturally takes its cue from the everyday pronunciation of the word (virtually the same as *close*) rather than the full *th* version we use when we are being very careful.

Headgear

Hat

titfer A cut-down version of rhyming slang **tit-for-tat**, which dates from the late 19th century and has since gone out of use. Titfer itself is first recorded in 1930, and transcended its rhyming slang origins in the middle years of the 20th century to become a widespread light-hearted British colloquialism for 'hat'.

> People are often astonished when I tell them that all duchesses say 'tit fer' rather than 'hat'.
> —Christopher Sykes 'What U-Future?' [written humorously from the perspective of 2055], in *Noblesse Oblige*, edited by Nancy Mitford (1956)

> The old lady made a show . . . Lil Pratt forgot to fill her mouth. . . . She'd not seen a titfer like that since the film of the mountain people in the Dardanelles, made after World War One.
> —*U. Holden* (1976)

Fat was a popular rhyme in the early 20th century (**ball of fat**, **bladder of fat**, and the Australian **barrel of fat**), possibly in allusion to the greasiness of a much-worn hat. **Ball and bat** was also quite widely used at that time; it was superseded by titfer in Britain, but survived rather longer in the US. American and Australian rhyming slang have also used **this and that**.

God forbid First recorded in 1936, and rhyming with *lid*, a British slang synonym of *hat*. Often spelt **Gawd forbid**, to give the genuine Cockney flavour:

> Why don't you take off your gawd-forbid? We're passing the Cenotaph.
> —James Curtis *The Gilt Kid* (1936).

penny-a-mile Rhyming with another slang term for 'hat', *tile*, now virtually obsolete. First recorded in the late 19th century, the rhyme survived into the 1920s, but it's since moved on to another application, 'smile' (see *A smile* at **BEHAVIOUR, ATTITUDES, AND EMOTIONS**).

More specific items of headgear to be rhymed are the cap and the bowler hat:

Cap

The bizarre 19th-century **baby's pap** perhaps recalled the often shapeless caps of the period; the equally obsolete **game of nap** is based on a type of card game popular in the late 19th and early 20th centuries (*nap* was originally an abbreviation of *Napoleon*).

Bowler hat

In the first two-thirds of the 20th century, when bowlers were the preferred headwear of the archetypal British city gent, **steamroller** often stood in. Also sometimes heard was **bottle of cola**: this apparently originated at the beginning of the century as **bottle of Kola**, *Kola* being the brand name of a type of British soft drink manufactured by the firm R. White, but it soon became associated with the other, somewhat more universal brand name *Coca Cola*.

Coats

Coat

There's a maritime flavour to much of the rhyming slang for *coat*. Dating back to at least the mid-19th century is **I'm afloat**, which generally refers to a heavy winter overcoat. As with much frequently used rhyming slang, the end (in this case *float*) was jettisoned for brevity, leaving **I'm a** (It's cold out—you'll need your I'm a). In American English it metamorphosed to **eye me float**. Variants on the same theme, which also date back to the 19th century, are **all afloat** and **bucket afloat**. The latter, which perhaps nods to the colloquial use of *bucket* for a clapped-out boat, came to be reinterpreted as **bucket and float**, a usage apparently current around the First World War period. In the 20th century, American English has come up with **ivory float**—probably suggested by the advertising slogan of 'Ivory' soap (a US brand of soap), 'It floats'; and Irish English has expanded the range of nautical allusion with **Glasgow boat**—presumably a reference to a vector for Hiberno-Glaswegian communication.

More earth-bound alternatives include the now superannuated **John O'Groat** (taking a small liberty with *John O'Groats*, the name of the locality popularly (though erroneously) considered to be the most northerly point in mainland Britain) and **pound note** (actual pound notes first appeared in Britain in the mid-19th century, but their demise at the hands of the pound coin (introduced in 1983) marked the point of no return for their rhyming status), and also **Quaker oat**, from the name of a porridge-like British breakfast cereal with a black-garbed Puritan on the packet, and perhaps with a subliminal comparison between the effects of the cereal and the warmth of the overcoat. In the early to mid-20th century **nanny goat** had a vogue, commonly abbreviated to **nanny** (Yes, guvnor, it [i.e. a raincoat] is my old nanny all right.) *The Blue Lamp* (1949)). Closest to the classic rhyming slang formula, though, is **weasel and stoat**, which in practice is generally **weasel**.

Jacket

'Coat' in rhyming slang usually refers to an overcoat. When the shorter garment needs to be specified, there are three options:

fag packet, or just **fag**. Decidedly only a Briticism; *fag*'s connotations of homosexuality would have made it a non-starter in North America.

steam packet. Current in the 19th century, but long since obsolete. A quite different sort of *packet*, of course, and one which picks up the nautical theme again: a steam packet was a steam-powered mail-boat (originally as maintained to carry 'the packet' of State letters and dispatches).

tennis racket. Reportedly often shortened to **tennis**, which makes it sound like a French word for a sports jacket ('*le tennis*').

Trousers and their supporters

Trousers

The key rhyming word for *trousers* is *houses*, which at first sight may not seem to fit very well. But this is 19th-century Cockney, and with a pronunciation of /ˈtraʊzɪz/, or even /ˈtrɑːzɪz/, *houses* falls into place (J. D. Brayshaw gives something of the flavour in Slum Silhouettes (1898): An' as fer 'is rahnd-the-'ouses, they 'ad a crease right dahn 'em). Of all its combinations, the oldest and deepest ingrained is:

round the houses First recorded in the middle of the 19th century, and already then featuring as a familiar piece of rhyming slang:

> Philip intimating that, as soon as he had put on his *trousers*, he would blacken Bill's eyes, roared out, 'Wait till I've togged my 'round-the-houses', and then I'll cook your 'mince-pies' for you'.
> —Augustus Mayhew, *Paved with Gold* (1858)

Probably suggested not by any literal notion of circumambulating the house, but by the expression *round the houses* 'circuitously'.

Like most common rhyming slang, **round the houses** is regularly abbreviated, but this leads us into uncertain territory. Some sources give **round the's**, or **round de's**, as the shortened form, but much more often encountered is **round me's**. This presupposes a full form **round me houses** (presumably for **round my houses**), which is in fact recorded in Ducange Anglicus's *The Vulgar Tongue* (1857) and does appear elsewhere in print (Still 'e kept on dancin'—another one went 'pop', He said 'I'm goin' ter keep on till me "round-me-'ouses" drop'. Weston and Lee *Knees up, Mother Brown!* (1939)). Round my houses lacks a certain internal logic, and Julian Franklyn, in his *Dictionary of Rhyming Slang* (1961), suggests that round me's evolved (presumably by some sort of dissimilation) from /ˈrɑːn ni/, an eroded pronunciation of round the. On that reasoning, round my houses would be a later invention, coined to account for the *me*. But such a phonetic development is not entirely convincing. However round me's arose, it progressed still further, in Australian and South African slang, to **rammies** (first recorded in 1906):

> Old Bill watched the youngest jackeroo disrobing . . . 'If I was you, young feller,' he said, 'I'd leave them rammies on.'
> —*Bulletin* (Sydney) (1933).

In American slang, the shortening process is yet more radical: to **rounds**.

Other *house* rhymes:

council houses This term for a dwelling built or provided by a local authority did not come into the language until the 1920s, providing a useful *terminus a quo* for the rhyming slang use.

Rowton houses A Rowton House was a sort of cheap but respectable lodging-house which provided accommodation for the homeless in Britain in the first half of the 20th century. It was named after the philanthropist Montague William Lowry-Corry, 1st Lord Rowton, who erected the first of them in London in 1892.

terrace An Australianism, dating from the 1940s. In Australian English, *terrace* is used literally for 'terrace(d) house'.

Also Australian are:

petrol bowsers A *petrol bowser* was originally a petrol pump in Australian English, taking its name from a US firm that manufactured them, S. F. Bowser & Company, Inc. By the 1940s the word was also being applied to a petrol tanker for refuelling aircraft, tanks, etc. The rhyming slang usage is first recorded (in the frequent shortened form **petrols**) in the chronicles of Barrie Humphries (1971):

> This *randy* Australian bastard passed out cold even before I could get him out of his petrols.

dead wowsers A *wowser* in Australian English is someone who puts a damper on things, a puritanical spoilsport.

Back to Britain for **Callard and Bowsers**, named after a firm manufacturing toffee and other confectionary, and usually shortened to **Callards**.

Pants

The use of *pants* (short for *pantaloons*) for 'trousers' originated in the US in the middle of the 19th century, and has never really transplanted successfully to British English, so *pants*/'trousers' rhymes are mainly American (though with some Australian use too):

fleas and ants Perhaps with a subliminal memory of the 'ants in the pants' notion (not recorded until the 1930s). Another *ant* rhyme sometimes associated with trousers is **insects (and ants)**, but this more commonly refers to underpants (see UNDERWEAR).

uncles and aunts Depending for its rhyme on the American pronunciation of *aunt*, as does the distinctly odd **bull's aunts**, which may be elucidated by a reported Australian rhyming usage of **bull-ants** (literally 'bulldog ants').

song and dance Likewise presupposing US *dance* /dans/.

Jeans

Jeans did not begin to become a universal teenage uniform until the 1950s (although they actually originated in the 19th century). Tinned baked beans had come on the scene in Britain in the 1930s, so a rhyme beckoned. **Baked beans** for *jeans* seems to date from the 1960s (perhaps with half an eye to the cowboy's stereotypical diet and attire as a linking factor), as does the less common but similarly inspired **tin of beans** (when used, generally shortened to **tins**). A different bean came on the scene in the 1970s, in the form of **string beans**—*string bean* being a mainly American term for a bean, such as a French bean or runner bean, whose pods are eaten. Away from the bean scene, **Milton Keynes** (from the name of the Buckinghamshire new town founded in 1967) has done some *jeans* duty in the late 20th century.

Flares

Flares as a term for wide-bottomed trousers—that is, trousers whose legs flare below the knee—came in in the early 1960s, when the garment itself started to become fashionable. The earliest rhyme to catch on seems to have been **Grosvenor Squares**, after the square in southwest central London where the US Embassy is situated (and scene of a notorious anti-Vietnam War protest and riot in 1968). This was soon followed by **Lionel Blairs**, commemorating the British dancer and all-round entertainer of that name (1931–) (who wore his flares with style and who also provided a rhyme for *chair*—see HOUSEHOLD MATTERS). After the 1970s flares became deeply naff, and their rhymes survived only as terms of ridicule. A subsequent comeback coincided with the rise to power of Tony Blair (1953–), British prime minister from 1997, and the temptation was irresistible—**Tony Blairs** it was, or more often **Tonys**:

> 'Ace pair of Tonys', said the cabby to a friend the other evening. 'Eh?' he replied. What the man meant to convey as his appreciation for my friend's pair of flared trousers. The Labour leader has made it into the lexicon of Cockney rhyming slang.
> —*Daily Telegraph* (1994)

Cords

The use of *cords* for 'corduroy trousers' seems to date back to the 18th century, but rhyming slang **House of Lords** is a post-Second World War development.

Bags

harolds Apparently a facetious shortening and alteration of an earlier **Harry Taggs**, which is where the rhyme comes in. **Harry Tagg** was originally theatrical rhyming slang for *bag*, in the luggage sense. It is not clear when trousers entered the equation, but *bags* as a colloquialism in this sense was in vogue between the mid-19th century and the mid-20th century. The identity of Harry Tagg, if such a man ever really existed, is also a mystery.

Strides

Strides as a term for 'trousers' seems to have originated in late 19th-century British criminal slang, but in the 20th century it was particularly prevalent in Australian English. The rhyme **jekyll and hydes** takes its cue, with no particular relevance, from Robert Louis Stevenson's tale of good and evil, *Dr Jekyll and Mr Hyde* (1886). It is regularly curtailed to **jekylls**:

> Is that oil all over your jekylls?
> —Tony Hoare *Minder* (1984)

A late 20th-century alternative is **Herbie Hides**, in honour of the British boxer Herbie Hide (1971–), who held the WBO heavyweight title from 1997 to 1999.

Braces

Until the advent of tight waistbands in the mid-20th century, trousers generally needed external help to keep them up, and most men wore braces. Horse-racing venues lent themselves conveniently to a rhyme: in Britain it was **Epsom races** (from the track in Surrey where the Derby and other classics are run) or **Ascot races** (usually shortened to **Ascots**), in Australia **Flemington races** (from Flemington Racecourse in Melbourne, setting of Australia's premier horserace, the Melbourne Cup). As a non-sporting alternative there was **airs and graces**.

Belt

For the more modern alternative of the belt, there is the rather mysterious Australian **dark felt**.

Flies

From the days of buttons come two rhymes originally used in the singular for the six-legged variety: **meat pies** and **Nellie Blighs** (see ANIMALS).

Gents' Natty Suitings

Suit

whistle and flute One of the most familiar of all pieces of rhyming slang, both in its full form and in its frequent abbreviation **whistle**:

> Half-Nelson lives for clothes. . . He never keeps a whistle more than a month.
> —Allan Prior (1960)

> Here's the money I owe you, and a twoer on top for the whistle that got ruined in yesterday's fracas.
> —Tony Hoare *Minder* (1984)

First recorded in Brophy and Partridge's *Songs and Slang of the British Soldier, 1914–18* (1931), but probably a good deal older than the First World War.

Variations on the *flute* theme include the equally appropriate **piccolo and flute** (the piccolo being the flute's higher-pitched cousin), and the American **fiddle and flute** (first recorded in 1919), branching out alliteratively from the woodwind section. The latter is generally shortened to **fiddle**:

> Hey, you look sharp in the new fiddle.
> —*Boots Malone* (film) (1952)

bag of fruit An American alternative to the flute thing.

Waistcoat

In the heyday of rhyming slang, three-piece suits were the rule, and most men would have worn a waistcoat as a matter of course. No shortage of rhymes for the garment, therefore, but they reflect a strong transatlantic usage split. In Britain, the usual term is *waistcoat*; hence:

Charlie Prescot To 21st-century eyes not a convincing rhyme, but in the 19th century (when it is first recorded) and in the early 20th century *waistcoat* was generally not given its full phonetic value as /ˈweɪstkəʊt/, but eroded to /ˈweskət/ or /ˈweskɪt/. This would have rhymed well enough with *Prescot*. There is no evidence to suggest who Charlie Prescot was, if such a person really existed. The fact that in rhyming slang he has two less-often-heard-of brothers, **Billy Prescot** and **Jim Prescot**, and even a military uncle, **Colonel Prescot**, suggests he was called into being for the sake of his rhyme.

Charlie Prescot is recorded in American English, too, but in North America the more usual term for a waistcoat is *vest*. That is the hook for **east and west**, and also for **Sunday best** (unusually close semantically, but there is no suggestion that the expression is reserved only for one's smartest waistcoat).

Shirts and Collars

Shirt

Dirt is the operative word when it comes to rhyming *shirt*: **dig and dirt**, **dinky dirt**, **roll me in the dirt**, **throw me in the dirt**, and, longest lived of all, **dicky dirt**. An existential comment on the perennial condition of men's and boys' shirts? Perhaps, eventually, but it seems likely that the ultimate starting point of this little word-family was actually not *dirt* but *dicky*.

Dicky (or *dickey*) was familiar from the early years of the 19th century through to the mid-20th century as a term for a detachable shirt front, a now obsolete item of apparel that cut down on laundry bills (His rusty, moth-bedevilled business suiting and wrinkled dicky suggested extremes of dreadful indigence.

Lawrence Durrell *Bitter Lemons* (1957)). It was one of a clutch of similar sartorial uses of *dicky* whose common factor seems to have been 'a covering garment, offering protection rather than for show'. As long ago as the 18th century it was being applied to a woman's petticoat (Of all her splendid apparel not a wreck remained . . . save her flannel dicky, *The Minor; or history of George O'Nial Esq.* (1787)), and it also turns up as the name of various types of aprons and bibs (in 19th-century Yorkshire dialect a leather apron was a plain *dick*—of which more in a moment). There is even an isolated record of *dicky* being used in late 18th-century slang for an entire shirt, albeit a tattered or worn-out one. It has always been assumed that the source of all these *dickies* is the personal name, the pet-form of *Richard*; but given the 'covering' factor and the Yorkshire *dick*, another candidate might be Dutch *dek* 'covering, roof, cloak, horse-blanket' (which is also where English got *deck* from).

So we might imagine a scenario where *dicky* was already a word for a shirt or shirtlike garment, and was transformed into rhyming slang with the alliterative addition of *dirt*. Once established, the first element was open to elaboration and mutation (roll me in the dirt is first recorded as long ago as 1859, in John Hotten's *Dictionary of Modern Slang*). The variants dig and dirt and dinky dirt are recorded in early 20th-century American English.

The one *dirt*-free alternative available is **Uncle Bert**, often shortened to **uncle** (as in 'Where's my clean uncle?'). There are reports of the derived Uncle Bertie being used for *shirty* in the sense 'angry'.

Collar

The impulse to rhyme *collar* faded with the demise of the men's detachable shirt collar. It has not quite died out, but its heyday was the late 19th and early 20th centuries. Probably its most successful manifestation was the curious **holloa, boys, holloa**—virtually an entire sentence, which goes well beyond the usual morphological bounds of rhyming slang formation. It is said to come from a poem attacking the 17th-century would-be regicide Guy Fawkes. Latterly the archaic spelling *holloa* has tended to be replaced by the more up-to-date *holler* (**holler, boys, holler**), which for authenticity's sake is often spelled *'oller*. And in actual usage, the phrase is more than likely to be shortened to **'oller, boys**.

The other main collar-option is **Oxford scholar**, which reportedly never caught on with the working classes, but had some currency in higher social circles. Possibly it was held back by the fact that it was also rhyming slang for *dollar* (five shillings).

Then there is **half-a-dollar**, which apparently dates from the late 19th century. With the habitual dropping of the final element and further phonetic erosion, it generally manifests itself as a Cockney pronunciation of *Arthur*. Nowadays it is used, if at all, mainly with reference to a dog's collar.

Tie

Peckham Rye By far the best established of the rhyming slang versions of *tie*, it dates from the 19th century. It is the name of an area in Peckham, in the southeast London borough of Southwark. The word *rye* comes from Old English *riþe*, meaning 'stream', but Peckham Rye is now a road, and that is probably what the area takes its name from. Nowadays, though, it is most closely associated with a large open space in the area, common land from ancient times, and since the 1890s demarcated and officially designated 'Peckham Rye Common'. All in all a suitable place to be immortalized in London rhyming slang, situated as it is less than three miles southeast of the Elephant and Castle.

pig's fry A culinary reference that betrays its age: *fry* is a now largely superseded term for various internal parts of an animal (liver, pancreas, etc.), or a medley of these, prepared for the table (typically, as the name suggests, by frying). American rhyming slang has the alternative **lamb's fry**, which is usually a specific euphemism for 'lamb's testicles'.

Fourth of July Ostensibly an Americanism (4 July being Independence Day in the USA), but the only evidence of its use is in British English. It first appeared around the First World War period, and the supposition is that it arose from contact with US troops serving in Europe.

And finally, an unusual piece of double rhyming slang, which denotes both collar *and* tie: **swallow and sigh**. It seems to have been mainly used in theatrical patois. One explanation preferred for it is that it is what you do if you are wearing a tight collar and tie.

Pockets and their contents

Pocket

Locket seems a not inappropriate rhyme word for *pocket*—the sort of thing that could easily be slipped into a pocket. Hence **chain and and locket** and **penny locket**, which appear to date from the 19th century. Hence also **Lucy Locket**, after the nursery rhyme character: 'Lucy Locket lost her pocket, Kitty Fisher found it; Not a penny was there in it, Only ribbon round it' (the originals of both Lucy and Kitty were reputedly courtesans of Charles II's time, but the nursery rhyme is not recorded before the first half of the 19th century).

Undoubtedly the most successful *pocket* rhyme, though, is **sky rocket**, first recorded in 1879 and still going strong towards the end of the 20th century:

> Ten trouble-free runs . . . and you're back in England with five thousand quid in your skyrocket.
> —Berkeley Mather, *Snowline* (1973)

In everyday parlance commonly reduced to **sky**, which also dates back to the 19th century:

> Said 'ee found it [i.e. a gun] on the rattler [i.e. the tube train]. Put it in 'is sky when 'ee got off at Leicester Square.
> —Peter Hill *Washermen* (1979)

> I bring you tidings of great joy, Terence. A wedge in your sky, wonga in your wallet.
> —Leon Griffith *Minder* (1979)

> 'One hundred pounds is still one hundred pounds.' 'Not when the price is two hundred pounds, it's not, and certainly not when you've got Liberia's deficit in your sky rocket.'
> —*Lock, Stock, and Two Smoking Barrels* (1998)

Criminals with a professional interest in pockets favoured the term— hence *skyman* 'pickpocket'.

A rival briefly popular in the 1950s was **Davy Crockett**, from the name of the celebrated US frontiersman (1786–1836). It undoubtedly took its cue from the 1956 Walt Disney film *Davy Crockett, King of the Wild Frontier*, which was heavily promoted, with a range of tie-in products (notably a fake coonskin hat), and provoked a short-lived craze.

An old word for 'pocket' (and one with a shared ancestry) is *poke*, and this was rhymed as **Barney Moke**. It was mainly a pickpockets' term, and actually more often denoted 'wallet' than 'pocket'.

Handkerchief

In the mid-19th century, a *handkerchief* was colloquially an /ˈaŋkətʃə/, so the contemporary rhyming slang **Charley Lancaster** (from an unknown original) fitted better than it seems to to modern eyes. In the 20th century, Australian English took up the theme with **Jackie Lancashire**.

The abbreviation of *handkerchief* to *hanky* appears to have happened around the end of the 19th century, and a rhyme was waiting for it in the form of **Widow Twankey**, from the name of the washerwoman and hero's mother in the pantomime *Aladdin* (traditionally played by a man). Generally shortened to **widow**.

Women's dresses

Dress

Women's outer clothing goes largely ignored by rhyming slangsters, but *dress* has yielded **more or less**—based, it has been claimed, on the idea that you see more or less depending on the current fashion in hemlines and décolletage. Less common has been **Daily Express**, from the name of the British daily newspaper.

Frock

From the late 19th century to roughly the middle of the 20th century, a woman's dress was generally a *frock* in British English, and this found its rhyme in **almond rock**—previously, and much more commonly, used for *sock*.

Bustle

The bustle, a pad or framework artificially expanding the proportions of the female posterior, was fashionable in the middle years of the 19th century, which coincides with the public career of Lord John Russell (1792–1878), British prime minister 1846–52 and 1865–6. He had the dubious privilege of eponymizing this prosthesis as the **Lord John Russell** (first recorded in 1859), or more casually the **Johnny Russell**.

Underwear

To begin in the nether regions: rhyming slang, moving with the times, accommodates swiftly changing usage in this area—from the *bloomers* and *drawers* of the 19th and early 20th centuries to the *knickers* of the later 20th, taking in *pants* on the way:

Bloomers

The image is strictly knee-length and impenetrable, and if the rhyming slang survives, it is only in facetious use: there is **Montezumas**, after the last emperor of the Aztecs, and also the rather racier **wicked rumours**.

Drawers

Similarly at the functional rather than the glamorous end of the spectrum. In the 19th century the rhyme was **early doors**. Australian English produced **Maggie Moores** (usually **Maggies** for short) in the 20th century, and in Britain in the 1950s there was an irresistible urge to rhyme **Diana Dors**, the curvaceous blonde (1931–84) who was the British answer to Marilyn Monroe (she also figured in similarly inspired children's rhymes of the period: 'Diana Dors has no drawers, Will you kindly lend her yours?'; there is no evidence that her real surname, Fluck, has been exploited for rhyming slang purposes).

Knickers

Alan Whicker (1925–), the roving British televison reporter with the suave moustache and the distinctive nasal twang, can hardly have expected to be immortalized as a word for women's underpants, but so it is: **Alan Whickers**, familiar enough to be often shortened to **Alans**. Less commonly heard is the much put-upon **Bill Stickers**, who began life as a paster-up of posters, but became personalized via the frequently encountered warning 'Bill stickers will be prosecuted'.

Clickety-clicks, exploiting existing rhyming slang clickety-click for *six*, takes care of the shortened form *knicks* (which itself dates back to the late 19th century).

Underpants

As with *pants* = 'trousers', *ants* figures strongly in *underpants* rhymes, and with perhaps an even more marked suggestion of 'ants in the pants'. Both **insects and ants** and **beetles and ants** are 20th-century coinages (*pants* did not begin to be used for underwear in the modern sense until the 20th century), and both are commonly abbreviated—to **insects** and **beetles**.

On the upper part of the body, one may feel the need of a vest to keep out the chill—not to be confused with *vest* = 'waistcoat', which is the favoured interpretation in US English (see **WAISTCOAT**). *Vest* rhymes all have a dated air, reflecting an earlier age of universal vest-wearing; the *bra* rhyme, on the other hand, could scarcely be more up to date. It is all on its own, though, and together with a solitary rhyme for *stays* emphasizes yet again the marginalization of women's concerns in the world of rhyming slang:

Vest

Brig's rest Applied mainly to the extremely itchy and comfortless undergarment supplied to inmates of HM Prisons in the early years of the 20th century: usually cited with a capital *B*, but there is no hint of a real person behind the name—more likely it comes from *brig* 'military or naval prison'; *rest* is probably an ironic reference to the lack of it when wearing the garment in bed.

little grey home in the West Much used among troops in the trenches and elsewhere during the First World War. It is the title of a song, lyrics by Wilmot D. Eardley and music by Hermann Löhr, which was a hit in 1911.

Wild West A term for the lawless frontier of the western US since the middle of the 19th century.

Bra

ooh la la The suggestion of French naughtiness gives away the rhyme's age—not one for the 21st century.

Roseanne Barr From the American actress (1952–) who starred in her own TV comedy series *Roseanne* (first broadcast in 1988). Her generous bosom adds point to the rhyme.

Stays

Bryant and Mays Back to the days when whalebone and laces provided an engineering solution for the elegant management of the female form. This type of corset found its rhyme in the name of a celebrated British firm of match manufacturers, responsible among other brands for 'Swan Vestas'.

And to finish up with, a general term:

Undies

Eddie Grundies Eddie Grundy provides the comic relief in the BBC radio soap opera *The Archers*, and over the years has become something of a folk hero.

Reg Grundies An Australian rhyme, celebrating the television producer Reg Grundy (1924–), who was responsible for, among other gems, the soap opera *Neighbours*. Commonly abbreviated to **grundies**, **reginalds**, or **reggies**:

> One night after a big day on the grog, Arthur has got out of bed and walked out onto the balcony dressed in his Reg Grundies.
> —M. Colman *In a League of their Own* (1994)

Pyjamas

panoramas One of the relatively small class of single-word rhyming slang, and reportedly used mainly in the context of chivvying children into bed. Perhaps based on the BBC television current-affairs programme *Panorama* rather than on any general concept of a wide view.

Footwear

Boots

In the 19th and early 20th centuries the boot was as salient an item of footwear as the shoe, and received a lot of attention from early rhyming slangers: **German flutes** dates from the mid-19th century and apparently continued in use in the US into the 20th century (**piccolos and flutes** is a rarely heard variant on the same rhyme).

King Canutes seems to have enjoyed some currency in the early 20th century; while the obsolete **Burdett Coutts** commemorates the name of the philanthropist Baroness Burdett Coutts (1814–1906), amongst whose largesse was the handing out of free boots to the deserving but bootless poor.

daisy roots Undoubtedly the most durable *boot*-rhyme has been **daisy roots**, first recorded in 1859 and still recognized if not much actively used at the end of the 20th century. It came to wider attention in the Lonnie Donegan song 'My Old Man's a Dustman' (a hit in Britain in 1960), which offered a rationale for the rhyme: . . . He's got such a job to pull them up that he calls them daisy roots. The term was exported to the US, Australia, and South Africa, and in the early 20th century sometimes apparently metamorphosed mysteriously to **daisy recruits** (or **recroots**). In practice it has often been applied to shoes as well as strictly boots.

> Your toes is poking out of your daisy-roots.
> —*Gen* (1943)

Shoes

Shoes themselves have been just as enthusiastically rhymed, and amongst the offerings have been **how d'you dos** (dating from the mid-19th century), **canoes** (usually connoting capacious shoes for the larger foot), **five to twos** (perhaps with a glance at the angle of a standing person's feet), **one and twos** (first recorded in the 1920s, and often shortened to **ones**), **Ps and Qs** (commandeering the earlier phrase denoting politely conventional behaviour), **bottles of booze**, **rhythm and blues**, and **St Louis blues** (often shortened to **St Louis**).

Slippers

The threesome of standard 19th- and early 20th-century footwear is completed by the homely slipper. **Pair of kippers** (or simply **kippers**) evokes two down-at-heel slippers side by side, but its olfactory connotations are less than flattering. The early 20th-century **Jack the Rippers** (later revived as **Yorkshire rippers**) was applied to the slipper mainly in its role as an instrument of corporal punishment at school and in the home. **Yankee clippers** (from *clipper* 'sailing vessel') probably exploits the boatlike shape of slippers (compare **canoes** for 'shoes').

Sandals

Sandals have been **Roman candles** (often **Romans** for short, which picks up on the image of the thonged sandal of Classical times) and, when the name was still widely recognized, **Harry Randalls**, commemorating a British music-hall comedian of the late 19th and early 20th centuries.

Trainers

Trainers are late arrivals at the heel-bar, but already they have inspired **struggle-and-strainers** (recalling the effect of exercise on their wearers) and the more prosaic **tea-strainers**. The eponymous **Claire Rayners**, inspired by the well-known British journalist and agony aunt Claire Rayner (1931–), is first recorded in 1997. (The subjects' response to becoming rhyming slang is rarely known, but Rayner is on record as taking 'an atavistic pride in having entered Cockney rhyming slang' (*The Times* (2001).) Also reported in use is **Gloria Gaynors**, from the name of the popular American singer Gloria Gaynor (1947–), best known for her 1979 hit 'I Will Survive'.

Hosiery

Stockings

reelings and rockings A coinage of the 1950s, when not the least of the attractions of the new rock 'n' roll for male onlookers was the extensive glimpses of stocking afforded by the female dancers' pirouettes. The inspiration was Chuck Berry's hit song 'Reelin' and Rockin' (1958).

Silas Hockings A theatrical usage of the early 20th century, based on the name of the now long-forgotten author Silas Hocking (1850–1935). At the turn of the 20th century he was reputedly the biggest-selling novelist in Britain.

Socks

Rocks is the mainstay of *socks* rhymes, appearing in combinations both logical and bizarre. The best established is **almond rocks** (from the name of a type of sweetmeat popular in the latter part of the 19th century), habitually shortened to **almonds**. **Peppermint rocks** carries on the confectionary theme. A variation on it was **army rocks**, where *almond* became *army* to denote specifically army-issue socks during the First World War, and the same articles sold and worn as war-surplus for many years afterwards. The name-like forms **Bobby Rocks** (Australian), **Charlie Rocks** (American), and **Joe Rocks** (Australian) were probably a response to bafflement at almond rocks.

Other *socks* rhymes:

curly locks Another Australianism (Australians seem fond of rhyming *socks*), exploiting an established cliché.

Oscar Hocks An American alternative, first recorded in the 1920s. The identity of Oscar Hock has not survived:

> 'Oscar Hocks. Oscar Hocks.' Clean socks every night.
> —Malcolm Braly *It's Cold out There* (1966)

Tilbury Docks Tilbury Docks, on the north bank of the Thames in Essex, opened in 1886, and by the end of the 20th century were London's main port, the docks in 'Dockland' having all closed. They might seem to provide a natural East End rhyme, but in fact it was the Navy that took the term up with enthusiasm (perhaps Tilbury was too much of a rival for London dockers to domesticate it). It was reportedly popular with the London Fire Brigade in the first half of the 20th century, but thereafter gradually went out of use— handicapped, no doubt, by the fact that Tilbury Docks is also rhyming slang for *pox* (i.e. VD) (see ILLNESS). (The same disability applies to **Nervo and Knox** (see ILLNESS), which originally, in the 1940s, was a rhyme for *socks*.)

Tights

It is the women's garment, called into being in the 1960s when stockings could not cope with what the miniskirt revealed, that has attracted rhymes, not the earlier unisex theatrical garment favoured by ballet dancers and Shakespearian gents: hence, both from the 1970s, **fly-by-nights** (from the earlier *fly-by-night* 'nocturnal decamper, dubious operator') and **Snow Whites** (from the winsome Grimm/Disney heroine, and apparently with no restriction as to the colour of the tights).

Spats

Spats, short gaiters worn by men to protect their shoes from mud, were essentially a 19th- and early 20th-century phenomenon, and their rhymes are but a memory:

thises and thats First recorded in the first decade of the 20th century, but long since obsolete.

Wanstead Flats From the name of an open area, 113 acres in extent, between Wanstead and Forest Gate in East London, originally the southernmost portion of Epping Forest.

Assorted Accessories

Gloves

turtle doves First recorded in the 1850s, and well enough established to be usually used (in the days when gloves were a standard component of everyday outerwear, not just an extra for especially cold days) in the shortened form **turtles**

> 'Turtle doves' for gloves, and so on, normally associated with cockneys, is neither confined to the metropolis, nor to the shift-for-a-living class.
> —Iona and Peter Opie, *The Lore and Language of Schoolchildren* (1959)

Scarf

Half is a straightforward rhyme for *scarf*, and it turns up in **half and half** and **one and (a) half** (the indefinite article is commonly elided in speech). Written examples often come the Cockney with *arf* instead of *half*. As an alternative there is **tin bath**, frequently shortened to **tin** (in which guise it reportedly often forms a pair with **titfer** as necessary gear when braving the cold outside); it relies, of course, on the 'Cockney' pronunciation of *bath* as /bɑːf/. All the rhymes seem to cover the full *scarf* spectrum, from the working man's muffler to the silkiest ladies' head-covering.

Umbrella

The umbrella inspires rhymes with female names—perhaps coined by females, since the stereotypical male rhymer, being a simple working man, scorns to carry one. The oldest is **Isabella**, first recorded in the mid-19th century. In the 20th century, *Ella* came into favour, although the family relationship was uncertain: it could be **Aunt Ella** or **Cousin Ella**.

Button

leg of mutton From the days when mutton (rather than mutton dressed up as 'lamb') still featured regularly on the English diet. Ray Puxley in his *Cockney Rabbit* (1992) notes the comic potential of the frequent abbreviation **leg**, as in 'Mum, my leg's come off, can you sew it back on for me?'

An alternative version in US slang is **hook of mutton**, a mysterious phrase whose underlying meaning has never been satisfactorily deconstructed.

Len Hutton After Yorkshire and England opening batsman Sir Leonard Hutton (1916–90), who became something of an icon after making the then world record Test score of 364 against Australia at the Oval in 1938.

Jewellery

tomfoolery First recorded in 1931, and remaining tenaciously in use since then—mainly amongst those who make a profession of trying to steal jewels. Its shortened form **tom** (first recorded in 1955) has cut itself free from its rhyming roots and become part of standard British underworld slang:

> I wouldn' be surprised if you both done a stretch fer knockin' orf some ole bloke's tom-foolery.
> —Michael Harrison *Reported Safe Arrival* (1943)

> What d'you do with the tom and money you had out of Manor Gardens this afternoon?
> —G. F. Newman *Sir, You Bastard* (1970)

> Once inside a house they go straight to the master bedroom. 'You turn it over hunting for the Tom.'
> —*Sunday Times* (1999)

A ring

Frank Thring An Australian rhyme of the 1970s, often applied specifically to a wedding ring.

ting-a-ling Like its cousin *ding-a-ling*, in non-rhyming slang a euphemism for *penis*.

A diamond

Simple Simon From the hero of the nursery rhyme 'Simple Simon met a pieman, going to the fair'. First recorded in US rhyming slang, in 1928. Generally applied to a diamond set in a ring:

> I do not see any Simple Simon on your lean and linger.
> —Damon Runyon *Cosmopolitan* (1929)

Money and Commerce

As an argot of the street and of markets, rhyming slang is in constant touch with buying and selling and doing deals, and over the past century and a half it has built up an impressive vocabulary of money. The effects of inflation have made themselves felt, though. In the 19th century and the first two-thirds of the 20th century, pre-decimal days in Britain, humble shillings and pennies and even subdivisions of pennies were not to be sneezed at, and all had their rhymes. By the end of the 20th century, however, it was much higher amounts that were attracting slang—*Hawaii* for '£50', for example (from the 1970s US television detective series *Hawaii-Five 0*), and *Placido* for '£10' (almost an example of rhyming slang at one remove: it's short for *Placido Domingo*, the name of the celebrated Spanish operatic tenor, but *tenor* for *tenner* scarcely merits the description 'rhyme')—and where slang went, rhyming slang was not slow to follow.

Money

No great insight into human nature is needed to account for the prevalence of *honey* as a rhyme word for *money*: over the years it has cropped up in **bread and honey** (probably not the source of the originally US slang *bread* for 'money', which seems to have been suggested by *dough* 'money'), **pot of honey**, **sugar and honey** (often shortened to **sugar**), and simply **honey** (US slang, first recorded in 1859 and surviving into the 20th century: I drew the honey from his poke [= wallet]. A. H. Lewis *Confessions* (1906)). Easily the most successful and long-lived, though, has been **bees and honey**, first recorded in 1892 and keeping going well into the late 20th century:

> D'you reckon we'd waste good bees and honey on a slump like you for nothing.
> —Jeffrey Ashford *Counsel for the Defence* (1960)

Honey does not hold a monopoly, though:

Bugs Bunny From the Warner Bros. cartoon rabbit of that name, who first appeared on screen in 1940. The rhyme appeared in the 1950s, and is often shortened to **Bugs** or **Bugsy**.

Gene Tunney A New Zealand rhyme of the 1960s, based on the name of the US heavyweight boxer Gene Tunney (1898–1978).

tom and funny In use in Britain in the 19th century, but in the 20th it survived only in South African English.

Rather more versatile in its rhymes is *cash*:

Arthur Ashe Based on the name of the black US tennis player Arthur Ashe (1943–93), Wimbledon men's singles champion in 1975. A rhyme reputedly favoured by secondhand-car dealers.

bangers and mash A colloquial alternative to sausage and mash:

> She [Martine McCutcheon] landed the part [of Eliza Doolittle in *My Fair Lady*] and, in the argot of her origins, went from being boracic lint to having some bangers and mash.
> —*Sunday Times* (2001)

dot and dash A rhyme of the 1950s and 1960s, from the short and long signals used in the Morse Code system.

Henry Nash If there was a real Henry Nash, his identity has not survived.

Knotty Ash A 1980s rhyme, based on Knotty Ash, the district of Liverpool immortalized in the comic world of Ked Dodd (for the relevance to money, see KEN DODD below).

oak and ash Reputedly originally theatrical slang.

Oscar Asche An Australian and New Zealand rhyme, based on the name of the Australian actor Oscar Asche (1871–1936) and first recorded in 1905:

> Billee Hughes will pay zee Oscar Asche.
> —*Rising Sun* (Melbourne) (1929)

It has long since died out, but its shortened form **Oscar** (first recorded in 1917) remained in circulation towards the end of the 20th century:

> I can do with the oscar, but I don't know if I can draw any more photos.
> —Barry Humphries *Bazza Pulls it Off* (1971)

pie and mash Ray Puxley in *Cockney Rabbit* (1992) reports that 'in the cab and courier industry a "pie and mash job" is a fare or job that is not on account'.

sausage and mash A rhyme dating from the late 19th century. Often shortened to **sausage** (and as such functioning as a verb as well as a noun—see *goose's neck* at CHEQUE), and it has been speculated that that lies behind the expression *not a sausage* 'nothing at all'. However, the earliest recorded examples of the phrase (from the 1930s) have no particular connection with money.

smash First recorded in the mid-19th century, and perhaps owing something to the earlier non-rhyming slang *smash* 'counterfeit money'.

Other slang or colloquial synonyms for *money* to have been rhymed include: *dosh*, a term of American origin revived in British English towards the end of the 20th century and rhymed in the 1990s as **rogan josh** (**rogan** for short), after the popular Indian takeaway dish, or as **orange squash**; *dough*, a long-standing colloquialism, which became **cod's roe**; *loot*, rhymed in the mid-20th century as **whistle and toot** (often shortened to **toot**, an unusual case of abbreviation by removal of the initial element—perhaps due to competition from whistle = whistle and flute 'suit'); *readies*, standing for 'ready cash in the form of banknotes', and first recorded in the 1930s, which ties in chronologically with the rhyme **Nelson Eddies**, after the popular American singer Nelson Eddy (1901–67) who starred in many films of that period; *screw* 'wages', rhymed in Australian English as **kangaroo**, but much more commonly encountered in the shortened form **kanga**, first recorded in 1969 (Your daughter's got a bit of kanga, but, hasn't she? . . . Kanga? . . . Cash. That's what they say in the bush. E. Hanger *2D and Other Plays* (1978)); and *wad*, a term for a bundle of banknotes which was popularized in the more general sense 'money' in the late 1980s by the Harry Enfield character 'Loadsamoney', and which found a rhyme in **Ken Dodd**, after the zany Liverpudlian comedian Ken Dodd (1931–), who made a connection with money in the public imagination when he got into difficulties with the Inland Revenue.

British Currency

A farthing

One quarter of an old penny, in circulation in Britain until 1961. Its antiquity shows up in its rhyme, **Covent Garden** (from the fruit, vegetable, and flower market formerly in the centre of London), which relies on the long defunct pronunciation /ˈfɑːdən/.

A halfpenny

In the 19th century, copper coins were known in British slang as *browns*. The rhymes based on this seem to have been applied mainly to the halfpenny, although there was some use for 'penny' as well. Chief among these was **Camden Town**, the name of the North London borough which, when the rhyme is first recorded in the 1850s, was already a fairly well built-up suburb. A less common alternative was **Kentish Town**, from the area just to the north of Camden Town which likewise was thoroughly incorporated into London by the middle of the 19th century. Both were commonly shortened to **town**.

A penny

Abergavenny A 19th-century rhyme, based on the name of the town on the edge of the Brecon Beacons in South Wales.

Jack Benny Commemorating the American comedian Jack Benny (1894–1974), who built stinginess and penny-pinching into his comic persona.

Kilkenny A late 19th-century rhyme, based on the name of the city and county in Leinster, in the Republic of Ireland.

Reginald Denny A rhyme current in the 1940s and 1950s, from the name of the British film actor Reginald Denny (1891–1967).

All the above related to pre-decimalization, 240-to-the-pound, 'old' pennies, and the same goes for the various rhymes based on slang synonyms for *penny*: *copper*, which produced the rhyme **clodhopper**; *stiver*, a term of Dutch origin dating from the 18th century, which was the basis of **coal-heaver**, usually shortened to **heaver**; and the mysterious *win*, used for 'penny' between the mid-16th century and the early 20th century, which was rhymed as **nose and chin**. See also *brown* at **A HALFPENNY**.

Twopence

In the slang of the late 17th, 18th, and early 19th centuries, 'twopence' was *deuce*. This was often rhymed as a **bottle of spruce** (spruce, or spruce beer, being a sort of beer-like drink made from the leaves and twigs of the spruce tree, which cost around twopence a bottle).

Threepence

Australian slang of the 20th century used *trey* (or *trey-bit*) for a 'threepenny coin' (it was based on the gamblers' word *trey* for 'three'). This inspired a trio of Aussie rhymes based on the surname *Gray*: **Alma Gray**; **Dolly Gray** (first recorded around the time of the First World War, and no doubt based on the name of the heroine of a song popular among soldiers at that time, 'Goodbye Dolly, I must leave you'); and **Dora Gray**.

In Britain in the 19th century, *threepence* was often worn down to *thrums*, and that was rhymed as **currants and plums**.

Fourpence

In the underworld cant of the late 16th century the sum of fourpence (for which a coin existed at that time—a groat) was termed a *flag* (that may have come from Middle Low German *vleger*, the name of a coin of low denomination). It survived into the 19th century, no doubt given a boost by the fact that fourpenny coins were again minted in Britain between 1836 and 1856, and around that time the rhyme **castle rag** was coined for it.

Sixpence

The sixpence's affectionate nickname *tanner* is the basis of most of its rhymes:

Goddess Diana A mid-19th-century rhyme, after the Roman goddess Diana, virgin huntress. Despite efforts to preserve it, *tanner* didn't survive long enough after the 1971 decimalization of British currency to inherit the rhyme that was surely awaiting it, **Princess Diana**.

lord of the manor Dating from the middle of the 19th century, and in use until the demise of the sixpence, usually in the shortened form **lord**.

sprasi Anna A curious formation which combines a rhyme on *tanner* with an entirely different slang term for 'sixpence', *sprasi*.

tartan banner In use in the first two-thirds of the 20th century.

Australian and New Zealand slang for 'sixpence', *zac* (perhaps from Scottish *saxpence*), produced the rhyme **hammer and tack** (often **hammer** for short).

A British colloquialism for 'sixpence' was **kick**, usually used in combination with shilling amounts (thus 'two and a kick' was two shillings and sixpence). First recorded in the street argot of the early 18th century, this was not conventional rhyming slang, but no doubt phonetic similarity played a part in its development.

A shilling

Abraham's willing Recorded in the mid-19th century, but it didn't survive into the 20th.

I'm willing A 20th-century successor to the previous entry.

John Dillon A New Zealand rhyme of the 1930s, based on the name not of a person but of a race-horse.

potato pillin A coinage of the 1930s, representing a rather desperate attempt to shoehorn *peeling* into a rhyme with *shilling*. A more 'Cockneyfied' version was **tater pillin**.

rogue and villain Probably the most widespread of *shilling*-rhymes, first recorded in 1859 and still around when the shilling disappeared in 1971:

> Come, cows and kisses, put the battle of the Nile on your Barnet Fair, and a rogue and villain in your sky-rocket.
> —J. W. Horsley *Jottings from Jail* (1877)

Thomas Tilling A rhyme of the 1920s and 30s, based on the name of a firm running buses and coaches. Often **Thomas** for short.

Colloquially, a shilling was usually a *bob* (the word dates from the late 18th century), and that had its share of rhymes too:

doorknob Current in the late 19th and early 20th centuries.

kettle on the hob Dating from the late 19th century, and often abbreviated to **kettle**. It also serves as a rhyme for the male first name *Bob*.

one for his nob From an expression used in the card game cribbage, denoting an extra point for holding the jack of the up-turned suit.

touch me on the nob or **touch my nob** A 19th-century rhyme, presumably exploiting *nob* 'penis', which was extant at that time (the 20th-century version *knob* has also been imported into the rhyme). In its pared-down form **touch me** it survived well into the middle of the 20th century.

In Australian and New Zealand slang, a shilling used to be a *deener* (an adoption from British slang, and probably ultimately from Latin *denarius*).

This was rhymed from the 1920s to the 1960s as **riverina**, from the name of a district in southern New South Wales.

Half a crown

In Australian English, the *half* of *half a crown* (the sum of two shillings and sixpence) was rhymed as **poddy calf**, which means literally 'a hand-fed calf'.

Five shillings

In the mid-19th century, when there were four US dollars to the pound sterling, five shillings came to be known in British slang as a *dollar*. This formed the basis of two rhymes: **shirt and collar** (sometimes **shirt collar**), which was in use from around the 1850s to the 1930s (there's no evidence it has any connection with *lose your shirt* 'to lose all your money on a bet'); and **Oxford scholar** (**Oxford** for short), first recorded in 1937 but reportedly in use in Southwest England as far back as the 1870s:

> 'We'll say a quid deposit, returnable on return of the hat, and a straight charge of an Oxford for the loan. Right?' 'Right.' The young man handed over his Oxford scholar.
> —Anthony Burgess *The Doctor is Sick* (1960)

In Australia and New Zealand after the decimalization of the currency, Oxford scholar was applied to a literal *dollar*.

Ten shillings

In mid-20th-century British slang, ten shillings (half of a pound) was a *half*, which proved more amenable to rhyming than *ten shillings*:

cow and calf Probably the original form, but soon joined by **cow's calf**. That was generally shortened to **cow's**, and plain **calf** was also used.

shower bath *Bath* pronounced /bɑːf/, of course; but it was usually omitted anyway, and **showers** (with the additional *s*) used on its own. A favourite of the racecourse fraternity.

Rhymes based simply on *ten* were **Big Ben** and **cock and hen** (see *Ten* at **NUMBERS**).

A pound

The word *pound* itself has been rhymed with **hole in the ground** (generally shortened to **hole**); **lost and found** (previously used for 'ten pounds'—see *lost and found* at **TEN POUNDS**); and **merry-go-round** (usually just **merry**). A more important and fruitful source of rhymes, though, is the colloquial synonym *quid*:

fiddley-did An Australian rhyme, first recorded in 1941, and often shortened to **fiddley**:

He would like to be home right now, putting a couple of fiddleydids on a little horse.
—R. Bielby *Gunner* (1977)

saucepan lid First recorded in 1951. Usually plain **saucepan**.

teapot lid Usually shortened to **teapot**.

yid An Australian rhyme of the early years of the 20th century. An unusually brief coinage, but perhaps the stereotyped connection between Jews and money gave extra impetus to its use. Its frequent transformation to **yit** or **yitt** might betray a measure of guilty conscience about its use. Often in *half a yid* = 'ten shillings'.

Some other rhymed *pound* synonyms: *nicker*, which in the 1930s produced **cow's licker** (the usual process of abbreviation was blocked by cow's 'ten shillings'—see *cow and calf* at TEN SHILLINGS); and simply *one* (for *one pound*), rhymed in late 19th-century Australian English as **John Dunn**.

From the days when pounds were *sovereigns* comes the rhyme **Jimmy O'Goblin** (or **Jemmy O'Goblin**). First recorded in theatrical slang at the end of the 19th century, it survived well into the 20th, and came to mean simply 'pound':

> He had won five Jimmy-o-goblins at ten to three at Chester.
> —Evelyn Waugh *A Handful of Dust* (1934)

> Her first husband left her half a million. Yes, sir, five hundred thousand jimmy o'goblins.
> —C. Smith *The Deadly Reaper* (1956)

In the past it was often shortened to **O'Goblin** (Come now, your Grand Grace, is it a deal? Four hundred and fifty chinking o'Goblins a week for one hall a night. P. G. Wodehouse *Swoop* (1909)), and in Australia to **Jim** (The racehorse they have just bought in Bourke for fifty jim. A. E. Yarra *Vanishing Horsemen* (1930)).

Four pounds

Backslang for *four* is *rouf*, or *roaf*—hence the rhyme **French loaf**. In its more conventional form, *four* is sometimes rhymed as **dirty whore** (see *Four* at NUMBERS).

Five pounds

The standard colloquialism *fiver* gets the lion's share of the rhymes: **deep-sea diver** (a coinage of the 1970s); **Lady Godiva** (after the 11th-century wife of Earl Leofric who rode naked through the streets of Coventry to persuade her husband to lower taxes); and **sky diver** (literally, 'a parachutist').

There are plenty of alternatives, though: **half a cock** (*cock* is short for cock and hen—see at TEN POUNDS); **Lincoln's Inn** (a late 19th-century rhyme based on slang *fin* 'a fiver' (which probably came, via Yiddish, from German *fünf* 'five'), and taking the name of one of the Inns of Court in central London); **Tiny Tim** (based on *flim* 'a fiver', and inspired by the tear-jerking invalid boy in Dickens's *A Christmas Carol*); **man alive** (rhyming with *five*); and, most influential of all, **Jack's alive** (also rhymed on *five*), long defunct itself but preserved since the 1950s in assorted shortened forms—**jack**, **jacks**, and **jax**:

> 'That one,' says the dealer from Islington, 'that one we know she died in; so it'll cost you a jax.' . . . Five quid for a shroud; cheap at the price.
> —*Guardian* (1968)

> 'Couldn't lend me a Jack's, Terry, could you?' 'Sure.' He gave the DS a fiver.
> —G. F. Newman *Sir, you Bastard* (1970)

> From under a pottery sugar jar . . . protruded two jacks.
> —Kenneth Royce *The Miniatures Frame* (1972)

Ten pounds

In the 19th century, **lost and found** stood for 'ten pound'. That has long since died out, although the rhyme was revived in the 20th century for a single *pound* (see at A POUND). Roughly contemporary were **Big Ben** and **cock and hen**, rhyming on *ten* (see *Ten* at NUMBERS). Tenners were perhaps rare enough until the late 20th century not to inspire a rhyme, but rhymers made up for it in the 1990s with **Ayrton Senna** (**Ayrton** for short), based on the name of the Brazilian racing driver Ayrton Senna (1960–94).

Twenty pounds

Colloquially, twenty pounds is a *score*, which in rhyming slang becomes an **apple core** (a coinage of the 1950s) or a **Charlie Clore** (based on the name of the British financier Charles Clore (1904–79), who in the 1960s became a byword for vast wealth).

Twenty-five pounds

Pony is long-standing slang for 'twenty-five pounds', and in the mid-19th century it was rhymed as **macaroni**.

A thousand pounds

Bulging salaries in the City of London in the 1980s necessitated frequent references to *grand*, slang for 'a thousand pounds', which was insouciantly rhymed as **bag of sand** (**bag** for short).

Change

home on the range An Australian rhyme, quoting a line from the popular American song 'Give me a Home where the Buffalo Roam': 'Home, home on the range, where the deer and the antelope play'. It was written in the early

1870s, the words probably by Brewster Higley and the music probably by Dan Kelly, and it's now the state song of Kansas.

kitchen range A rhyme from the early part of the 20th century, when kitchen ranges—a type of multiple cooking stove—were still in use.

Finance

A bank

The favourite *bank* rhyming word is *tank*: **iron tank**—expressive of impregnability; **shovel and tank**—recalling the days when bank tellers had little shovels for gathering up coins; and—the oldest of the trio—**tin tank**. To put alongside these are the long obsolete **chain and crank**; **J. Arthur Rank**, popular enough for a while to be shortened to **Arthur**, but driven out of use by a less respectable application of the rhyme (see *J. Arthur Rank* at MASTURBATION); and **rattle and clank**.

A cheque

Assorted birds' necks have been popular with rhyming slangsters when it comes to cheques: **chicken's neck**, **duck's neck**, and—most widely used— **goose's neck** (popular enough to be shortened to **goose's**—to cash a cheque in rhyming slang is to *sausage a goose's* (see *sausage and mash* at MONEY)). Another favoured *neck*-rhyme is **pain in the neck**, often abbreviated to **pain**.

Some alternatives to *neck*:

Duke of Teck, and his wife the **Duchess of Teck**. Generally shortened to **duke** and **duchess** respectively. Prince Francis of Teck was a member of the royal house of Württemburg. In 1866 he married Princess Mary Adelaide, first cousin of Queen Victoria, and in 1871 he was created Duke of Teck in the British aristocracy. Their daughter Mary became queen consort of George V.

Gregory Peck Dating from the 1950s, and in frequent use throughout the rest of the 20th century, often in the shortened form **Gregory**. After the US film actor Gregory Peck (1916–).

total wreck In use in America and Australia in the mid-20th century.

A loan

Darby and Joan In use in Australia from the 1940s. From the name of the archetypal old married couple, who first put in an appearance in an 18th-century ballad.

To borrow

Rhymed as **tomorrow**, implying a fatalistic or cynical attitude to the probable day of repayment. Someone who is *on the tom* is trying to cadge money. There are a couple of colloquial alternatives to *borrow*. *Tap* (as in 'tap someone for a fiver') has been rhymed as **Andy Capp** (from the name of the strip-cartoon character, a put-upon, virulently politically incorrect, flat-cap-wearing working man, invented by Reg Smythe in 1956 and featuring regularly thereafter in the *Daily Mirror*); as **cellar flap** (an early 20th-century rhyme); and as **rip rap** (first recorded in the 1930s). Like **tomorrow**, the last of these has been nominalized—a borrower is *on the rip-rap*. To *cadge* is to **coat and badge**, a mid-19th-century rhyme inspired by *Doggett's Coat and Badge*, the name of a prize awarded to the winner of an annual rowing race for Thames watermen (again, turned into a noun—a borrower is *on the C and B*).

Credit

In Australian slang, someone who bets on credit is betting *on the* **Murray cod**—a rhyme on *on the nod*. A Murray cod is a type of large freshwater fish that lives in the Murray River in southeastern Australia.

Wages

greengages First recorded in 1931, and often shortened to **greens** (which was already in circulation as slang for 'money'):

> The money? Greengages we call it, greengages–wages. You'll be surprised. In a lot of places it's a fiver a night.
> —*Guardian* (1964)

rock of ages First recorded in 1937, and based on the words of the hymn 'Rock of Ages, cleft for me' (1776) by Augustus Montague Toplady. Often contracted to **rocks**:

> If there's no *rock of ages* (wages), there may well be a *bull an' cow* (row).
> —Peter Wright *The Language of British Industry* (1974)

In Australian English, the alternative term *pay* is rhymed with **Zane Grey**, after Zane Grey (1875–1939) the writer of western fiction (including *Riders of the Purple Sage*).

An advance on wages is colloquially termed a *sub*, which gets rhymed as either **rhubarb** (reflecting a former 'Cockney' pronunciation /ˈrʌbʌb/) or **rub-a-dub**.

Tax

beeswax Usually applied to income tax, no doubt with a nod to the rhyme bees and honey 'money'.

sealing wax The Australian version of the rhyme.

Rates

garden gates The portal of the Englishman's home and castle on which these exactions were made in the days before Council Tax.

Shares

Rupert Bears A coinage of the 1980s, based on the cartoon bear who appeared in a comic strip in the *Daily Express* from 1920. Often shortened to **Ruperts**, which may conjure up for some the stereotypical upper-middle-class stock broker.

Pawn

bullock's horn A late 19th-century rhyme which didn't survive long into the 20th century. Almost always shortened to **bullock's**.

Commerce

A shop

Mrs Mopp A coinage of the 1940s, based on the character Mrs Mopp, a cleaner, in the BBC radio comedy programme *ITMA* of that decade. By extension, *shopping* was **Mrs Mopping**.

A customer

In the world of rhyming slang, customers are generally *punters*, a choice of vocabulary reflected in the rhymes:

Billy Bunter From the name of the fat schoolboy in stories written between 1908 and 1961 by 'Frank Richards' (Charles Hamilton, 1875–1961). Mainly a betting-shop usage.

gezunter Presumably a variation on *gazunder*, a euphemism for 'chamber pot'. Usually applied to the sort of punter who lays bets.

Hillman Hunter From the name of a type of saloon car introduced in Britain in 1966. Invented by second-hand car dealers, but extended to any sort of customer regarded as a 'mug'—from the targets of double-glazing sellers to prostitutes' clients.

Price

curry and rice An Australian rhyme, dating from the 1950s. An alternative version is **fried rice**.

nits and lice The British preference, applied mainly to the 'price' on a horse or dog—that is, the odds offered by a bookie. Nits are the eggs of hair lice.

snow and ice A minor 20th-century rhyme.

Profit

bottletop The rhyme is based on *cop* in the sense 'to acquire for yourself', but it's used as a noun, meaning 'something gained'.

Robertson and Moffatt An Australian rhyme from the 1940s, based on the name of a Melbourne department store (in was on Bourke Street, right next door to Buckley and Nunn, possible source of another piece of Australian slang—*Buckley's chance* for 'no chance at all'). Usually shortened in front of the customers to **Robertson**.

A till

jack and jill From the nursery rhyme 'Jack and Jill went up the hill to fetch a pail of water':

> Don't you get cold. Go on, you get back to the old jack and jill.
> —Leon Griffith *Minder* (1979)

A bill

jack and jill A further exploitation of the nursery rhyme (see *jack and jill* at A TILL). Applied especially to utility bills (gas, electricity, etc.).

rhubarb pill A late 19th-century rhyme. Rhubarb pills were laxatives, and the rhyme implies an analogous evacuation of the purse.

A tip

fish and chips Not very convenient for the singular form, but in practice usually reduced to **fish**.

sherbet dip After a type of sweet which could be sucked, dipped into sherbet powder (a flavoured mixture of sugar, tartaric acid, and bicarbonate of soda), and sucked again.

A slang synonym for *tip* is *drop*, which has received the rhyme **lollipop**.

A market pitch

hedge and ditch Applied to a place where a market trader sets up his or her stall, and also to a bookie's pitch at a race course. A late 19th-century rhyme.

A costermonger

split asunder First recorded in 1859, but long since obsolete.

A door-to-door salesman

mozzle and brocha From the phrase on the mozzle and brocha, rhyming on *on the knocker*, which is slang for 'selling from door to door'. Its main components are from two Yiddish words, *mazel* 'good luck' and *brocha* 'a blessing'. Over time its application broadened out to neighbourly cadging: someone asking to borrow the proverbial cup of sugar would be said to be 'on the mozzle'.

An alternative rhyme for *door-to-door* is **forty four**.

A catalogue

cattle dog A 20th-century Australian coinage which is part play on words, part rhyme.

The Absence of Money

Poor

on the floor An apt metaphor as well as a rhyme. Sometimes 'double-rhymed' to **on the Rory** (see *Rory O'More* at **FLOOR**).

Broke

coal and coke A rhyme from the late 19th century, when it was originally **coals and coke**.

heart of oak or **hearts of oak** A long-standing metaphor for 'a stout courageous spirit' or 'a courageous man', first recorded on rhyming duty in the mid-19th century.

Skint

boracic lint A rhyme so widely known that it, and especially its abbreviation **boracic**, have passed into common colloquial parlance:

> She [Martine McCutcheon] landed the part [of Eliza Doolittle in *My Fair Lady*] and, in the argot of her origins, went from being boracic lint to having some bangers and mash.
> —*Sunday Times* (2001)

> 'He's boracic,' said someone. 'He's out grafting.'
> —D. Raymond *He Died with his Eyes Open* (1984)

First recorded in 1959. The original boracic lint was lint (a type of soft material used for surgical dressings) impregnated with the mild antiseptic boric acid. The literal significance of *boracic* has been so lost sight of that versions such as **brassic** or **brassick** sometimes appear. A rare alternative is

pink lint, and towards the end of the 20th century **After Eight Mint** (**After Eight** for short) enjoyed some currency (after a brand of 'sophisticated' chocolate-covered after-dinner mints introduced by Rowntree & Co in 1962).

Free

Occasionally rhymed as **yet to be** (reflecting a healthy scepticism towards the possibility of free lunch). *Buckshee* 'free', an adaptation of *baksheesh* 'a gift of money', fortuitously rhymes with *free*, but can't be regarded as true rhyming slang.

Work and its Lack

Ordinary people's working lives are the seedbed of rhyming slang, but it's the particularities of individual occupations that provide the seeds. Rhyming slangsters do not worry themselves overmuch with work as an abstract concept. Nor—apart from a few *scab*-rhymes—do they give any attention to the vocabulary of trade unions and strikes. This is on the whole the language of independent grafters, not massed labour forces.

It's the fear of being out of a job that cuts deep, and that concern is reflected in the rhymes: ten for *dole* alone. The unemployment of the 1920s and 1930s has left its mark on rhyming slang. And behind it, the spectre of vagrancy—the life of a tramp, begging for food and money.

Work

The earliest of *work*-rhymes, **Russian-Turk**, conflates Britain's two enemies of the mid-19th-century Crimean War, betraying at once a hostile attitude to the interruption of leisure. A later war provided the inspiration for **Dunkirk** (from the mass evacuation of British forces from the French port of Dunkerque in 1940), while the *Turk* theme has been carried on in **terrible Turk** (from an expression applied in the late 19th and early 20th centuries to an implacably forceful person). The Australian rhyme **dodge and shirk** smacks of cynicism, and the British **smile and smirk** is at best ambiguous (it's usually reduced to **smile**, and can be used as a verb as well as as a noun). The latest addition to the list (from the 1990s) is **Captain Kirk**, from the name of the skipper of the starship *Enterprise* (played by William Shatner) in the US televison sci-fi series *Star Trek*.

For those for whom work is *graft*, an alternative rhyme is available: **George Raft**, from the name of the American film star George Raft (1895–1980), who specialized in mean-eyed gangster roles.

A job

couple of bob Usually used in the context of looking for work, with the implication of hoped-for payment (*bob* is 'a shilling').

knocker and knob Perhaps based on the idea of looking for work from door to door.

A pension

stand to attention Originally military slang, referring to an ex-serviceman's pension, but latterly a general term. Generally shortened for convenience to **stand to**.

A shirker

office worker With not the subtlest irony, manual-working rhyming slangsters give their opinion of the exertions of pen-pushers.

A scab

Rhymes for this term denoting 'a strike-breaker' are all Australian: **hansom cab** (now betraying its age) and two members of the McNab family—**Sandy McNab** (first recorded in the 1920s) and **Jack McNab**. The shortened form of this, **Jack**, has been applied since at least the 1940s specifically to members of the Permanent and Casual Waterside Workers' Union, a dockers' union viewed by others as blacklegs.

In Charge

The boss

dead loss Accurately reflecting the workers' opinion of many bosses. (*Dead loss* in the sense 'someone or something useless or hopeless' emerged from the Second World War RAF slang.)

Edmundo Ros A rhyme from the 1960s, immortalizing the Latin American band-leader Edmundo Ros (1910–). Almost always shortened to **edmundo**.

Joe Goss Used in both the US and Australia, and possibly based on the name of the late 19th-century American prizefighter Joe Goss.

pitch and toss First recorded in the 1940s, and based on the name of an old game involving throwing coins at a mark and then tossing them for 'heads' or 'tails'.

The chief

chunk of beef An Australian rhyme, often shortened to **chunka** or **chunker**.

joint of beef The traditional British version.

For other *chief*-rhymes relating specifically to the chief warder of a prison, see *A prison officer* at CRIME AND PUNISHMENT.

The master

lath and plaster A mid-19th-century rhyme, relic of the days when bosses were still called 'the master' (and walls were still built from laths and plaster).

A foreman

Joe O'Gorman A 19th-century rhyme from the building trade, conjuring up the stereotypical Irish navvy. His brother **Billy O'Gorman** often stood in for him.

Dismissal

The sack

last card of the pack Usually shortened—if you've 'drawn the **last card**', you've been dismissed. A rhyme which eloquently mixes the convention of 'getting your cards' with the idea of a last chance gone.

   pedlar's pack Which lies in wait for those who lose their job. First recorded in the 1970s.

   Roberta Flack From the name of the popular American singer Roberta Flack (1937–   ).

   tin tack The best established rhyme in this area, dating back to the late 19th century.

The push

Shepherd's Bush From the name of the area of West London, to the north of Hammersmith, said to be so called from a shepherd's practice of watching his sheep while sitting in a thorn bush. Usually shortened to **Shepherd's**.

Unemployment

The dole

The dole came into institutionalized use as a term for 'unemployment benefit' in Britain only after the First World War, and so rhymes for it date from the 1920s at the earliest. The most popular rhyming word for it is *roll*. **Sausage roll** (one of the first attempts) and **jam roll** (a later version, first recorded in the 1970s) both suggest the sort of fare affordable by someone reliant on the State. The 1950s brought the inevitable **rock and roll**, and **toilet roll** offers the irresistible opportunity to abbreviate to **toilet**, which slots neatly into the expression *on the dole*.

Dole's rhyme with /kəʊl/ provides a range of options. The early **cob of coal** (*cob* means 'a lump') signifies the pittance to be had from the dole; it was defunct by the 1960s. The curious **con and coal** seems to be an alteration of an earlier **Con and Col**, apparently a combination of two different abbreviations of the name *Colin*. Taking a divergent route are **Nat King Cole** (after the African-American popular singer and pianist Nat 'King' Cole (1919–65)) and **Old King Cole** (from the inappropriately merry old soul of the nursery rhyme):

> Any more like you and there'd be four million on the Old King Cole.
> —Leon Griffith *Minder* (1979)

If none of the above appeal, the Australians have a couple of alternatives: **horse and foal** and—suggesting the enforced leisure of unemployment— **strum and stroll**.

The labour exchange

Generally shortened for convenience to *labour*, and that was the recipient of the rhyme: **beggar my neighbour** (from the name of a type of simple card game). This in turn was abbreviated, to **beggar**, so that to be 'on the labour' (i.e. on the dole) was to be 'on the beggar'.

Vagrancy

A tramp

Perhaps the earliest rhyme was **halfpenny stamp**, generally reduced to **halfpenny** (pronounced /ˈheɪpni/), which summed up the tramp's probable financial resources. An unexplained variation on this was **half stamp**.

Lamp provided two alternatives in **hurricane lamp** (usually **hurricane** for short) and **paraffin lamp** (whose abbreviation **paraffin** was a dig at the stereotypical drink of tramps and dossers).

A beggar

peg-legger Originally a colloquialism for someone with a peg-leg (i.e. a wooden leg)—a one-legged man. Current in the 1930s and 1940s.

The spike

The 'spike' was the casual ward of the workhouse, where the homeless could find accommodation. The word was rhymed, unadventurously, with Mike, which in due course became **Mickey**.

At Leisure

Rhyming slangsters don't spend all their time grafting. The extensive vocabulary of alcoholic products (see **ALCOHOL AND OTHER DRUGS**) suggests that much of their free time is occupied down the pub, but there is plenty of time in rhyme-land for other leisure pursuits—parties, the pictures, dancing, watching the telly, even reading a book.

Fun

The best way of enjoying yourself is with a good laugh, or with a *lark*, in the now quaint-sounding vocabulary of the pre–21st century. Rhymers embraced the term, producing **Bushy Park** (from the large park to the north of Hampton Court Palace); **Joan of Arc** (from the name of the French national heroine (*c.*1412–31); mainly used now for *lark* in the extended sense 'a state of affairs'—as in 'Bugger this for a Joan of Arc'); and **Noah's Ark** (a late 19th-century rhyme).

A party

gay and hearty An Australian rhyme, usually curtailed to **gay**. It seems not to have survived the spread of the 'homosexual' meaning of *gay* in the 1970s:

> The mere mention of . . . gay, booze-up, turn, rort, do, will have his ears pricked like fish-hooks.
> —*Kings Cross Whisper* (Sydney) (1965)

> The most important point is whether or not the lounge will accommodate a gay. In other words, can 200 . . . drinking, singing, fighting . . . , dancing, chundering people fit into the lounge?
> —*Swag* (Sydney) (1968)

  hale and hearty The British version of **gay and hearty**, first recorded in the 1970s. All good clean fun.

  moriarty Probably just a general application of the surname *Moriarty*—there's no evidence for a specific derivation from Sherlock Holmes's arch-enemy Professor Moriarty ('the Napoleon of crime') or from the character Count Jim Moriarty played by Spike Milligan in the 1950s radio comedy 'The Goon Show'. Often shortened to **mori**:

> 'You having a little Moriarty?' 'Yes, have some champers.'
> —Leon Griffith *Minder* (1981)

Russell Harty A rhyme popular in the 1980s, celebrating the British television chat-show host Russell Harty (1934–88).

A toy

girl and boy Appropriate, if not exactly imaginative.

Dancing

A dance

Isle of France A translation of French *Île de France*, the area of northeastern France in which Paris is situated—so perhaps an allusion to stereotypical Parisian gaiety. First recorded in the 1850s, but it hardly made it into the 20th century.

South of France A late 19th-century rhyme. It applies to both an instance of dancing and a social or commercial event at which people dance.

treble chance The most recent of these rhymes, with the same range of application as South of France. It comes from the name of a type of combination bet on the Football Pools, which was introduced around the middle of the 20th century.

Tap dancing

cellar flap A late 19th-century rhyme, from the days when every music-hall bill contained a tap dancer or two. The idea behind it seems to have been of dancing on a space no bigger than a cellar trapdoor.

Music

A tune

stewed prune A rhyme dating from the 19th century, used in the context of ad-hoc singsongs round a pub piano or a mouth organ.

Hymns

hers and hims An Australian rhyme. The second element wouldn't pass muster with a strict rhyming slangster.

A piano

goanna An Australian alternative to **joanna** (a goanna is a type of large Australian lizard). First recorded in 1918:

> Grabbed the grand goanna and lowered it down in a lifeboat, see. They get ashore, load the piano on a truck and hides it.
> —F. Hardy *The Yarns of Billy Borker* (1965)

joanna From the female forename *Joanna*. One of the earliest known rhymes (it's first recorded in 1846, in the form *joano*), and one of the longest lasting:

> All the time a party down below was bangin' out a song called 'Bedelia' on a old johanner.
> —A. M. N. Lyons *Clara* (1912)

> The old Jo-anna intrudes its amateurish thumpings.
> —*Listener* (1972)

An organ

The word *organ* attracts rhymers to the Morgan family. Its most illustrious member to be included is **Captain Morgan**, a reference to the pirate captain Henry Morgan (1635–88) who became something of a folk hero. He's been joined by his more obscure relative **Joe Morgan**. From the Irish branch of the family comes **Molly O'Morgan**, old enough to have been originally applied specifically to a street barrel organ, but latterly, like these other rhymes, inclusive of all organs, musical or not.

A violin

Violin isn't much of a rhymer's word, but *fiddle* cries out for **hey-diddle-diddle**—from the title of the 18th-century nursery rhyme 'Hey! diddle diddle! The cat and the fiddle' (*diddle-diddle* was originally an imitation of the sound of a violin). It also serves for the 'fraud' sense of *fiddle* (see *Fraud* at **CRIME AND PUNISHMENT**).

Whistle

Partick Thistle Based on the name of the Scottish football league team (Partick is in Glasgow), and used as both noun and verb.

A song

ding-dong First recorded, in this sense, in 1859, but by the end of the 19th century it had also become a double rhyme, standing in for *sing-song* 'a communal singing session'. The original simple sense survived, though, into the 21st century:

If you want to hear our Martine sing a ding dong, you'd better get your Wilson Pickett for the National.
—*Sunday Times* (2001)

To sing

highland fling First recorded in the 1950s. A singer is a **highland flinger**.

   mangle and wring Generally applied (especially in the abbreviated form **mangle**) to someone who isn't making a very good job of a song. In this instance probably a back-formation from the agent noun **mangle and wringer** 'a singer'.

And the singer may need:

A microphone

Yorkshire tyke Rhyming a common nickname for a Yorkshireman with *mike*.

The Theatre

The stage

greengage Theatrical slang since at least the end of the 19th century, and in use up to the present day in the shortened form **green** (*on the green* is 'on stage'):

> We speak of . . . the stage as the 'green-gage'.
> —*Evening Standard* (1931)

> If a modern producer asks his stage-manager to summon down a man from the flies, we might well hear the cry: 'Bill, come down on the green a minute.'
> —*Times Literary Supplement* (1957)

A box

artful fox A late 19th-century rhyme which didn't long survive the 20th.

   Charles James A shortened version of the name of Charles James Fox (1749–1806), the great Whig statesman and orator. A late 19th-century rhyme which clung on into the 1930s, and suggests a longer historical perspective than obtains in the 21st: who today would make new rhymes with William Gladstone and Lord Salisbury?

A play

night and day First recorded in the 1850s, as both a noun and a verb (meaning 'to go to the theatre'). Long obsolescent.

An actor

Max Factor From the name of a leading cosmetics brand. Originally used literally, but it has increasingly come to be applied metaphorically to people who 'put on an act'—for example, footballers who fall over in the opposing penalty area when there's no one else about.

And for performers who fail to find favour, there's always the risk of the **Richard the Third** (the '*bird*'—i.e. booing and catcalls from the audience).

The Circus

A clown

Charlie Brown Applied to both a real circus clown and, metaphorically, someone who plays the fool. There's more than one 'real' Charlie Brown who might lie behind the rhyme, including the inept cartoon character created in 1950 by Charles M. Schultz for his *Peanuts* comic strip, and the sarcastic dummy used by the English ventriloquist Arthur Worsley, popular during the 1950s and 1960s. But in this case the inspiration is fairly clear: 'Charlie Brown', the 1959 hit song by Jerry Leiber and Mike Stoller, which contains the line 'He's a clown, that Charlie Brown'.

Jim Crow A rhyme somewhat precariously based on *saltimbanco*, a now obsolete term of Italian origin for a street-clown or busker. Recorded in the mid-19th century, and itself probably based on the refrain of an old plantation song, 'Wheel about and turn about and jump Jim Crow', which was a popular staple with 'Nigger minstrel' performers in the early 19th century.

The Cinema

The pictures

fleas and itches An Australian rhyme, alluding to the vermin infesting cheap cinemas. First recorded in 1967, it sometimes comes in the form **fleas and itchers**, a slightly closer approximation to Australian /ˈpɪtʃəz/:

> When not too tired, a man was able to visit . . . the open-air fleas-n' itches.
> —D. O'Grady *A Bottle of Sandwiches* (1968)

A club

rub-a-dub The original recipient of the rhyme was probably *pub* (see *Pub* at ALCOHOL AND OTHER DRUGS), but it also has a long-standing connection with nightclubs, drinking clubs, and working men's clubs.

While you're inside, take care you do nothing to offend:

A bouncer

half ouncer A pre-decimal rhyme, which has a verb to go along with it: **half-ounce** 'to beat up'.

And if it's that sort of club, you can watch:

A stripper

herring and kipper Decidedly uncomplimentary, and not improved by its usual abbreviation to **herring**.

Television

Television is scarcely rhyme-friendly, but in the informal world of rhyming slang, *telly* will do just as well:

custard and jelly A rhyme dating from the 1960s, incorporating two items featuring frequently in many rhyming slangsters' afters in that era. Readily shortened to **custard**.

Marie Corelli A rhyme from the early days of television, when the romantic novelist Marie Corelli (1855–1924) was still sufficiently well remembered to provide it.

Mother Kelly Another early rhyme, inspired by the owner of the doorstep in the popular sentimental song 'On Mother Kelly's Doorstep' (1925) by George A. Stevens.

Ned Kelly First recorded in the 1970s, and based on the name of the celebrated Australian bush-ranger and outlaw Ned Kelly (1857–80)— although the rhyme itself is not restricted to Australian English.

Roger Mellie A ready-made rhyme by courtesy of the magazine *Viz*, in which 'Roger Mellie, the man on the telly' is a regular strip-cartoon character:

> Armchair racing fans are in for a treat this afternoon with 11 live races on the Roger Mellie.
> —*Sporting Life* (1997)

In the 1950s and 1960s, *the box* (short for *goggle box*) was a popular and somewhat condescending synonym for *television*, and a rhyme was available for that too: **Nervo and Knox**. It was based on the names of Jimmy Nervo

(1890–1975) and Teddy Knox (1896–1974), one of a number of comic pairings who made up the Crazy Gang, a British variety combo of the middle years of the 20th century which appeared on the box from time to time.

Reading

A book

The modest but respectable number of rhymes for *book* encourages thoughts of self-improvement, a flourishing literary culture amongst the rhyming classes, and so on—but all is not quite as it seems. A *book* is also a record of bets made (as in *bookmaker*), and a couple of the rhymes below are implicated in that racier usage. It should be remembered, too, that in common late 19th- and early 20th-century usage a *book* could be any publication with the pages permanently fixed together, even with as little as a staple—so that what we would now think of as a magazine might be referred to as a *book*:

Captain Cook Commemorating Captain James Cook (1728–79), the Yorkshire-born navigator and explorer who claimed the east coast of Australia for Britain. It seems originally to have been a general rhyme, but it gradually moved firmly into the horse-racing camp.

docker's hook An Australian rhyme, whose natural habitat is the racetrack, not the library. A docker's hook is a short metal hook used by dock workers for grappling and pulling bales, crates, etc.

jackdaw and rook A theatrical rhyme, incorporating the use of *book* to mean 'the libretto of a musical play'.

Joe Hook A rhyme dating from the 1930s. A seldom heard variant was **Joe Rook**.

Rookery Nook From the name of a popular Aldwych farce, written by Ben Travers and first performed in 1926. The rhyme itself dates from the late 1920s.

A newspaper

Johnny Raper An Australian rhyme, based on the name of a well-known Rugby League footballer in Sydney in the post-World War II period.

linen draper A rhyme dating from the mid-19th century, when the term *linen draper* for 'a seller of linen and other cloth' would still have been generally familiar, but it survived well into the 20th:

> It might be just as well to keep under cover for a little until perhaps the linen-drapers gave him the office [i.e. a hint] that the chase had not been taken up.
> —James Curtis *The Gilt Kid* (1936)

Widely abbreviated to **linen**.

skyscraper A general rhyme for *paper*, but 'newspaper' is a frequent application.

A small and exclusive club of newspapers have their own specific rhymes:

Captain Grimes Coined in the 1980s for *The Times* of London. Presumably a reference to or memory of the dubious schoolmaster Captain Grimes in Evelyn Waugh's *Decline and Fall* (1928).

Currant Bun A 1980s appropriation to *The Sun* newspaper of what had since the late 19th century been a rhyme for the plain old *sun*:

> The tabloids are on her [Sophie, Countess of Wessex's] case full time. . . And the worst the currant bun has managed to come up with since is that Sophie strips nekked at a tanning clinic. What the hell did they think she'd do? Wear a British warm and balaclava like the Royal family?
> —*Odds On* (1999)

> It was . . . the Currant Bun that won it for 'Tone' [i.e. Tony Blair] in June and luxuriated in its role of the UK's 'most politically influential paper'.
> —*Observer* (2001)

Jim Gerald An Australian rhyme for any newspaper with *Herald* in its name. An arbitrary choice, not based on any particular Mr Gerald:

> I see there's a bloke who claims to be thirty-third cousin of the Tsar, and says he's an authority on Russia, writing his memoirs for the Jim Gerald.
> —*Overland* (1956)

> Melbourne's evening newspaper was, and sometimes still is, called the Jim Gerald (Herald) which would simply confuse the Cockneys.
> —*Bulletin* (Sydney) (1974)

News

bottle of booze A late 20th-century rhyme, frequently applied to the television news.

nails and screws An Australian contribution.

A photo

kipper and bloater First recorded in the 1970s, and generally shortened to **kipper**. The rhyme confirms a 'Cockney' pronunciation /ˈfəʊtə/ (or more likely /ˈfəʊʔə/) for *photo*.

And to get into the theatre, the cinema, a concert, or any other public leisure event, you'll almost certainly need:

A Ticket

bat and wicket Current mainly around the turn of the 20th century, and applied particularly to tickets for the music hall.

leg before wicket A cricketing term which comes with its own ready-made abbreviation, **l.b.w.**—used much more commonly than the full form. Used literally, and also substituted in expressions like *that's the ticket* 'that's just what's wanted': *that's the l.b.w.*

Wilson Pickett First recorded in the 1970s, and based on the name of the US soul singer Wilson Pickett (1941–):

> If you want to hear our Martine sing a ding dong, you'd better get your Wilson Pickett for the National.
> —*Sunday Times* (2001)

Scouting for Boys

For many youngsters, the Scouts has since the beginning of the 20th century been an absorbing way of using leisure time, and its popularity is reflected in rhymes that are almost as old as the movement itself:

A Boy Scout

Brussels sprout An unflattering but long-lived rhyme, which kept going throughout the 20th century. Commonly reduced to **brussel**.

tea grout Less common than Brussels sprout. In the days before tea bags, grouts were the used tea leaves left in the bottom of the cup or teapot.

A Wolf Cub

witchetty grub An Australian rhyme, based on the name of various insect larvae that are used as food by Native Australians.

Sport

Your average rhyming slangster is not, frankly, a runner, a jumper, or a kicker of balls. Not for him the agonies of training (the rhyme for *train* says it all—**struggle and strain**). If the relatively small amount of sporting terminology to have been converted into rhyming slang is anything to go by, the main physical exertion he will go in for is removing his wallet from his pocket to pay the bookie on the racecourse or the dog track. The exhilaration of gambling is the lure (see GAMBLING), not the cultivation of physique or the tribal loyalties of fandom—with possibly the occasional excursion to the snooker table or the dart board. So the scenario is: the Sport of Kings, Cockneys on Epsom Downs on Derby Day, pearly kings and queens, Prince Monolulu, the banter of bookies and punters, with perhaps a touch of razor gangs and *Brighton Rock* thrown in:

Racing

A race

belt and braces A collective term for 'the races'—i.e. horse races.

   Charlie Chase An Australian rhyme, based on the name of the US silent-film comic Charley Chase (1893–1961), and often shortened to **charlie**. Some metaphorical use, as in *not in the charlie* 'out of contention'.

Trotting races

red hots An Australian rhyme from the 1950s, based on *trots* (trotting involves horses moving at a fast trot, pulling a light vehicle on which the driver sits):

> It's not often I'd consider giving the red hots a miss on Saturday night—especially when I've got a couple of certainties.
> —*Herald* (Melbourne) (1979)

> He got a phone call at the 'red hots' to tell him he'd better get home in a hurry.
> —P. Keenan *Dead Certs and Dog Food: Australia's Funniest Racing Yarns* (1995)

A winner

hot dinner Perhaps suggesting what the winnings will enable the successful punter to afford. An even more celebratory alternative is **Christmas dinner**.

A racecourse

iron horse Despite the specific rhyme, it can refer to a dog track as well as to a horse-racing venue.

A jockey

hickey-hockey An Australian rhyme (and rather a feeble one), dating from the 1920s.

The paddock

smoked haddock A rhyme with some currency around the middle of the 20th century.

The post

holy ghost A rhyme for the starting post of a race, usually shortened to **holy**.

See also *A punter* and *The Tote* at GAMBLING and *Dog* and *Horse* at ANIMALS.

A Game

Mickey Spillane An Australian coinage of the 1950s, rhyming (approximately) on the name of the US crime novelist Mickey Spillane (1918–).

A Pitch

hedge and ditch A general rhyme for a pitch, regardless of the game played on it—but in practice, most often applied to football and cricket pitches.

A Goal

sausage roll An Australian rhyme of the 1960s, used mainly in the context of Australian Rules football. Usually shortened to **sausage** (kicked a sausage John Meredith *Learn to Talk Old Jack Lang: A Handbook of Australian Rhyming Slang* (1984)).

Cricket

Bat

this and that Variously claimed as both a noun and a verb.

A four

George Moore An Australian rhyme of the 1970s, possibly based on the name of the Australian jockey George Moore (1923–):

> Cosier had eight Georgie Moores and two Dorothy Dixers in his knock of 65.
> —Hibberd and Hutchinson *The Barracker's Bible* (1983)

A six

Dorothy Dix An Australian rhyme of the 1970s, still in use in the 21st century. It was based on *Dorothy Dix*, the pen-name of the US journalist E. M. Gilmer (1870–1951), who wrote a popular syndicated question-and-answer column (the name was already current in Australian slang as a term for a parliamentary question planted in order to give a minister the chance to make a prepared reply). Sometimes altered to **Dorothy Dixer**, on the model of *sixer* 'a six', or simply shortened to **Dorothy**:

> He still laughs loudly about hitting . . . a 'Dorothy Dix'—or 'Dorothy' for short—over the fence.
> —*Age* (Melbourne) (1979)

> That is a Dorothy—and a big one at that.
> —Richie Benaud *One-day Cricket* (Channel 4) (2001)

A turning wicket

In cricketers' jargon, a pitch that takes spin is a *turner*. This is rhymed with **bunsen burner**, from the laboratory gas burner named after the German chemist Robert Bunsen. Usually abbreviated, so a pitch that turns more than average is 'a raging **bunsen**':

> I adjusted to the wicket pretty quickly. I was expecting the pitches to be real bunsens but they weren't that bad.
> —Marcus Trescothick *Observer Sports Monthly* (2001)

Out

salmon-trout A variation on *salmon and trout*, which has several different rhymes to its credit (see e.g. *Gout* at ILLNESS and *Stout* at ALCOHOL AND OTHER DRUGS):

> As far as I'm concerned it was absolutely salmon-trout.
> —Jeff Thomson *Test Match Special* (BBC Radio Four) (2001)

Boxing

A boxer

The more complimentary rhyme, **typewriter**, is based on *fighter*—but it's more often used metaphorically, for a courageous or persevering person. Australian slang rhymes more brusquely on *pug* (from *pugilist*). The result: **steam tug**.

Swimming

Swimming being a particular aptitude of Australians, it's not surprising that they have produced the two extant rhymes for *swim* (the noun): **dark and dim**, and **tiger tim** (**tiger** for short—from the name of the children's cartoon character Tiger Tim created in 1904 by Julius Stafford Baker).

Billiards and Snooker

Chalk

Lambeth Walk A mid-20th-century rhyme, applied to the chalk used on cue tips. It comes from the Cockney song (written by Furber and Gay) and dance of that name, first performed by Lupino Lane in 1937 and popular in Britain during the Second World War.

For the rhymes attached to the various coloured balls in snooker, see *Colour* at THE SENSES.

Darts

horses and carts A 20th-century rhyme, generally shortened to **horses**.

A double

rasher and bubble Applied to a hit in the outer ring, which scores double. The reference is to a dish of bacon and bubble and squeak (fried leftover potatoes and greens).

Chalk

careless talk From the British Second World War anti-gossip slogan 'Careless talk costs lives'. It refers to the chalk used for marking up the score in darts.

Gambling

Your rhyming slangster is always game for a **national debt**—a 'bet' (or a **grumble and mutter**—a 'flutter'). His natural recreational habitat is the racecourse and the dog track (see **SPORT**), where the banter of punters and bookies is as fertile ground for rhymes as the lingo of his workplace is. And the occasional game of cards doesn't come amiss either. The opportunism of the rhymes sits well with a world where chance rules, where fortune rests on the toss—or **iron horse**—of a coin (this is *toss* as /tɔːs/, of course, securing the rhyme, not the more genteel /tɒs/, and iron horse can be used as a verb as well as as a noun).

Racing

The Tote

canal boat An occasionally heard alternative to nanny goat.

   nanny goat A rhyme for the state-owned mass betting system first recorded in 1961, and often reduced to **nanny**:

> The poor old ailing Tote—the Nanny Goat, as they call it.
> —*Daily Mail* (1970)

A tip

egg flip An Australian rhyme based on the name of the alcoholic drink made with beaten egg. A *tipper* (an occasional variant on *tipster*) is correspondingly rhymed as **egg-flipper** (first recorded in the 1960s).

   In Australian slang a tip, or more broadly any piece of inside information, is also a *drum* (from the idea of jungle drums passing on information), which rhymers have turned into **deaf and dumb** and **Tom Thumb** (after the diminutive fairy-tale character).

A tout

salmon and trout A 1930s rhyme for a person who seeks out information about the runners in a race (e.g. by spying on the training rides) and sells it to bookies.

A punter

See *Billy Bunter* and *gezunter* at **A CUSTOMER**.

A win

nose and chin In use since at least the early 20th century. The punters' expression *on the nose*, signifying that a bet is laid for a win (as opposed to a place), may well be based on the shortened version **nose**, which would take it back into the 19th century.

For rhymes on *book* in a betting sense, see *A book* at **AT LEISURE**.

Cards

Coldstream Guards After one of the five regiments of British Foot Guards.

feet and yards Usually reduced to **feet**.

Wilkie Bards A rhyme in vogue from the 1920s to the 1950s, when the name of the British music-hall comedian Wilkie Bard (1874–1944) was familiar to people.

For an individual playing card, the rhyme **Prussian guard** is sometimes used.

King

gold ring A general rhyme for *king*, but most commonly applied to the playing card.

highland fling First recorded in the 1960s, and used in cards only.

ting-a-ling Used exclusively for the card—which is perhaps just as well, as in US Black English slang it means 'penis'.

Queen

Mary Green Usually used in shortened form—the queen is 'the Mary'. There's no known connection with any real woman of that name, although no doubt the abbreviation was encouraged by the presence of Queen Mary (consort of George V) from 1910 to 1953.

Trey

Vicar of Bray *Trey*, an old word for the 'three' at cards (and dice), was given this rhyme in the late 19th century. The original Vicar of Bray was a parson of Bray in Berkshire who by switching his religious allegiance to match that of the reigning monarch was able to remain in his job for a lengthy period during the 16th century.

See also *Threepence* at **MONEY AND COMMERCE**.

Ace

cat's face A coinage of the 1940s.

Joker

tapioca From the starchy grain widely used in former times for making fairly unappetizing puddings.

The Four Suits

The four playing-card suit names all inherit rhymes from their more literal counterparts:

Clubs

rub-a-dub-dub See *A club* at **AT LEISURE**.

Diamonds

Simple Simon See *A diamond* at **CLOTHING**.

Hearts

jam tart Commoner in this sense than in the literal anatomical one. See *The heart* at **THE BODY AND ITS PARTS**.

Spades

lemonade A rhyme shared with *spade* 'a black person' (see *Spade* at **ETHNIC AND NATIONAL GROUPS**), but it's not clear which got it first.

Dice

Mice is the favoured rhyme-word for *dice*—combinations include **cats and mice**, **white mice**, and, most popular of all, **rats and mice**, first recorded in 1932:

> We used to play dice with them. . . Rats and Mice the game was called.
> —F. D. Sharpe *Sharpe of the Flying Squad* (1938)

If mice are too alarming, the alternatives are **block of ice** and **choc ice**.

Bingo

George and Ringo From the names of two Beatles, guitarist George Harrison (1943–2001) and drummer Ringo Starr (1940–)—who always seemed to come third and fourth when the quartet's names were given separately. An appropriate rhyme for the 1960s, when bingo was becoming a big-money industry in Britain, but it survived long after that:

> Down in Victoria Beckham [Peckham] do they really go out for a couple of games of George and Ringo before treating themselves to a quick port and Lennon?
> —*Sunday Times* (2001)

A card

The three known rhymes for a *bingo card* were first recorded on the same occasion, being used by a caller in the Army during the First World War (when the game went by the name 'housey housey'): **bladder of lard**, **Prussian guard** (also sometimes used for a playing card), and **six months' hard** (referring to a sentence of six months' hard labour).

For the number-rhymes of bingo callers, see NUMBERS.

Football Pools

April fools The shortened form inherits the plural—all hopeful rhymers regularly do the **Aprils**.

Betting

A stake

Joe Blake An occasional betting-shop rhyme.

Evens

Major Stevens A military rhyme for when the odds are one to one—not based on any known person, living or dead.

Odd

Tommy Dodd Originally, in the mid-19th century, the rhyme was applied to the 'odd' man in the coin-tossing game 'odd man out', the player who lost out, and also to the game itself (Not long ago a returned tradesman . . . allowed himself to be induced to play at Tommy Dodd with two low sharpers. A. Steinmetz *The Gaming-Table* (1870)). In the 20th century the pluralized form **Tommy Dodds** came to be used for betting odds.

And if you want to bet on credit, in Australian English you can bet on the **Mary Lou**, a rhyme dating from the 1920s and based on slang *bet on the blue* 'to bet on credit'.

Communication

The golden age of rhyming slang coincided with the telephone era. The days when people wrote **never betters** left scarcely an impression (that's the only rhyme on record for *letter*, and it's Australian), and the Internet has yet to make any significant contribution, perhaps because much of its jargon is unpromising territory for rhymes (although the incongruous **British Rail** has been spotted for *e-mail*).

But before all these alternative modes and electronic aids came the unmediated human voice—just talking. Which is what rhyming slang is all about.

The Voice

By far the commonest rhyme for 'voice' is **Hobson's choice**, in use long and widely enough to be instantly recognizable in its cut-down form **Hobson's**:

> Her Hobson's (rhyming slang for voice) is one of the most vibrant in the business.
> —*Observer* (1960)

> The landlady, Queenie Watts, throws her Hobsons (*Hobson's choice* = *voice*) so hard that on a clear night you could hear it in Canning Town.
> —*New Statesman* (1961)

First recorded in Eric Partridge's *Dictionary of Slang and Unconventional English* (1937), it exploits a long-standing but now little used English expression meaning 'no choice at all'. That dates back to the 17th century, and supposedly relates to a Cambridge tradesman of the early part of that century called Tobias Hobson (some sources refer to him as Hodgson or Jobson). He ran a business delivering parcels and goods, and didn't mind hiring his horses out for a consideration—but you had to take the one nearest the stable door or go without. No negotiation was possible—hence 'Hobson's choice'.

Probably unconsciously following this model was **Housewives' Choice**, based on the name of a morning radio record-request programme for the housebound housewives of the 1940s, 1950s and 1960s, originally broadcast on the BBC Light Programme in 1946.

Other *voice*-rhymes:

let's rejoice An Australianism of the 20th century.

Rolls Royce Based on the name of the quietest of cars, but the implication is of a superior and well-upholstered singing voice.

Walter Joyce Recorded in the 1880s in the work of George Sims, a late 19th-century chronicler of Cockney life, but the identity of the subject seems not to have survived.

Speech

Not all who use rhyming slang are on the right side of the law, and it shows in the rhymes relating to 'talking'—many of which often imply 'passing on information about criminal activities to the police'.

Speak

bubble and squeak Reputedly dating from the late 19th century, and based on the name of the dish of fried leftover potatoes and greens (which itself came from the sound of the cooking). Generally reduced to **bubble**, and as such often used as a noun: to 'put the bubble in' is to give information to the police (this is sometimes interpreted as a rhyme based on *squeak* 'to betray someone by informing against them', but 'rhymes' on identical words—*bubble and squeak/squeak*—are generally avoided, and it's more likely to be the original *speak* rhyme).

Talk

The most successful of all *talk* rhymes has long since cut itself adrift from its original rhyming root, so much so that most people no longer realize where it came from. **Rabbit and pork** is of no great antiquity (it's first recorded in the early 1940s), but its curtailed form **rabbit** spread rapidly out from its Cockney base in the 1960s, 1970s, and 1980s, particularly via television comedies and advertisements, to become a widely recognized colloquialism—so much so that the speech of the street has felt the need to reclaim it by disguising it as *bunny*. The usual application is to tedious or incomprehensible prattle.

It seems to have started out as a noun, meaning 'talk' in general or 'a conversation' (We only allow ourselves a second to remember that rabbit-and-pork is talk. *Spectator* (1960)), but its abbreviated form has become more verb than noun:

> A girl reporter from Rolling Stone rabbits on idiotically about the Maharishi.
> —*Guardian Weekly* (1977)

Other rhymes have been based on *pork*—**pickled pork** (in use from the late 19th century to the 1930s) and **roast pork** (which achieved some success as a verb in the shortened form **roast**)—but none has ever challenged the primacy of **rabbit**.

As alternatives to the *pork* strategy there are **ball of chalk**, or just **ball** (more commonly a rhyme for *walk*) and **Duke of York** (mainly 19th century). Both are, or were, used as verbs.

A talker

Johnnie Walker Sometimes applied to a police informant, but usually it's simply someone who gabbles incessantly and tiresomely. The implication is clearly of a tongue loosened by too many whiskies (*Johnnie Walker* being a brand dating back to the late 19th century).

Say so

The sarcastic use of 'I should say so!', implying disbelief or indignation, has spun off a rhyme that has taken on an independent existence of its own: *I should* **cocoa**. Severance of its rhyming roots often shows itself in alternative spellings:

> 'She says you paid her a pound a week for the best part of nine months,' Dover went on. Mrs. Gomersall laughed scornfully. 'I should co-co!' she chortled.
> —Joyce Porter *Dover Three* (1965)

First recorded in the 1930s, it does exist in the more conventional two-part format (**coffee and cocoa** and **tea and cocoa**), but it's not clear that either of these predates the shorter version.

The alternative **kiko** gained some currency in the 1940s and 1950s, reflecting a 'Cockney' pronunciation of *say so* as /sʌɪ səʊ/.

Swear

For this very specialized form of communication, two rhymes are available: **Lord Mayor** (from the days when youngsters might be told off for 'Lord Mayoring'; the London link is obvious) and **rip and tear** (despite some overlap in meaning, there is no connection with *let rip*).

Dumb

red rum First recorded in the 1970s, and inspired by Red Rum, the horse which became a popular hero in Britain after winning the Grand National steeplechase three times, in 1973, 1974, and 1977.

A word

There is not much call for a general rhyme for *word*. It's useful only in very specific contexts. Easily the best known is **dicky-bird** (sometimes **dicky** for short), first recorded in the 1930s. It exploits a nursery term for 'a bird' which dates from the mid-18th century. It's occasionally used for *word* in the sense 'a promise' (I give yer me dicky. Michael Harrison *Reported Safe Arrival* (1943)), and thespians employ the abbreviated **dickies** for the words they have to learn:

> While discussing the new arrival, one of our number asked the inevitable question surrounding any actor of particularly mature years. 'But can he still do the dickies, darling?' The 'dickies' are the words. He was asking in his oblique way if the ancient recruit would still be able to remember his lines. Or if he'd even be able to learn them in the first place.
> —*Guardian* (2001)

But by far its commonest habitat is negative expressions of the type 'never said a dicky-bird', implying taciturnity or uncommunicativeness:

> Didn't say a dicky bird, the poor girl didn't.
> —M. Benney *Low Company* (1936)

A seldom heard alternative formulation is **early bird**.

A different stretch of territory is staked out by **Richard the Third** (more usually plain **Richard**), which denotes a promise or oath—as in 'He gave me his Richard'.

Rhyming slang

Yes, there is rhyming slang for *rhyming slang*: Australian English offers **old Jack Lang**, an unidentified personage, perhaps the hero of a long-forgotten anecdote famous for his prodigious use of rhymes.

Information

ike In use in the 1930s ('E passed the ike, that there was somethink on there. J. G. Brandon *Dragnet* (1936)) and only conjecturally of rhyming origin. *Ike* is also slang for 'a Jew', and in that context it's short for *ikeymo* (from *Isaac Moses*), which could have provided the basis for a rhyme on *info*.

Tom Thumb An Australian rhyme dating from the 1940s, exploiting the diminutive fairy-tale character. It's based on 'the *drum*', long-standing Australian slang for 'a piece of reliable inside information':

> I need the Tom Thumb on that cook. Albert Knox. What do you know about him?
> —R. G. Barrett *Leaving Bondi* (2000)

The telephone

The clear favourite amongst British *phone* rhymes is **dog and bone**. First recorded in 1961, it exploits a natural pairing that has since perhaps faded out in the days of tinned dog-food. There may also be a memory in it of the line 'Nick-nack paddywhack, give the dog a bone', from a traditional nursery song. It has achieved some degree of permanence, both in its full form and shortened to **dog**:

> Get on the dog; invite old Arthur down here for an evening on the river.
> —*Minder* (1983)

The rhyme on *bone* was anticipated, though probably not inspired, by the earlier US **switch and bone**, recorded in 1944. It also crops up in the univerbal **hambone**, in **jelly-bone**, which is unusual in providing a rhyme for the initial as well as the final part of its model, and in **rag and bone** (for an example, see the entry for eau de Cologne below).

Orthographically and phonetically (though not, of course, etymologically) *bone* is also present in **trombone**, which probably comes closest to dog and bone in popularity, and has been one of the more successful of single-word rhymes (probably because of a perceived logical connection with *blower* 'telephone'):

> I can't wait to see Daley's boatrace. He'll be on the old trombone in two minutes.
> —Leon Griffith *Minder* (1979)

Names have offered convenient rhymes, too. An obvious candidate was **Molly Malone**, eponymous heroine of the ballad about the Dublin cockle-and mussel-seller. A male variant is **Mike Malone**, and US rhyming slang offers **Maggie Mahone**, completing an Irish-inspired triad. **Al Capone** is not American but Antipodean, and dates from the 1930s (most of which decade the Chicago gangland boss spent in jail); it's recorded as New Zealand prison slang in 1997. There is also some evidence of use for **Darby and Joan**, the archetypal old married couple, who first put in an appearance in an 18th-century ballad.

Eau de Cologne was coined at a period when that fragrant fluid was still frequently dabbed on wrists and temples, but survives in the 21st century:

> One day you might need someone, and you'll go 'Eek!', and then you'll look at the book, and that's my phone number, and you're on the eau de cologne, or even the rag and bone, and I'll sort it out for you.
> —Jimmy Saville **BBC2** (2000)

The obligatory shortened form has often been rationalized to **odour** (not quite the mot juste, but within the same semantic ballpark), or even (revealing a sharply Anglicized pronunciation of the full form) realized as **odie**.

Blower

Blower as a colloquialism for 'telephone' dates from the 1920s. Its rhyme **Percy Thrower** commemorates the gardening expert Percy Thrower (1913–88) who pioneered gardening programmes on British television in the 1950s, notably with the BBC's *Gardening Club* (1955–67), and became synonymous with horticulture in mid-20th-century Britain.

And for those who still prefer to put it in writing, there is:

The pen

Bill and Ben The names of the two 'Flowerpot Men', children's puppets made out of bits of garden pottery who had their own highly successful television programme in the 1950s. They continued to have a cult following long after they left the screen (not least for their much-imitated gobbledegook language), and this helped to keep alive a pairing well suited to rhyming slang.

    cock and hen Dating from the 19th century, but seldom heard in the 20th.

    Dirty Den From the nickname of an obnoxious character (in full Den Watts) played by Leslie Grantham in the BBC television soap *EastEnders*. Impeccable Cockney credentials.

The Post

For those who stick to the good old-fashioned *post* there's **tea and toast**. If you prefer *mail*, there's the more up-to-date **Jimmy Nail**, in honour of the Geordie actor and singer (1954–) who made his name in the 1980s television drama series *Auf Wiedersehen, Pet*.

Transport and Travel

When rhyming slang was young, you either went by train or used real horse power, or you walked. As transport technology evolved, it encompassed such novelties as trams, buses, bicycles, underground trains, and of course cars. But there's one travel medium rhyming slangsters never really seem to have got to grips with—the air. There's a distinct lack of rhymes relating to aircraft (although *plane* presents no great challenge to rhymers), and **Wilbur Wright**, the rhyme for *flight*, harks right to the pioneering days of the conquest of the air (it commemorates Wilbur Wright (1867–1912), the US aviator who with his brother Orville was the first to make a controlled powered flight in an aeroplane, in 1903; it's generally shortened to **wilbur**).

On the Road

A road

frog and toad One of the most familiar pieces of 'Cockney' rhyming slang, first recorded in the 1850s and still referred to in the late 20th century and into the 21st: Jimmy said yeah, they'd be hitting the old frog and toad any minute themselves. Joseph O'Connor *Cowboys and Indians* (1991). Usually shortened to **frog**. Julian Franklyn in his *Dictionary of Rhyming Slang* (1960) suggests that travelling on a road out into the country (not so far away in the 19th century) would have been one of the few opportunities Londoners got to see frogs and toads. The pseudonymous 'Ducange Anglicus', in his *The Vulgar Tongue* (1857), put forward an even more convoluted (and fairly unconvincing) explanation—that *frog* here refers to the horny pad on the bottom of a horse's foot, and that *toad* was originally *toed*, the past form of the verb *toe*.

If the road is little more than a *track*, it can be rhymed as **hammer and tack** (first recorded in the 1920s, and usually shortened to **hammer**). And in the 19th century, tramps, vagabonds and footpads referred to the road as the *toby*; in rhyming slang that became **George Robey**, after the English music-hall comedian George Robey (1869–1954), known as the 'Prime Minister of Mirth'.

A street

channel fleet An Irish rhyme.

field of wheat Rhyming slang is not without irony: little could be ru... removed from a congested, choking city street than a field of wheat. First recorded in 1859.

plate of meat In use in the 19th century, but more familiarly applied to the feet that tramp the unyielding streets of the city (see *Feet* at **THE BODY AND ITS PARTS**).

The gutter

bread and butter As often used metaphorically ('the lowest level, destitution') as literally.

A car

jamjar First recorded in 1934, and in vigorous enough use in the 21st century to serve as the name of an Internet company selling cars: *jamjar.com*. Motor cars seem to have inherited the rhyme from tram cars, for which there is some evidence it was in use at the end of the 19th century, and in the Second World War R.A.F. slang it was applied to armoured cars. In South African English in the 1960s it was abbreviated to **jammy** or **jammie**.

> Parking this dreadful great orange-and-cream jamjar . . . slap under a no-parking sign.
> —Robin Cook *The Crust on its Uppers* (1962)

la-di-dah Coined at a time when car-ownership was the preserve of the higher social classes, and continuing to connote particularly a swanky new motor.

shaun spadah A long forgotten rhyme based on the name of Shaun Spadah, the horse which won the Grand National in 1921.

A motor

Rhymes for *motor* 'a car' date from the first decade of the 20th century, when cars were new-fangled and expensive and also the object of some scorn, and when *motor* was a widely used abbreviation of *motor car* or *motor carriage*. The earliest effort seems to have been the facetious and unwieldy **tea for two and a bloater** (a bloater being a lightly smoked herring). Rhyming ideas never got further than *bloater*, but a shorter version came along in **Yarmouth bloater**, a nod to Great Yarmouth, the Norfolk seaport famous for its smoked fish. A later third option was **kipper and bloater**.

Wheels

This is *wheels* in the colloquial sense 'one's own personal transport, typically a car' (first recorded in the 1950s). Its rhyme, **jellied eels**, could scarcely be more authentically 'Cockney'. 'Have you got jellied eels?' is an enquiry about whether you have your own transport.

A Rolls Royce

The name of royal concubine Camilla Parker Bowles (1947–) offered too apposite a rhyming opportunity to be missed, and sure enough in the 1990s the toffs' *Rolls* attracted numerous variations on the theme: **Camilla Parker**, **Parker Bowles**, **Parker**, and even the full **Camilla Parker Bowles**.

A taxi

Joe Baxi An ephemeral rhyme based on the name of the US heavyweight boxer Joe Baxi (1919–77), who achieved brief fame in Britain when he crossed the Atlantic in 1947 to fight the British heavyweight champion Bruce Woodcock.

Slapsie Maxie Another boxing-inspired rhyme, from Australia and New Zealand, based on the name (plus nickname) of the US boxer 'Slapsie' Maxie Rosenbloom (1904–76). Current in the 1930s.

A cab

flounder and dab Dating from the middle of the 19th century, when it referred to a hansom cab, and long obsolete in Britain, although there is some evidence that it survived into the era of motorized taxis in the USA. A dab, like a flounder, is a type of flatfish.

mab A mid-19th-century rhyme. *Mab* used to be a slang word for 'prostitute', and it was also a name—short for *Mabel*.

Sandy Macnab A rhyme dating from the 1940s, and not based on any particular Sandy Macnab—simply a generalized Scotsman.

smash and grab Based on a term for a type of robbery from shop windows first recorded in 1920s—no doubt with half an eye to the 'daylight robbery' of taxi fares.

A cabbie

Westminster Abbey A favourite destination for the tourists who provide so many of London taxi-drivers' fares.

A lorry

Annie Laurie Mainly an army usage, current during the First World War period, and based on the name of the heroine of a popular ballad. An unadventurous rhyme, but usually disguised by being reduced to **Annie**.

sad and sorry A rhyme with some limited 20th-century currency.

A truck

Donald Duck An Australian rhyme of the 1960s, after the cantankerous

Walt Disney cartoon character of that name. Almost always shortened to **donald**.

   goose and duck Some reported mid-20th-century usage among dock-workers (who might have been supposed to favour its more scabrous use—see *Sexual intercourse* at **SEX**).

A van

Peter Pan Commemorating the eternally youthful hero of J. M. Barrie's play *Peter Pan* (1904)

   pot and pan Generally just **pot**, for convenience:

> And get Antioch Dood to collect the pots -. 'Pots' are lorries, from rhyming slang, pots and pans vans.
> —Jonathan Gash *The Tartan Sell* (1986)

A tram

Rhymes for *tram* are circumscribed by the period (roughly from the 1880s to the 1930s) when electric trams regularly ground their way around the inner-city streets of Britain. More recent attempts to reintroduce the vehicle have not been successful enough to encourage a revival of the rhymes. Most of those were based on *jam*: **bread and jam** (recorded in American and Australian usage as well as British); **jar of jam** (current in the 1930s); and **plain and jam** (in use in the 1910s and 1920s, and exploiting the contrast between plain doughnuts and the more luxurious and expensive jammy ones). An occasional alternative was **baa-lamb**.

A bus

swear and cuss An appropriate evocation of the response of London passengers to the lateness, crowdedness, discomfort, etc. of their buses.

   trouble and fuss Another heartfelt coinage which encapsulates, haiku-like, the attitude of the rhymer to the rhymed.

A coach

cockroach First recorded in the immediate post-Second World War period, when holiday-makers in Britain took to the roads in large numbers. The coaches they travelled in were evidently not models of hygiene.

A charabanc

A predecessor to the terms *coach* or *motor coach*, which began to replace it in the 1940s, it was regularly shortened colloquially to *charra*, which was the basis of the rhyme: **bow and arrow**.

A sulky

big and bulky A late 19th-century Australian rhyme (a sulky is a type of horse-drawn carriage).

A bike

clever Mike Possibly inspired by the tricks of a stunt rider.

   dirty tyke A variation on the usual *Mike* theme. *Tyke* is an opprobrious term for a man or boy.

   Iron Mike Based on the nickname of the bruising US boxer and former world heavyweight champion Mike Tyson (1966–).

   Pat and Mike A 19th-century rhyme, using two stereotypical Irish names.

A pram

jar of jam The word *pram* emerged in the 1880s, and it attracted this rhyme (possibly inherited from *tram*—see above) in the following century.

A garage

horse and carriage A gracious nod to the internal-combustion engine from the days of the hippomobile (in the early days, garages had been termed 'motor-stables'). The Anglicized pronunciation /ˈgarɪdʒ/ for *garage* was already well established by the time the rhyme was coined.

To park

skylark A usage dating from the 1950s. It seems to be a reapplication of a rhyme already in use for the noun *park* 'a recreational open space'.

A traffic warden

gay gordon A rhyme based on the dance of that name—it's not clear whether there was originally also intended to be any imputation of homosexuality.

The clutch

Lord Sutch An automotive outing for the British pop singer turned politician 'Screaming Lord' Sutch (real name David Sutch) (1940–99), who as leader of the 'Monster Raving Loony Party' enlivened many a by-election campaign in the last quarter of the 20th century.

The Railways

A train

Rain is the not very imaginative leitmotiv of the majority of *train*-rhymes, most of them Australian: there's **hail and rain** (a British rhyme, in use between the 1920s and the 1970s); **roaring rain** (an Australian rhyme, perhaps inspired by the mighty sound of a locomotive at full tilt); **shower of rain** (another Australian contribution); and **thunder and rain** (similarly antipodean).

Some non-*rain* alternatives:

John Wayne A tribute to the Hollywood star John Wayne (1907–79), perennial hero of westerns. A rhyme of the middle years of the 20th century.

Mary Blaine or **Mary Blane** A 19th-century rhyme, long since defunct. Like *train* itself at that time, it was used as a verb as well as as a noun, meaning 'to travel by train'. The identity of Mary Blaine, if there was such a person, is not known.

struggle and strain An evocation of a steam locomotive trying to make it up a steep incline.

A railway line

ball of twine A 20th-century Australian rhyme.

The tube

Oxo cube Apparently a post-Second World War rhyme, and usually shortened—many Londoners know their underground railway as 'the **Oxo**'. The reference is to the name of a brand of stock-cube, which was registered as a trademark in 1899.

A guard

Christmas card A general rhyme for various types of *guard*, but perhaps most commonly applied to the sort responsible for a train.

A station

constipation A relatively unusual single-word rhyme, albeit of several syllables. Perhaps a coinage of a frustrated commuter, stuck in a station in one too many motionless trains.

poor relation A rhyme from the early part of the 20th century, when only the well-off had cars, and the hoi polloi had to travel by train.

salvation Another single-word rhyme, from the late 19th century. It didn't survive long into the 20th.

On the Water

Rhyming slang being in the main an urban phenomenon, the majority of rhymes relating to ships come not from sailors and the sea but from dockers (especially London dockers), stevedores, longshoremen, and other river workers.

A boat

frog in the throat In use in the First World War period, but it seems to have died out since then. The original, 'literal' meaning, 'temporary hoarseness', is first recorded in 1909.

   hat and coat Applied in particular to refrigerated cargo ships—the joke being that the docker needs to wear his hat and coat while unloading them.

I'm afloat An appropriate but not sparklingly original rhyme, dating from at least the middle of the 19th century. Largely the preserve of dock workers and longshoremen.

   nanny goat In use during the Second World War, but with its subsequent application to the *Tote* (see *The Tote* at **GAMBLING**) the nautical usage has faded into the background.

A ship

halfpenny dip A London dockers' rhyme, first recorded in the mid-19th century and current into the 20th. The reference is to a lucky dip in a sweetshop, into which for the price of a halfpenny (/ˈheɪpni/) you could plunge your hand and pull out a sweet.

   old whip A sailor's rhyme for the ship he is currently serving on.

A barge

Davy Large A dock workers' rhyme, dating from the late 19th century. Davy Large was a real person, a London docker employed by the firm Scruttons Ltd., who went on to become well known as a trade-union official.

Fuel

Oil

ruin and spoil Rhyming slangsters not being known for their green credentials, this rhyme was probably not inspired by the environmental effects of spilled oil.

Diesel

pop goes the weasel From the name of a popular song and dance that originated in the 1850s, often decoded as 'pawning the flat-iron'. A rhyme mainly used in the road-haulage industry.

Travel

A ticket

Ticket-rhymes mainly cover admission to a place of entertainment (see *A ticket* at **AT LEISURE**), but they are also used for travel tickets.

A fare

grey mare A rhyme dating from the days of horse-drawn transport, in the late 19th century, but extending forwards into the days of trams and then buses, and also applied to train fares.

A suitcase

crowded space Not a reference to most people's case-packing technique— the rhyme was used by thieves who made a speciality of stealing cases from railway stations and other crowded spaces.

On Foot

A walk

A small cluster of *chalk*-rhymes, dating mainly from the late 19th century, not only denote a literal 'walk' but also figure largely in the metaphorical *take a walk!*—that is, 'go away, get lost!': **ball of chalk** (the most familiar and widely used, often shortened to **ball** and employed in that guise as a verb as well as as a noun); **pennorth of chalk**; and **powdered chalk**. The Australian member of the family, **stick of chalk**, appears only to have been used literally.

Some alternative formulations:

guy A late 19th-century coinage, based on **Guy Fawkes**, the name of the 16th-century English conspirator and incendiarist (1570–1606), but a somewhat forced rhyme. Extended in use from a literal 'walk' to any journey or expedition.

pickle and pork or **pickled pork** An Australian rhyme of the 1940s and 1950s.

whisper and talk A late 19th-century rhyme, usually shortened to **whisper**.

To walk

Duke of York A 19th-century rhyme of short life-span.

A footpath

oats and chaff First recorded in the 1850s, and apparently surviving into the 1930s. The rhyme depends on 'Cockney' *path* /pɑːf/.

And hopefully to be avoided:

A Crash

Jack Flash Probably inspired by the 1968 Rolling Stones' song 'Jumping Jack Flash', with no doubt an allusion to excessive speed as well.

sausage and mash A taxi drivers' rhyme, first recorded in the 1950s.

Time and Tide

The average British rhyming slangster takes a fatalistic attitude to seasons and climes. Deeply ingrained folk memories of gloomy skies and dank chilly air are reflected in the choice of rhyming subjects: rhymes in the general area of 'coldness' greatly outnumber those for 'heat', and *rain* is by some way the most frequently rhymed meteorogical term.

Temperature

Cold

brave and bold A late 19th-century rhyme, which failed to survive more than a couple of decades into the 20th.

Cheltenham Short for **Cheltenham Gold**, which itself was based on the name of the Cheltenham Gold Cup, a celebrated English steeplechase first run in 1924.

potatoes in the mould A bizarre late 19th-century rhyme, referring not to an artistic shape made from mashed potato but to potatoes still in the ground. Still in use, not in its impossibly long full form, but pared right down to the Cockney **taters**.

soldiers bold Apparently a development of the rhyme **soldier bold**, used for 'a cold' (see *A cold* at ILLNESS).

warriors bold A variation on the **soldiers bold** theme. Julian Franklyn in his *Dictionary of Rhyming Slang* (1960) gives a circumstantial account of a sighting of it 'by R. A. Hadrill, Esq., who came upon it (*c.*1955) in a Turkish bath where it was used by all the attendants with reference to the plunge pool. They in turn had picked it up from a bookmaker.'

Chilly

Uncle Willie First recorded in the 1920s, and surviving into the latter part of the 20th century.

Nippy

George and Zippy A 1980s rhyme from the names of two puppet characters on the children's television programme *Rainbow*. George was a hippo and Zippy a creature of indeterminate species with a zip for a mouth.

A draught

George Raft From the name of the American film star George Raft (1895–1980), who specialized in mean-eyed gangster roles. In the middle to later years of the 20th century, complaints of 'a right old George Raft in here' were commonly to be heard.

Hot

peas in the pot A late 19th-century rhyme, almost always reduced to **peas**. The sole rhyming representative of 'heat'—and in practice it's far more often been used metaphorically (for sexual attractiveness, high skill, etc.) than literally.

Weather

hat and feather Occasionally reduced to **hat and**, but mainly used in its full form.

Rain

allacompain A 19th-century rhyme first recorded in 1859, and probably either a mishearing of or an eroded form of **all complain**—a natural enough town-dweller's reaction to rain. Long since defunct.

Andy Cain A rhyme popular in the late 19th and early 20th centuries. It's never been traced to any particular individual.

France and Spain A late 19th-century rhyme whose life-span was considerably extended by the rain-sodden trenches in France in the First World War. In use it underwent severe phonetic erosion to **frarny**.

King of Spain An Australian rhyme of the 20th century.

Mary Blaine or **Mary Blane** First recorded in 1859, and long since obsolete. A purely arbitrary rhyme, not based on any particular person.

pleasure and pain A 20th-century rhyme implying a schizophrenic attitude to precipitation.

A shower

fairy bower An Australian rhyme of inordinate tweeness. For the sort of shower people deliberately stand under, see *Toilette* at HOUSEHOLD MATTERS.

Snow

buck and doe According to Ray Puxley in *Cockney Rabbit* (1992), the phonetic reduction of **buck and doe** to /bʌkən ˈdəʊ/ gives a deliberately expletive impression.

come and go Sometimes reduced, ambiguously, to **come**. Perhaps its most frequent manifestation is verbal, in the present participle form—as in 'It's really coming and going out there!'

to and fro A less common alternative to come and go.

Thunder

stand from under An adaptation of an injunction by building workers, fire fighters, etc. to those standing below when something is to be lowered—or thrown—to the ground. Not much use as a warning itself, as the lightning that would have caused the damage has preceded it.

Wind

Jenny Lind From the name of the Swedish soprano (1820–87) who was immensely popular in the 19th century, and was known as the 'Swedish nightingale'. Also applied to stomach 'wind' (see *Wind* at **IN THE LAV**).

Windy

Rawalpindi From the name of the city in northeastern Pakistan. In use in the 1940s and 1950s.

In the Sky

The sun

Bath bun In use since the 1970s, although it had been employed from much earlier as a rhyme for *son* (as have all the other *bun*-rhymes below, and also pie and one—see *Son* at **RELATIVES AND FRIENDS**).

currant bun The most widely used present-day *sun*-rhyme, first recorded in the late 19th century, and since the 1980s also applied to the British tabloid newspaper *The Sun*:

> A few glasses of Moët . . . and some pâté de foie gras, 'cos I'm a champagne and liver sausage sort of person, and watch the old currant bun setting behind the Docklands arena. Paradise.
> —John Sullivan *Only Fools and Horses* (1991)

Dick Dunn A late 19th- and early 20th-century rhyme based on the name of the bookmaker and well-known racecourse personality Richard 'Dick' Dunn (died 1905).

hot cross bun An Australian contribution, and perhaps the most apposite of the various *bun*-rhymes, adding the element of heat to the element of roundness.

old Jamaica rum A naval rhyme, dating from the 19th century and largely redundant by the middle of the 20th. Not a perfect rhyme, but it was usually reduced to **old Jamaica** anyway.

penny bun A rhyme from the early part of the 20th century, when buns could still be had for a penny.

pie and one From a familiar order in a caff or pie shop—'one' being a single portion of mashed potato.

The moon

silver spoon Rhyming *moon* with *spoon* is not exactly original, but the *silver* part is at least apt. Usually reduced in use to *the silver*.

Aurora Australis

roaring horsetails Not strictly rhyming slang for this Australian term for the Southern Lights, more a joky folk-etymologizing substitution.

Days and Times

Time

Harry Lime A rhyme current from the 1950s to the 1970s, from the name of the anti-hero of the film *The Third Man* (1949) (screenplay by Graham Greene, who in 1950 published a novel based on it). The elusive Lime, played in the film by Orson Welles, memorably summed up the Swiss nation's contribution to civilization as the cuckoo clock.

lemon and lime From the popular fruit drink.
nickel and dime A US rhyme, first recorded in the 1930s.
See also *Imprisonment* at **CRIME AND PUNISHMENT**.

A week

bubble and squeak First recorded in the 1970s, and generally shortened to **bubble**.

A day

blue and grey Possibly an allusion to the colours of clear and clouded skies.
load of hay First recorded in 1859, but it doesn't seem to have survived into the 20th century.

In Australia in the late 19th century, *the other day* was rhymed as **my mother's away**.

A minute

cock linnet A standard component of Cockney folklore, the small singing bird kept in a cage—made famous particularly by the lines 'Off went the van with my old man in it, I followed on with my old cock linnet' in the 1919 music-hall song *Don't Dilly-dally on the Way* (written by Fred W. Leigh and Charles Collins, and made famous by Marie Lloyd).

Morning

gypsy's warning A pessimistic rhyme, exploiting an expression which means 'a cryptic or sinister warning'.

   Kathleen Mavourneen An Australian rhyme, based on the name of the eponymous heroine of the sentimental ballad. Inspired by its refrain 'It may be for years, it may be for ever', Australians use *Kathleen Mavourneen* metaphorically to mean 'for a very long time', and also 'an indefinite term of imprisonment', and perhaps some idea of an interminable morning lies behind its rhyming application too.

   maids adorning First recorded in 1859, and long since defunct.

Night

black and white The first half is self-evidently more appropriate than the second, but it's generally not abbreviated. First recorded in the late 19th century, and perhaps partially inspired by the name of a brand of whisky.

   take a fright First recorded in 1859, and reflecting a long tradition of night as a time of fear. Long superseded.

   Tom Right A mid-19th-century rhyme, perhaps indicating, Julian Franklyn suggests in his *Dictionary of Rhyming Slang* (1960), that night is the right time for criminal activity.

Late

Harry Tate From the name of the English music-hall comedian Harry Tate (1872–1940). While he was still a familiar figure, in the first half of the 20th century, it was in wide use, and even evolved semantically to denote incompetence or amateurishness.

   tiddler's bait That is the original form, but it can also appear as **tiddley bait**, and be shortened to **tiddler's** or **tiddley**. The inspiration is the catching of small fish, the youthful rhyming slangster's introduction to the world of angling.

Later

alligator A rhyme which enjoyed a vogue in the late 1950s, thanks to the success of R. C. Guidry's song 'See you later, alligator, After a while, crocodile' (1957). The valedictory exchange (slightly altered to 'in a while') became a children's and teenagers' mantra, and for a time **alligator** on its own was used as a goodbye formula.

hot potato An Australian rhyme, relying on the pronunciation /pəˈteɪtə/.

A clock

dickory dock A ready-made rhyme, lifted from the nursery rhyme 'Hickory dickory dock, The mouse ran up the clock'. First recorded in the late 19th century. The variant **hickory dock** has sometimes been used.

postman's knock From the children's game involving the forfeit of a kiss. Generally shortened to **postman's**.

tick-tock A fairly obvious and feeble rhyme. The usage can apply to watches as well as clocks, which suggests that its motivation may have been semantic appropriateness more than rhyme.

A watch

bottle of scotch A 19th-century rhyme, long disused. Julian Franklyn in his *Dictionary of Rhyming Slang* (1960) suggests that the rhyme may originally have been applied especially to Waterbury watches, a brand of pocket watch made in Waterbury, Connecticut, USA. If so, the compliment was returned, for Waterbury watch has been a rhyme for *scotch* (see *Whisky* at **ALCOHOL AND OTHER DRUGS**).

Gordon and Gotch From the name of a firm of book and magazine importers in Plaistow, East London. Usually shortened to **gordon**.

Location

A round-up of the (fairly cursory) attempts by rhyming slangsters to take cognizance of the world around them and their place within it:

The Wide World

The sky

Esurient rhymers look no further than *pie* for inspiration: **apple pie**, which emerged around the middle of the 20th century, and **shepherd's pie**, which is usually shortened to **shepherds** (Ray Puxley, in *Cockney Rabbit* (1992), suggests a connection with the predictive weather rhymes relating to shepherds and red skies, but the juxtaposition of ideas is probably coincidental).

The sea

coffee and tea Usually abbreviated to **coffee**.

housemaid's knee Apparently quite a recent coinage, first recorded in the 1970s.

River Lea From the name of a river that flows through Essex into the Thames in the eastern part of London—classic rhyming-slang territory. In use in the 19th century, but now apparently defunct.

Topography

The ground

penny a pound or **penny the pound** Dating back to the late 19th century, when a pound weight of many commmodities could be had for as little as a penny. Usually shortened to *the* **penny**.

safe and sound Perhaps reflecting the security of 'terra firma' (as opposed to being, say, up a ladder or at sea). Usually shortened to *the* **safe**.

A hill

Jack and Jill The obvious rhyme, after the boy and girl who went up one in the nursery rhyme.

    rhubarb pill An occasional outing for a rhyme much more usually applied to *bill* (see *A bill* at **MONEY AND COMMERCE**).

A river

bullock's liver A late 19th-century rhyme, long since disused.
    shake and shiver Used in both England and Australia, and usually reduced to **shake**.

A town

Imagination stretches little further than mostly unidentifiable members of the Brown family: there's **Joe Brown** (a 19th-century rhyme, predating the Lincolnshire-born 'Cockney' pop singer of that name (1941–)), and also **Jim Brown** and **Mother Brown** (probably from the 1939 song 'Knees up, Mother Brown!' by Weston and Lee, which became immensely popular in Britain during the Second World War, although conceivably the name in the song was inspired by an existing rhyme). The last two have mostly been used in the context of East Londoners' application of *town* to the West End of London. The Australian contribution to the mix is **penny brown**.

A street

See *On the Road* at **TRANSPORT AND TRAVEL**.

A park

Joan of Arc After the French heroine burnt at the stake by the English (*c.*1412–31).
    light and dark A rhyme dating from the late 19th century.
    Noah's Ark Of similar vintage to **light and dark**.
    skylark A more recent example, also used as a verb, meaning 'to park a vehicle' (see *To park* at **TRANSPORT AND TRAVEL**).

Position

The middle

hey-diddle-diddle or **hi-diddle-diddle** A 1950s rhyme, applicable in a general sense, although in practice probably most often applied to the centre of a dartboard. From the opening lines of the nursery rhyme, 'Hey diddle diddle, the cat and the fiddle, the cow jumped over the moon'.

A corner

Jack Horner From the nursery-rhyme character, 'little Jack Horner', who sat in the corner, eating his pudding and pie. But never as widely used as his alter ego Johnny.

Johnny Horner A popular rhyme, dating from the late 19th century and still in use a hundred years later—notably in the phrase *round the Johnny Horner* (In and out the corners, round the Johnny Horners Murray and Leigh *The Amateur Whitewasher* (1896)). Often shortened to **Johnny**. (Pubs being often located on street corners, 'going round the Johnny' became a euphemism for going for a drink.)

Cities

London

London itself isn't particularly amenable to rhyme, but its nickname 'the Smoke' (which dates from the second half of the 19th century) has produced **Old Oak**. And for revellers going up *West* (i.e. to the West End of London), there's **jacket and vest** (**jacket** for short), a rhyme popular especially in the pre-Second World War period.

Sydney

steak and kidney An Australian rhyme of long standing, first recorded in 1905.

Quality and Quantity

Abstractions don't as a rule much exercise rhyming slangsters. Practicalities are their usual stock in trade. But even in the most practical of worlds there are estimations to be made about size and weight, moral judgements to be formed about good and bad, right and wrong, pleasant and unpleasant. And from time to time they find their way into rhyme.

Good

Sad to say, in this imperfect world rhymes reflecting a positive judgement are well outnumbered by their opposites—indeed half of the actual rhymes on *good* are used to express the idea 'no good'.

Good

plum pud An Australian contribution.

   Robin Hood An appropriate application for the medieval English outlaw-hero who was the epitome of virtue—but a large proportion of its usage is in the expression *no Robin Hood* 'no good'.

   Wee Georgie Wood A favourable review for the diminutive early 20th-century British music-hall comedian. Usually shortened to **Wee Georgie**.

Nice

apples and rice Usually shortened to **apples** in literal use, but for the most part this is sarcastic—in which case it's used in full: 'Oh, very apples and rice, I must say!'

   apples and spice An Australian rhyme which has been overwhelmed and buried by the popularity of its shortened form **apples** in the expression *she's apples* 'everything's all right' (first recorded in 1943):

> Suddenly the engine leapt alive. . . 'She's apples, George.'
> —R. Beilby *No Medals for Aphrodite* (1970)

   sugar and spice An alternative to **apples and rice**, but without the sarcastic overtones.

Grouse

An Australianism of unknown origin meaning 'excellent', rhymed on

Mickey Mouse, the iconic cartoon mouse created by Walt Disney who first appeared in 1928:

> Yes, but it's real Mickey Mouse though.
> —R. T. Hoser *Indecent Exposures* (2000)

A smasher

gammon rasher First recorded in the 1970s.

Bad

Bad

Jack the Lad From the colloquial designation of a cocky chancer, which dates from the 1950s.

shepherd's plaid A rhyme current between the mid-19th century and the early 20th. Usually shortened to **shepherd's**.

sorry and sad Another 19th-century rhyme, with more survivability than shepherd's plaid.

No good

chunk of wood First recorded in 1859. The alternative version **chump of wood** was sometimes heard.

See also *Robin Hood* at GOOD.

Rotten

The rhymes all seem to retain at least a vestige of the word's original implication of putrefaction, but (with the apparent exception of Dolly Cotton) their main role is to suggest unfairness, disagreeableness, or just plain badness. The common factor is *cotton*, whose rhyming possibilities are extensively explored (although as far as is known the obvious target of *Dot Cotton*—long-term denizen of the BBC soap *EastEnders*, played by June Brown—has not yet been hit). The earliest recorded examples, from the first part of the 20th century, are **Dolly Cotton** and **Johnny Cotton**, together with their more respectable relative **Doctor Cotton**. These were all imaginary figures, but a real member of the family is **Billy Cotton**, commemorating the British band-leader (1899–1969) and star of the popular 1950s and 1960s radio programme *The Billy Cotton Band Show*. Inanimate members of the group are **needle and cotton** and **reels of cotton**. For Australians, who haven't formed the *cotton* habit, there's the alternative of **gone and forgotten**.

A bummer

A slang term for a bad or depressing experience which dates from the 1960s:

Joe Strummer In honour of Joe Strummer (1952–), a member of the late 1970s punk band 'The Clash'. Used adjectivally.

John Selwyn A metaphorical application of the earlier 'literal' meaning, 'a bad trip' (see *A Bad Reaction to Drugs* at **ALCOHOL AND OTHER DRUGS**).

A shocker

Barry Crocker An Australian rhyme, in dubious honour of the Australian entertainer and actor Barry Crocker (1935–). Often shortened to **Barry**:

> The New Zealanders had a 'Barry Crocker' of a year, also losing both of their games against South Africa.
> —*Canberra Times* (1998)

> A Barry now means a shocker, after Barry Crocker.
> —*Herald Sun* (2001)

Worthless

not worth a tiger tank A 1970s rhyme. The final element, rhyming with *wank*, was inspired by the slogan 'Put a tiger in your tank' advertising Esso petrol.

Right and Wrong

Right

Commonly (and in the case of **shiny and bright** almost exclusively) used in the context of 'all right', indicating general satisfactoriness:

harbour light Usually shortened to **harbour**—if everything's in order, it's 'all harbour'.

Isle of Wight From the island off the south coast of England.

shiny and bright The latter part is usually dispensed with—'all shiny'.

Wrong

Pete Tong From the name of the British disc jockey Pete Tong:

> You knew it was all going to go a bit Pete Tong when Burton rejected relocation to Australia . . . with a firm: 'No, we're staying in England!'
> —*Observer* (2001)

Size

Big

porky pig Suggestive of excessive size round the waist, but also used in ironic accusations of ungenerosity (as in 'That's very porky pig of you!').

Thin

needle and pin First recorded in the 1930s. Rhymes aren't usually so semantically appropriate.

Weight

love and hate Usually used in the context of attempted dieting and weight loss.

   pieces of eight Generally shortened to **pieces**, and used in the expression *do some pieces*—i.e. lose some weight.

Numbers

In the world of rhyming slang, **cucumbers** are of strictly practical relevance. There's not much call for arithmetical usage, even behind the till of the market stall. That particular rhyme for *numbers* is usually applied to telephone numbers, but for the most part, number rhymes operate in two specific contexts: craps, a gambling game played with two dice; and the patter of bingo callers. Ordinal numbers came into their own towards the end of the 20th century in designating the class of a university degree.

One

buttered bun The bingo caller's usual stand-by for 'one' is *Kelly's eye*, but if he or she feels a rhyme coming on, this is available. An alternative version is **buttered scone**, which presumably depends on a pronunciation of *one* as /wɒn/.

penny bun Dating from the early part of the 20th century, when buns could still be had for a penny, and used mainly in quoting racing odds: ten to one would be 'a cockle to a penny bun'.

First

The rhymes both designate a first-class degree.

Pattie Hearst A rhyme dating from around 1974, which was when Pattie Hearst (1954–), daughter and heiress of the US newspaper magnate William Randolph Hearst, achieved fame by first being kidnapped and then joining her captors to become an urban guerilla. Usually abbreviated to **Pattie**.

raging thirst A 1980s rhyme, generally shortened to **raging**. Probably inspired by the stereotypically permanent relationship between students and beer.

Two

In the days when bingo was housey-housey or lotto, **dirty old Jew** was a common callers' rhyme, but its rasping racism ill fitted it for post-Holocaust sensibilities. More acceptable in the 21st century are **Dr Who** (from the eponymous time-travelling hero of the BBC television science-fiction series, which was first broadcast in 1963) and **me and you**.

Two-two

Desmond From the name of Archbishop Desmond Tutu (1931–), South African churchman and Nobel Peace Prize winner. The phonetic similarity makes for a feeble rhyme, but the joke was too good to resist.

Three

Three itself seems not to have attracted any rhymes, but the gamblers' slang *trey* 'three' has yielded Vicar of Bray (see *Trey* at GAMBLING) and a few Australian rhymes for *threepence* (see *Threepence* at MONEY AND COMMERCE).

Third

The rhymes all designate a third-class degree.

Douglas Hurd From the name of the British Conservative politician Douglas Hurd (1930–), a man much too brainy to have deserved the rhyme. Usually shortened to **Douglas**.

George the Third A coinage of the 1980s, after the notoriously mad English king of that name who reigned 1760–1820. As the object of the substitution is the same word, it scarcely counts as a rhyme.

Richard the Third A further 1980s 'rhyme', no cleverer than George the Third. Usually curtailed to **Richard**, which at least has the merit of disguising the lameness of the word-play.

Four

dirty whore Some usage for 'four pounds (£4)', but it more commonly stands for *thirty-four* (see below).

George Moore A cricketing rhyme (see *A four* at SPORT).

knock on the door or **knock at the door** A bingo callers' rhyme.

Five

beehive Used mainly by bingo callers.

Jack's alive Some general use, but overwhelmingly this denotes five pounds or a five-pound note (see *Five pounds* at MONEY AND COMMERCE).

man alive Occasionally used for '£5', but mainly this is a bingo callers' rhyme.

Six

Captain Hicks The military or naval cousin of **Jimmy Hicks**—or sometimes the same person (see below). The context is certainly the same: craps or poker.

chopsticks A bingo rhyme, dating from the First World War period. An alternative formulation, apparently even earlier, is **chopping sticks**. It's not clear whether this is an alteration of **chopsticks** (probably for rhythmic purposes), perpetrated in defiance of meaning and etymology (chopsticks aren't used for chopping, and the word isn't related to English *chop*), or whether it represents a variant of Scots English *chapping stick* 'a stick for hitting people with'.

Dorothy Dix A cricketing rhyme (see *A six* at SPORT).

Jimmy Hicks A rhyme of American origin, used by crap and poker players, and first recorded in 1919. It doesn't seem to have been based on any particular individual, although a persona was invented for him as 'Captain Jimmy Hicks of the Horse Marines' (**Captain Hicks** is an alternative form of the rhyme, and it's sometimes shortened to simply **Hicks**):

> The dice showed three and three. 'Jimmy Hicks!'
> —S. V. Benet *The Beginning of Wisdom* (1921)

kick See *A sixpence* at MONEY AND COMMERCE.

pick up sticks A bingo callers' rhyme, based on the name of a game involving removing small sticks from a pile without disturbing the other sticks.

Tom Mix Often used to refer to the sum of six pounds. Inspired by the name of Tom Mix (1880–1940), US star of early western films.

Seven

God in heaven or **God's in heaven** A bingo callers' rhyme, first recorded in the 1940s. Latterly largely replaced by **gates of heaven**, first recorded in 1962. **Heaven** is also used on its own, but as it's mainly the preserve of crap players, it's probably an independent coinage (see also ELEVEN).

Eight

garden gate Mainly heard in bingo halls, but also used to refer to the sum of eight pounds. Bingo callers keep to the full form, but in a monetary context it's often shortened to **garden**.

Harry Tate Used in the days of housey-housey, when the name of the English music-hall comedian Harry Tate (1872–1940) was still familiar.

Nine

feel fine Mainly in financial contexts, to denote the sum of nine pounds—in which case it's commonly abbreviated to **feel**.

mother of mine A sentimental rhyme favoured by bingo callers.

yours and mine Another bingo rhyme.

Ten

Big Ben Some general usage, but mainly in Britain it stands for the sum of ten pounds (originally, in the first half of the 20th century, before inflation took effect, it was ten shillings). In the US, it signifies the score ten in the game of craps, but it seems unlikely that the rhymer had the tower of the Houses of Parliament in London, or its great bell, in mind. It was probably an alteration of the earlier *Big Dick* (with the same meaning), substituting one name for another:

> Crow tossed the dice, their roll stopped on ten. 'Big Ben, I've got it made then!'
> —Paul Crump *Burn, Killer, Burn!* (1962)

cock and hen A rhyme dating from the 19th century, and often applied specifically to ten shillings or ten pounds (latterly mainly the former, as Big Ben took over 'ten pounds'). In early use it frequently alternated with **cockerel and hen**, which over time became worn down to **cockle and hen**—**cockle** was a common shortening.

Uncle Ben A bingo callers' rhyme (perhaps inspired by the brand name of a type of rice).

water hen A general rhyme, dating from the 1960s.

Eleven

heaven Used by crap players—but confusingly, they also rhyme it with *seven*.

A dozen

country cousin In use mainly amongst the horse-racing fraternity. It dates from the late 19th century.

monkey's cousin A facetious alteration of the expression *monkey's uncle* (as in the exclamation 'Well I'll be a monkey's uncle!'), favoured by bingo callers. First recorded in the 1940s.

Thirteen

Dick Turpin A somewhat approximate rhyme, based on the name of the English highwayman Dick Turpin (1705–39). First recorded in the 1930s, and used especially by dart players.

Twenty-two

dinky-doo A bingo callers' rhyme, apparently dating from the First World War period. There are numerous spelling variations, and also a two-syllable version: **dink-do**.

Twenty-four

Pompey whore A bingo callers' rhyme (for private consumption, especially in the services, rather than in public halls), dating from the beginning of the 20th century but largely obsolete by 1950. *Pompey* is Portsmouth, a naval port in Hampshire with its full complement of professional sex workers (the name probably came either from the captured French warship *Le Pompée*, which was used as the guardship of Portsmouth Harbour from 1811, or from the exploit of Portsmouth-based sailors in climbing Pompey's Pillar in Alexandria in 1781).

Thirty-three

Gertie Lee An early 20th-century bingo callers' usage. Not modelled on any particular Gertie Lee, but chosen for its double rhyme (on *thirty* as well as *three*).

Thirty-four

dirty whore A bingo rhyme, but like **Pompey whore** (see above) mainly a services' usage rather than a general one. It dates from the First World War period and, like **Gertie Lee** (see above), rhymes both parts of its referent.

Forty-four

Diana Dors The rhyme is based on 'all the fours', standard bingo callers' jargon for *forty-four*. Diana Dors (1931–84) was a curvaceous blonde British actress who came to prominence in the 1950s.

  open the door A bingo rhyme first recorded in the 1940s.

Sixty-six

clickety-click Easily the best known of all bingo callers' rhymes, albeit not very precise phonetically. First recorded in 1919, it was a product of the First

World War period, when housey-housey (or 'house') was a popular way of whiling away the time among the troops:

> A game of 'house' was in progress, and a voice monotonously droned the numbers: ... 'clickety click'.
> —L. A. G. Strong *Sea Wall* (1933)

Index

Note: This index lists all rhyming slang words and phrases in the book. For terms associated with personal nouns (e.g. Stuart Diver, Tony Blairs) these are indexed on the first word of the phrase and not by surname.

Oxford Paperback Reference

The Concise Oxford Dictionary of English Etymology
T. F. Hoad

A wealth of information about our language and its history, this reference source provides over 17,000 entries on word origins.

'A model of its kind'

Daily Telegraph

A Dictionary of Euphemisms
R. W. Holder

This hugely entertaining collection draws together euphemisms from all aspects of life: work, sexuality, age, money, and politics.

Review of the previous edition
'This ingenious collection is not only very funny but extremely instructive too'

Iris Murdoch

The Oxford Dictionary of Slang
John Ayto

Containing over 10,000 words and phrases, this is the ideal reference for those interested in the more quirky and unofficial words used in the English language.

'hours of happy browsing for language lovers'

Observer

Oxford Paperback Reference

The Concise Oxford Companion to English Literature
Margaret Drabble and Jenny Stringer

Based on the best-selling *Oxford Companion to English Literature*, this is an indispensable guide to all aspects of English literature.

Review of the parent volume
'a magisterial and monumental achievement'

Literary Review

The Concise Oxford Companion to Irish Literature
Robert Welch

From the ogam alphabet developed in the 4th century to Roddy Doyle, this is a comprehensive guide to writers, works, topics, folklore, and historical and cultural events.

Review of the parent volume
'Heroic volume ... It surpasses previous exercises of similar nature in the richness of its detail and the ecumenism of its approach.'

Times Literary Supplement

A Dictionary of Shakespeare
Stanley Wells

Compiled by one of the best-known international authorities on the playwright's works, this dictionary offers up-to-date information on all aspects of Shakespeare, both in his own time and in later ages.

AskOxford.•com

Oxford Dictionaries Passionate about language

For more information about the background to Oxford Quotations and Language Reference Dictionaries, and much more about Oxford's commitment to language exploration, why not visit the world's largest language learning site, www.AskOxford.com

Passionate about English?

What were the original 'brass monkeys'? **Ask**Oxford.•com

How do new words enter the dictionary? **Ask**Oxford.•com

How is 'whom' used? **Ask**Oxford.•com

Who said, 'For also knowledge itself is power?' **Ask**Oxford.•com

How can I improve my writing? **Ask**Oxford.•com

If you have a query about the English language, want to look up a word, need some help with your writing skills, are curious about how dictionaries are made, or simply have some time to learn about the language, bypass the rest and ask the experts at www.AskOxford.com.

Passionate about language?

If you want to find out about writing in French, German, Spanish, or Italian, improve your listening and speaking skills, learn about other cultures, access resources for language students, or gain insider travel tips from those **Ask**Oxford.•com in the know, ask the experts at

OXFORD

Great value ebooks from Oxford!

An ever-increasing number of Oxford subject reference dictionaries, English and bilingual dictionaries, and English language reference titles are available as ebooks.

All Oxford ebooks are available in the award-winning Mobipocket Reader format, compatible with most current handheld systems, including Palm, Pocket PC/Windows CE, Psion, Nokia, SymbianOS, Franklin eBookMan, and Windows. Some are also available in MS Reader and Palm Reader formats.

Priced on a par with the print editions, Oxford ebooks offer dictionary-specific search options making information retrieval quick and easy.

For further information and a full list of Oxford ebooks please visit: www.askoxford.com/shoponline/ebooks/

Oxford Companions

'Opening such books is like sitting down with a knowledgeable friend.
Not a bore or a know-all, but a genuinely well-informed chum ... So far
so splendid.'

Sunday Times [of *The Oxford Companion to Shakespeare*]

For well over 60 years Oxford University Press has been publishing
Companions that are of lasting value and interest, each one not only a
comprehensive source of reference, but also a stimulating guide,
mentor, and friend. There are between 40 and 60 Oxford Companions
available at any one time, ranging from music, art, and literature to
history, warfare, religion, and wine.

Titles include:

The Oxford Companion to English Literature
Edited by Margaret Drabble
'No guide could come more classic.'

Malcolm Bradbury, *The Times*

The Oxford Companion to Music
Edited by Alison Latham
'probably the best one-volume music reference book going'

Times Educational Supplement

The Oxford Companion to Western Art
Edited by Hugh Brigstocke
'more than meets the high standard set by the growing number of
Oxford Companions'

Contemporary Review

The Oxford Companion to Food
Alan Davidson
'the best food reference work ever to appear in the English language'

New Statesman

The Oxford Companion to Wine
Edited by Jancis Robinson
'the greatest wine book ever published'

Washington Post

Oxford Paperback Reference

The Concise Oxford Dictionary of Quotations
Edited by Elizabeth Knowles

Based on the highly acclaimed *Oxford Dictionary of Quotations*, this paperback edition maintains its extensive coverage of literary and historical quotations, and contains completely up-to-date material. A fascinating read and an essential reference tool.

The Oxford Dictionary of Humorous Quotations
Edited by Ned Sherrin

From the sharply witty to the downright hilarious, this sparkling collection will appeal to all senses of humour.

Quotations by Subject
Edited by Susan Ratcliffe

A collection of over 7,000 quotations, arranged thematically for easy look-up. Covers an enormous range of nearly 600 themes from 'The Internet' to 'Parliament'.

The Concise Oxford Dictionary of Phrase and Fable
Edited by Elizabeth Knowles

Provides a wealth of fascinating and informative detail for over 10,000 phrases and allusions used in English today. Find out about anything from the 'Trojan horse' to 'ground zero'.

OXFORD

Oxford Paperback Reference

The Kings of Queens of Britain
John Cannon and Anne Hargreaves

A detailed, fully-illustrated history ranging from mythical and pre-conquest rulers to the present House of Windsor, featuring regional maps and genealogies.

A Dictionary of Dates
Cyril Leslie Beeching

Births and deaths of the famous, significant and unusual dates in history – this is an entertaining guide to each day of the year.

'a dipper's blissful paradise ... Every single day of the year, plus an index of birthdays and chronologies of scientific developments and world events.'

Observer

A Dictionary of British History
Edited by John Cannon

An invaluable source of information covering the history of Britain over the past two millennia. Over 3,600 entries written by more than 100 specialist contributors.

Review of the parent volume
'the range is impressive ... truly (almost) all of human life is here'
Kenneth Morgan, *Observer*

OXFORD

More Art Reference from Oxford

The Grove Dictionary of Art

The 34 volumes of *The Grove Dictionary of Art* provide unrivalled coverage of the visual arts from Asia, Africa, the Americas, Europe, and the Pacific, from prehistory to the present day.

'succeeds in performing the most difficult of balancing acts, satisfying specialists while ... remaining accessible to the general reader'

The Times

The Grove Dictionary of Art – Online
www.groveart.com

This immense cultural resource is now available online. Updated regularly, it includes recent developments in the art world as well as the latest art scholarship.

'a mammoth one-stop site for art-related information'

Antiques Magazine

The Oxford History of Western Art
Edited by Martin Kemp

From Classical Greece to postmodernism, *The Oxford History of Western Art* is an authoritative and stimulating overview of the development of visual culture in the West over the last 2,700 years.

'here is a work that will permanently alter the face of art history ... a hugely ambitious project successfully achieved'

The Times

The Oxford Dictionary of Art
Edited by Ian Chilvers

The Oxford Dictionary of Art is an authoritative guide to the art of the western world, ranging across painting, sculpture, drawing, and the applied arts.

'the best and most inclusive single-volume available'

Marina Vaizey, *Sunday Times*